An Introduction to Open Systems Interconnection

ADVANCES IN TELECOMMUNICATION NETWORKS SERIES
Wushow Chou, Series Editor

Local Area and Multiple Access Networks
Raymond L. Pickholtz

Telecommunications and the Law: An Anthology
Walter Sapronov, Editor

An Introduction to Open Systems Interconnection
Dennis A. MacKinnon, William A. McCrum, Donald A. Sheppard

OTHER BOOKS OF INTEREST

Computer Network Architectures
Anton Meijer and Paul Peeters

Spread Spectrum Communications, Volume I
Marvin K. Simon, Jim K. Omura, Robert A. Scholtz, and Barry K. Levitt

Spread Spectrum Communications, Volume II
Marvin K. Simon, Jim K. Omura, Robert A. Scholtz, and Barry K. Levitt

Spread Spectrum Communications, Volume III
Marvin K. Simon, Jim K. Omura, Robert A. Scholtz, and Barry K. Levitt

Elements of Digital Satellite Communication: System Alternatives, Analyses and Optimization, Volume I
William W Wu

Elements of Digital Satellite Communication: Channel Coding and Integrated Services Digital Satellite Networks, Volume II
William W Wu

Current Advances in Distributed Computing and Communications
Yechiam Yemini

Digital Transmission Systems and Networks, Volume II: Applications
Michael J. Miller and Syed V. Ahamed

Transmission Analysis in Communication Systems, Volume I
Osamu Shimbo

Transmission Analysis in Communication Systems, Volume II
Osamu Shimbo

Spread Spectrum Signal Design: LPE and AJ Systems
David L. Nicholson

Digital Signal Processing Design
Andrew Bateman and Warren Yates

Probability for Engineering with Applications to Reliability
Lavon B. Page

An Introduction to Open Systems Interconnection

Dennis MacKinnon

Software Kinetics Limited

William McCrum

Department of Communications
Government of Canada

Donald Sheppard

Protocols Standards & Communication Inc.

COMPUTER SCIENCE PRESS

An imprint of W. H. Freeman and Company
New York

This book is dedicated to Lindsay, Martha, and Patrick, who hopefully will read this book sometime in the future. It is they who will benefit most from the "vision" that OSI is bringing to life.

Library of Congress Cataloging-in-Publication Data

Printed in the United States of America

Computer Science Press

An imprint of W. H. Freeman and Company
41 Madison Avenue, New York, NY 10010
20 Beaumont Street, Oxford OX1 2NQ, England

1 2 3 4 5 6 7 8 9 0 RRD 8 9

CONTENTS

PREFACE

AN INTRODUCTION TO OPEN SYSTEMS INTERCONNECTION introduces and describes a "megatrend" in information processing and communications, which is making interconnection and interworking among computers possible on a global scale through international standardization. The goal of the standards developers is the elimination of the traditional computing Tower of Babel. Open Systems Interconnection (OSI) provides the framework and technical direction. The result is increased function and reduced costs for managing and distributing business information.

The introduction of OSI is a significant step in the quest for the elusive "wired world." It promises to change the way we use telecommunications and computer networks and this, in turn, promises to change our way of life. Anyone involved in or affected by communications or distributed processing (which is just about everyone these days!) needs at least a basic understanding of OSI and its capabilities. We expect this book to meet that need.

In 1977 the International Organisation for Standardization (ISO) and the International Telegraph and Telephone Consultative Committee (CCITT) predicted the need for a standardized communications architecture—a "reference model" for international standards—that would facilitate efficient interworking among systems from different technologies, manufacturers, administrations, nationalities, and enterprises. The architecture and the services, protocols, and supporting tools that have subsequently been specified are collectively referred to as Open Systems Interconnection.

OSI standardization, despite much early criticism, has proved to be very successful. A meeting of some 40 experts in Washington, D.C., in March 1978 started work that has yielded a set of proven standards covering most aspects of multivendor systems interconnection. International OSI standards meetings now attract over 350 professionals from all over the world to work on more than 50 separate projects.

Interconnection standards, however, are only the first step on the road toward fully interoperable systems and applications portability. Standards developers are now using the experiences of OSI to create important new standards in areas such as distributed processing, graphics, office systems, and databases. Open Distributed Processing heralds a new era of standardization that will become another major step forward in interoperable systems.

THE GOALS OF THIS BOOK

It is perhaps unfortunate that OSI standards come complete with their own set of special terms and concepts. The OSI "language" can be overwhelming to the uninitiated. Thus, it is a primary goal of this book to clarify OSI terms and concepts using, as much as possible, everyday language and familiar examples. We have chosen to use the ordinary "telephone application" as our primary example, even though OSI protocols are not actually used in today's voice networks. A list of acronyms has also been provided (in Appendix I) to allow quick reference.

We believe that three factors have made this book both necessary and timely. The first is the need to rapidly raise the general level of OSI awareness and understanding, and thereby to increase its acceptance into systems plans and designs. Our aim in this area is to assist with effective *technology transfer.* Next, the standards committees always need new volunteers to ensure a constant flow of ideas and to stimulate a high level of discussion and debate. Thus, we seek to generate *enthusiasm* and perhaps even to inspire *innovation.* Finally, many OSI products are either currently (or soon will be) available in the marketplace. Many of these will claim (more or less correctly) to conform to the OSI model and protocols. We wish to provide sufficient information about OSI to enable purchasers to place products into context and to reduce their reliance on vendor claims. This should provide the potential user with a measure of *technical confidence.*

We believe it is no longer feasible to put all there is to know about OSI into a single volume. Our focus in this book has been on the upper three layers (the Application, Presentation, and Session Layers), which are, we believe, the least well understood. The lower four layers, on the other hand, are concerned primarily with the telecommunications "subnetworks" that provide the pathways among communicating systems. There are, in our opinion, numerous excellent texts dealing with the many complexities of local and wide-area networks. Consequently, we have chosen to treat the lower layers at a conceptual level only.

It is our goal to enable the reader to analyze any communications function, activity, or product in terms of where it fits into the OSI architecture. This book defines standards that fit properly into an OSI Environment as well as it can be covered at this stage of OSI maturity. What this book does *not* do is to provide an engineering course on communications software programming or telecommunications network design.

We have discovered that it is somewhat difficult to guess just who will be most interested in this book. Systems planners will certainly require an understanding of OSI to maintain a good feel for where technology is going and to know what is reasonable and practical at any given time. Systems architects should be fully conversant with the concepts, principles, and capabilities of OSI; its impact on information systems designs is going to be dramatic. Software developers may wish to use this book as a stepping stone —their goal, of course, is to tackle all the gory details of the formal standards and the products that implement them. We also believe that systems managers should be concerned with OSI-based technology at a global level; they must recognize trends that can be exploited to gain competitive advantage and must be aware of the complexities that their technical professionals face in providing innovative solutions. Finally, we hope that we have also succeeded in making this book palatable to the proactive executive who wishes to keep his or her "finger on the pulse" of advances in communications.

THE ORGANIZATION OF THIS BOOK

We have organized the contents of this book into four major parts. The first part introduces the basic terminology and the *conceptual framework* for OSI. This will be of interest primarily to readers who are not familiar with ISO 7498 (Information Processing Systems—Open Systems Interconnection—Basic Reference Model) or its CCITT equivalent (Recommendation X.200). The second part covers OSI *services and protocols* in greater detail. The third part presents an Application Layer *protocol design methodology* and reviews the supporting tools and facilities that are becoming available to assist in this process. The critical area of testing for conformance to the standards is also introduced. Finally, we look toward the future of open systems standards and provide an *insight into the vision* that drives the many people who continue to work diligently in the standards committees.

Even though it may seem that we administer a very large dose of technical jargon, we have elected to take the perspective of the systems generalist rather than that of the telecommunications engineer. Our approach has been to focus on what OSI does to solve communications problems and how to make use of it, rather than just to describe OSI protocols in precise terms. Even though OSI could be treated primarily as a technical accomplishment, we like to think of it as a highly successful agreement among diverse communities of interest (individuals, companies, and countries). Ultimately, however, success will be measured by implementation, use, longevity, and cost–benefit, not by the completion of the standardization process. This book should be viewed as a roadmap, as it were a "hitchhiker's guide" to OSI, and not as an OSI encyclopedia.

In any book with as much technical complexity as this one, it is probably impossible to eliminate all errors or omissions. For anything unintentional that has crept in or been left out, we apologize and take full responsibility. It should, however, be remembered that successful standards are not static; evolution and growth will occur as user requirements change and as progress is made in the underlying technologies. Thus, there is bound to be some change over time, especially in the technical details, that will conflict with what we have written. The reader who requires precision and completeness down to the smallest detail is urged to obtain copies of the latest versions of the formal standards themselves. These are readily available from American National Standards Institute (ANSI) in the United States, the Canadian Standards Association in Canada, or from similar sources around the world—at a price, of course! To assist the reader in sorting out what to buy and also to provide a record of the reference material available at the time of writing, we have included a list of relevant OSI standards in Appendix II.

It is unlikely that a book like this could have been written four years ago, since the OSI upper layers had not stabilized and thinking was evolving quite rapidly among the experts. Obviously, nothing could ever have been written if the many millions of man-hours that the "standards industry" has invested in OSI had not occurred. In fact, our biggest challenge has been to keep up with, and participate in, the standardization process while taking the time to write about it.

ACKNOWLEDGMENTS

It is obvious to us that it would be impossible to acknowledge individually all those who have produced the technical material that is referenced in this book. We do believe, however, that the tremendous contribution to OSI of the various chairmen, convenors, rapporteurs, editors, and secretariats should not be forgotten. It was these people who kept everyone honest and friendly, made sure the paperwork got done, and in reality made it all happen. In particular, the chairman of the original SC16, Charles Bachman, the recently retired convenor of WG1, Hubert Zimmermann, and the recently retired SC21 chairman, Richard DesJardins, were an inspiration to most of us during the early days of the OSI dream. The current SC21 chairman, Paul Bartoli, and the secretariat, Lisa Rajchel, are doing an excellent job of keeping the spirits up, the paper moving, and the "wheels in motion."

The effort of ISO TC68, the ISO standards committee for banking and related financial services, to produce a banking application protocol design methodology helped motivate our efforts with this book and led us to recognize the general need for an introduction to OSI. The banking draft standard, DIS 9955, has provided much useful material, especially for Chapter 11.

We also thank our publisher for its considerable patience and the reviewers for their vote of confidence and suggestions. Most importantly, the long-term support and encouragement of our families has been critical to the completion of this book with a minimum of stress and strain.

Dennis MacKinnon
William McCrum
Donald Sheppard

CHAPTER 1

INTRODUCTION

Most people take the ability to communicate almost completely for granted. In fact, day-to-day communications is so commonplace and so natural that few of us ever think about the complexities involved or the difficulties that may arise. Facilities for communicating over short and long distances have become as essential to daily living as roads or electric power. It would be a very different world indeed if people and, more recently, computers were unable to "interconnect for the purpose of exchanging information" and were not at least partially "open" to mutual understanding.

Over the past 25 years computers and data communications have become increasingly important resources, to the point where some form of computer can now be found almost everywhere we turn. Musical Christmas cards, lifelike arcade games, airplane control systems, scientific computing systems, and telephone switches are only a few of the examples. Imagine how different the world would be if travel reservation systems, personal banking machines, electronic mail, word processing, and many, many other computer applications either did not exist or were prohibitively expensive. It would be much like turning off the power, only now it is "information power" instead of electric power.

Access to this information power has become so critical that no single organization or company can be allowed complete control over the processing, storage, or distribution of information. Hence, nonproprietary connectivity and interworking have become strategic requirements for social reasons as well as for corporate competition and personal interest. The day when everyone will have an "information-phone," an integrated services equivalent of today's familiar telephone, is emerging as a distinct possibility (France's Minitel and Canada's Alex are early examples). Standardization for widespread, global interconnectivity among information-phones is the enabling force that will allow large-scale information distribution to be achieved successfully and economically.

This book introduces and describes Open Systems Interconnection (OSI). OSI communication services go much further than what would be considered traditional telecommunications. Powerful capabilities for code conversion, file transfer and management, transaction processing, message handling, and global directories are examples of the advanced services included within the scope of OSI. The goal of this book is to paint a broad picture that will introduce OSI technology, place OSI standards into context, and act as a roadmap for more detailed studies.

Why has the importance of a standard communications architecture increased so dramatically over the past decade? At one level the change could be viewed simply as a natural reaction to the tremendous growth in computer processing requirements and the intense demand for information. The primary benefit of any communication system is that it increases the value of information by collecting and distributing it quickly, accurately, and securely. Information that is not available when and where needed rapidly becomes less useful, loses its importance, and consequently becomes considerably less valuable.

As the world generates more and more information, and as increasingly powerful computers become available to process and store this information, then managing, distributing, and formatting become important challenges. The scenario that used to be quoted for telephone networks (the idea that all of us would have to be operators if call switching were not automated) may soon also apply to the switching of "conversations" among computer applications. This book examines what is needed for systems to cooperate, or interwork, for the purpose of supporting useful applications in a distributed processing environment.

There is little doubt that terminology in the field of communications is proliferating, with additions to the vocabulary almost a continuous process. A glance at the Appendices illustrates the range of specialized terms and acronyms that are used in OSI standards. Many of these are now basic to any understanding of advanced networking. This book should prove useful as a cross-reference to OSI concepts and terminology.

There are four major parts in this book.

Part I focuses on the basic concepts and architecture of OSI and aims to raise the act of communicating to a more conscious level. The concepts and terminology behind the Basic Reference Model of Open Systems Interconnection (ISO 7498/X.200) are explained. The logical, engineering basis for OSI will become clearer as a result.

Part II introduces the services and protocols that have been defined for use in an OSI Environment. The emphasis in this part will be on the "interworking" aspects of communications provided by the Application, Presentation, and Session Layers. Concepts related to the assembly of physical circuits to form a reliable "transport-service" are summarized but not discussed in detail.

Part III introduces a step-by-step procedure for developing user-specific "application-protocols," taking into consideration the generic Application-

Service-Elements (ASEs) provided by OSI. Tools and techniques that are critical to the overall success of OSI standards are surveyed. Since only a relatively small number of people actually participate in the standards development process itself, it is essential that the supporting tools and techniques be properly demystified and explained in layperson's terms.

Finally, for those who are not satisfied with merely keeping pace with today's developments, Part IV provides a very brief glimpse into the future of Open Systems. Much work is currently being done in the International Organisation for Standardization (ISO) and the International Telegraph and Telephone Consultative Committee (CCITT). In March 1988 a new ISO Working Group was formed to create a reference model for distributed processing, formally called the Reference Model of Open Distributed Processing. Much, if all goes as planned, will be accomplished by the standards committees over the next three to five years.

Examples from everyday life can be a powerful way to illustrate OSI concepts and functions. For this reason the "telephone application" will be used for purposes of comparison. Despite its size and extensive use of networking, the real telephone system was not designed with OSI in mind and does not presently use OSI protocols. A second example, a simple credit card authorization, has also been selected as being representative of a typical computer transaction that *could* (but typically, again, does not) make good use of OSI services. Although these examples will break down if pushed to their limits, they do provide a very familiar context for most readers and can make some of the complexities a little less intimidating.

The following brief introductions to the examples serves to "set the scene" for their use in the remainder of the book.

1.1 THE TELEPHONE AS AN EXAMPLE OF OPEN COMMUNICATIONS

The telephone application provides the service of interconnecting two or more parties who wish to exchange "voice information" (i.e., two people who want to talk to each other). It is a highly distributed application that is potentially spread across a variety of resources in the "telephone system." The telephone system is nonstop, highly available, and typically boasts a very high quality of service (at least in Canada). The telephone itself acts as the interface between the person and the network (both of whom perform telephone application functions).

Telephones are available virtually everywhere, and are considered "open" because of their basic compatibility. Various physical resources are used in telephone systems (telephone sets, branch exchanges, answering devices, twisted copper wire, etc.), each of which contributes to the realization of the overall telephone application. Public and private telephone systems usually interconnect, as can systems of differing vintage or manufacture. The complete telephone system can be viewed as comprised of networks, switching devices, interface devices, and people.

The telephone system is a good example of a large-scale system that is multivendor, multiadministration, and multinational. Standards (although not OSI-based) have been instrumental in achieving low-cost, global connectivity among the users of the telephone system.

The telephone example, as defined for this book, is a simple two-party call. It involves a calling party (the caller, a person) who wishes to talk (exchange voice information) with a called party (another person). The caller chooses whom to talk to, initiates the call, and controls the progress of the resulting conversation.

The calling party makes a call by creating a "connection" to a called party. This connection, which exists for the duration of each call, is established first by taking the telephone off the hook, then by dialing a number that represents the telephone assigned to the called person (the presumed location of the person), and finally by saying "Hello" to the person who answers.

The person answering a telephone call may or may not be the called party (e.g., a secretary may intercept calls or an answering machine might be operating). It may even be necessary to call a common number and then to request an extension to reach the desired person. Thus, the correct telephone number does not guarantee the right connection.

Once a connection has been established between the desired parties, a conversation is possible. The parties most often know in advance what language to speak (in OSI terms, this is a preestablished "transfer syntax"). If they do not, a negotiation generally takes place (either explicitly or implicitly, through the first few words that are spoken) to determine if some acceptable language is available to both parties. When a language has been chosen, a meaningful conversation is possible—although often not guaranteed! Various topics may be discussed, sometimes using the same words in different ways. For example, the meaning of a word used in a casual conversation is often quite different from that of the same word used in a legal sense.

A conversation ends when either party hangs up the telephone (or occasionally, when a failure or severe degradation in quality of service occurs).

The following steps illustrate the use of the telephone system for the purposes of our example:

	Calling Party (M = Me)	Called Party (Y = You)
1.	M decides to call Y.	
2.	M may consult directory. M lifts the phone off hook. M checks for dial tone.	
3.	M dials the number for Y.	
4.		Telephone rings.
5.		X answers: "Hello, X speaking."

6.	*M* says: "Hello *X*." *M* confirms language of *X*. *M* asks: "Is *Y* there?"	
7.		*X* answers: "Yes, please hold."
8.		*Y* says: "Hello *M*."
9.	*M* confirms that it is *Y*. *M* confirms language of *Y*.	
10.	*M* initiates subject "1."	
11.		*Y* agrees to subject "1."
12.	*M* starts conversation.	*Y* starts conversation.
13.	Steps 10 to 12 are repeated for all desired subjects, with mixing of subjects and languages during the conversation if needed.	
14.	*M* asks: "Is that all?"	*Y* confirms: "Yes, that is all."
15.	*M* says: "Good-bye."	*Y* says: "Good-bye."
16.	*M* hangs up.	*Y* hangs up.

1.2 BANK CARD AUTHORIZATION AS AN EXAMPLE OF OPEN COMMUNICATIONS

Validating the identity of the holder of a bank card (the Cardholder) and determining restrictions on usage is a common business requirement in a banking environment. This type of transaction is usually called a Card Authorization Message and is normally combined with other messages in a point-of-sale credit application.

Card Authorization, which provides a good example of an application where interenterprise computer communications is essential, should be familiar to most of us. Since many banks must implement the same function and must cooperate to perform the task, considerable economies can result from standardization. ISO 8583 is the existing international banking standard that specifies the user messages required for bank card applications, including Card Authorization.

In a banking environment the Card Issuer "owns" and takes responsibility for cards that have been issued to its customers. The customer may use the card at a merchant or automated banking machine (the Card Acceptor) that is administered by another bank (the Card Acquirer) (see Figure 1.1). Hence, banks need to communicate for the purpose of authorizing the use of the card.

A Card Authorization occurs when a Card Acceptor (e.g., at the point-of-sale terminal) requests permission to proceed with a transfer of funds from

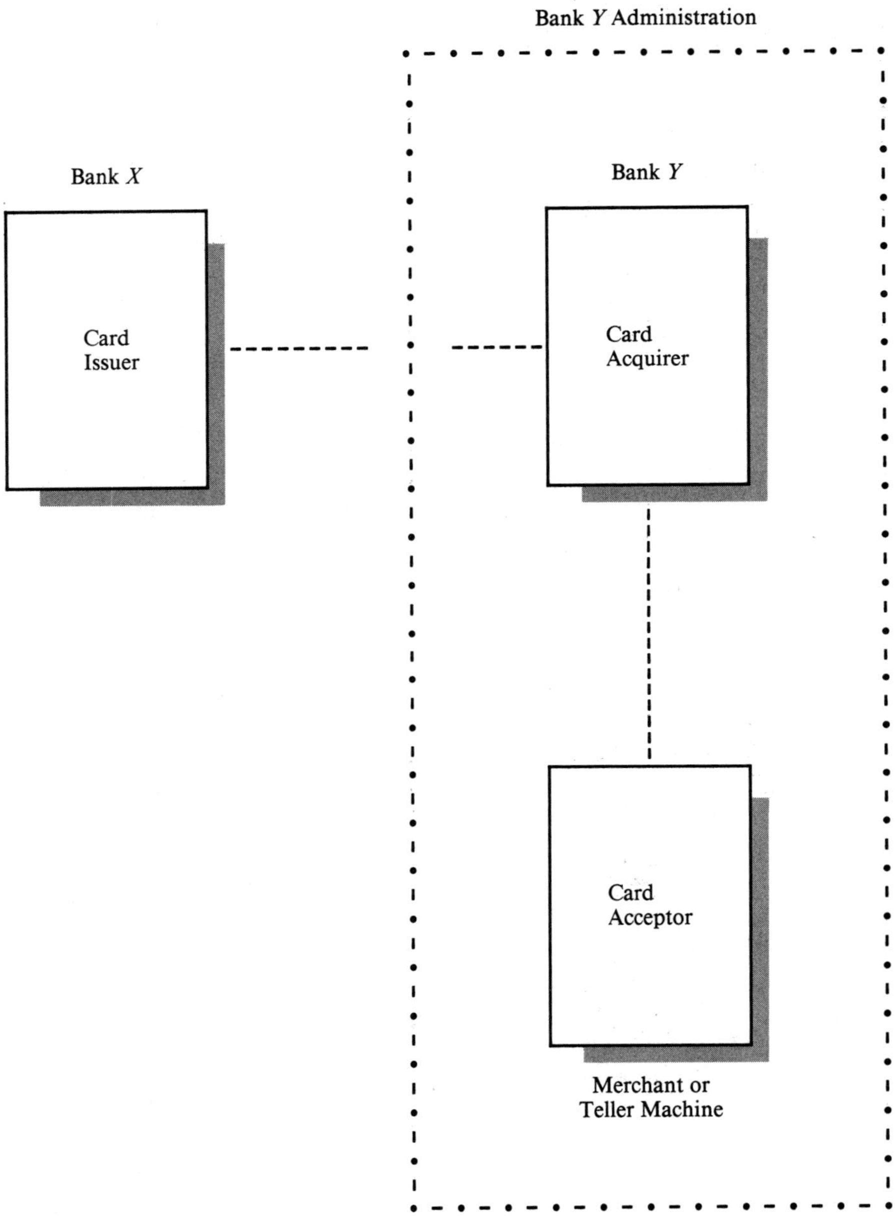

Figure 1.1 Bank card application.

the Card Issuer to the Card Acquirer. This request is generally routed through the retailer's bank (the Card Acquirer) prior to reaching the Card Issuer. A very simple interchange occurs: An Authorization Request is sent to the Card Issuer, and an Authorization Response is returned.

The following steps illustrate a Card Authorization activity for the purposes of our example:

	Cardholder	Card Acceptor	Card Acquirer	Card Issuer
1.	Present card.			
2.		Read stripe. Send request.		
3.			Forward request.	
4.				Receive request. Check account. Send reply.
5.			Receive response.	
6.		Receive response. Take action.		
7.	Remove card.			

CHAPTER 2

THE ROOTS OF OSI

Any introduction to OSI should begin with a historical perspective. This chapter provides a bird's-eye view of the problems OSI was intended to solve, identifies what makes OSI necessary and important, and suggests why things have turned out as they have.

Even though OSI was born and bred in the standards community, it has responded directly to the requirements of users and manufacturers. As is true for most technologies, change is a fact of life, with the tendency being toward increased complexity and greater sophistication. Communications technologies are no exception to this trend; OSI has served as a framework not only to harmonize and coordinate developments but also to accelerate the rate of change.

An understanding of standardization processes is also desirable. OSI is the product of a voluntary organization based on committees and consensus. This has an impact on the results and affects how progress is made.

Placing OSI in context will help to suggest answers to questions like these: *What* was the motivation for OSI in the first place? *What* is OSI expected to achieve? Is it headed in the right direction?

2.1 WHY DID OSI HAPPEN?

It can be said that OSI is the inevitable outcome of the digitization and computerization of business systems that has been happening since the 1960s. OSI may, for some observers, be primarily a reaction to the computing Tower of Babel that has resulted from an unregulated and highly competitive industry. On the other hand, OSI may become the "marriage certificate" in the long-forecasted marriage of computers and telecommunications.

Computers and networks are mutually supportive:

- Networks allow computers to send and receive the information they process and store.
- Processing components embedded in a network have become essential to the operation of high-speed, high-function integrated digital networks.

Optimizing the overall use of resources and managing the changing cost trade-off of processing versus communications versus storage is leading toward portable applications, distributed storage and function, and network-based operating systems. A gradual shift is occurring in the style of communications, as is illustrated by Table 2.1.

Nolan (*Harvard Business Review*, March/April 1979) identified six stages of growth in the corporate data processing function. An analogous model (illustrated in Table 2.2) can be postulated for the growth of the data communication function. This model identifies six stages in the evolution of corporate communications: from individual, independent physical circuits to an integrated, corporate-wide network utility.

For many companies the Initiation Stage (stage 1) for data communications occurred in the mid-1960s. Small numbers of data circuits were installed, primarily for connecting to Telex, teletype, or dumb terminals. Intercomputer communications did not exist. During this period little effort and no management attention was paid to planning, organizing, and operating the data communications facilities.

The early 1970s was an entrepreneurial period. It was a time of rapid expansion in the need for networking, the technical capabilities, and the number of incompatible products. The Contagion Stage (stage 2) can be characterized as a period of rapidly increasing costs, a lack of skilled personnel, and too many options. During this period, communications became a business and competitive issue, even though many people refused to believe it.

Table 2.1 The Evolution of Networking

Early Networks	Today's Networks
Small numbers of nodes	Large numbers of nodes
Single vendor	Multivendor
Few processing resources	Many processing resources
Large host, dumb terminal	All devices intelligent
Central control	Dispersed management
Internal to corporation	Interenterprise
National or local	Global
Periodic shutdown of services	Nonstop operations
Bandwidth dedicated	Bandwidth shared

Table 2.2 Stages of Communications System Growth

Stage of Development	Architecture	Management	Planning
1 Initiation	Individual circuits Point-to-point	No focus or attention Few trained personnel	None, carrier provided Reactive, Disjointed
2 Contagion	Many separate circuits	No automation	Individual plans for each application
	Various applications	Minimal control	Reactive, Disjointed
3 Control	Circuit consolidation Route optimization	Network control centers Test and support tools	Budgets and forecasting Tactical plans
4 Facility integration	Several, incompatible Bandwidth sharing	Network management centers Network administrative applications	Integrated planning Project management
5 Network resource administration	Uniform architecture Resource integration	Some network operations	Strategic and tactical planning
6 Integrated network utility	Uniform architecture Information integration Distributed/nonstop	Integrated, automated network management	Strategic and tactical planning

The inevitable result of stage 2 was more interest and involvement at senior management levels, with increased focus on organizing and staffing the corporate data communications department.

During the Control Stage (stage 3) costs were carefully scrutinized, networks were optimized, project management was implemented, control centers were established, and separate budgets were created. Some companies went so far as to defer implementing an application if telecommunications costs were too high. This period of rationalization proved beneficial not only because good business management was brought to bear on communications, but also because many new opportunities for communication services were identified.

Early implementations of communications-based data processing applications were typically done on an ad hoc basis with little or no systems integration and no long-range planning. Business requirements were usually restricted to supporting internal operations (with some exceptions, such as airline and bank networks). A variety of communications control procedures competed to attain de facto standard status. International standardization for basic communications functions was started. Interconnection of different systems was a costly proposition, if it was possible at all.

Technology history books will probably list the 1970s as the era of the proprietary communications architecture. Implemented during this time were Systems Network Architecture (SNA) from IBM, Digital Network Architecture (DNA) from Digital Equipment Corporation, and Distributed Systems Architecture (DSA) from Honeywell (now Bull HN), and a variety of others. The business reasons that motivated each vendor to adopt a structured, layered approach to communications were probably different. SNA is said to have been originally created simply to reduce the number of communications access methods that IBM had to support. The results, however, were similar. Users were able to regain control of their networks, then began to move into the Facility Integration Stage (stage 4) without fear of technical obsolescence or disruptive change. This paved the way for the full-scale shared networks of the 1980s.

Stages 1 to 4 are indicative of a computer-centered view of systems. Communications is considered a support resource for an application (much like a disk drive or printer) and plays an invisible role. At its worst, communications became an afterthought in the design process.

The Network Resource Administration Stage (stage 5) marks the beginning of a transition toward a network-centered approach to systems thinking. The network begins to take on an existence independent of any individual application or user. This can be compared to the public services (such as packet switching or electronic mail) that are offered by the telephone companies. The transition from stage 4 to stage 5 is an important milestone because it marks the beginning of fully "architected" communications.

By the time stage 5 is reached, the complexities and pitfalls of operating a network are well known, the business dependencies are clear, and the major opportunities for profit have been recognized. Planning and architecting have become important tasks, and a corporate commitment to move to a unified and consistent network architecture has been obtained. External connections that allow customer and supplier access to the corporate network may also become a requirement at this stage. The pressure to develop applications to assist in managing the network increases, and there is a growing desire to integrate components from several vendors.

A fully integrated network, defined as the Integrated Network Utility Stage (stage 6), provides a powerful communications utility that is positioned to meet the needs of advanced forms of distributed data processing. At this level of maturity the integrated corporate network should, in normal circumstances, be transparent to its users and be taken for granted (as is the telephone network, for instance). Since no real network, even in stage 6, is unchanging and error free, facilities for planning, organizing, and operating the integrated network are essential and will have been implemented. This includes support not only for failure and configuration control but also for functions such as capacity, security, contingency, and directory management.

Movement to stage 6 is stimulated by an increasing need for multivendor, multiarchitecture, multienterprise, multiapplication interworking. Typical applications include factory automation, electronic mail, electronic funds, library automation, public database access, and trade data interchange (invoices, waybills, etc.), most of which involve interenterprise exchanges of information. An example of a high-level conceptual architecture for a stage 6 banking communication system is shown in Figure 2.1.

Stage 5 and 6 networks require continuous operations. From a management perspective, the size, complexity, and distribution of many stage 6 networks precludes having to shut the network down for administrative purposes. Using the telephone application as an example, can you imagine having to shut down all the telephones in a city (or in an office building) just to add a new telephone set? In information-intensive industries like banks, which use a delivery network for access to customer accounts, severe difficulties occur when the network is unavailable for any significant period of time. In fact, a bank could be out of business in less than a week if all communications were unavailable. In this case, the quantity and quality of network resources has a direct impact on the success of the business and therefore on bottom-line profits.

Stages 5 and 6 are only now starting to be realized for even the most advanced users, although specialized, custom-built networks have been available for many years. A stage 6 integrated network is where OSI becomes a critical success factor. The migration to stage 6 will provide many challenges for suppliers and users throughout the 1990s.

2.2 JUST WHAT *IS* OSI, ANYWAY?

Open Systems Interconnection is three things:

- It is a *vision* for the future of computer communications.

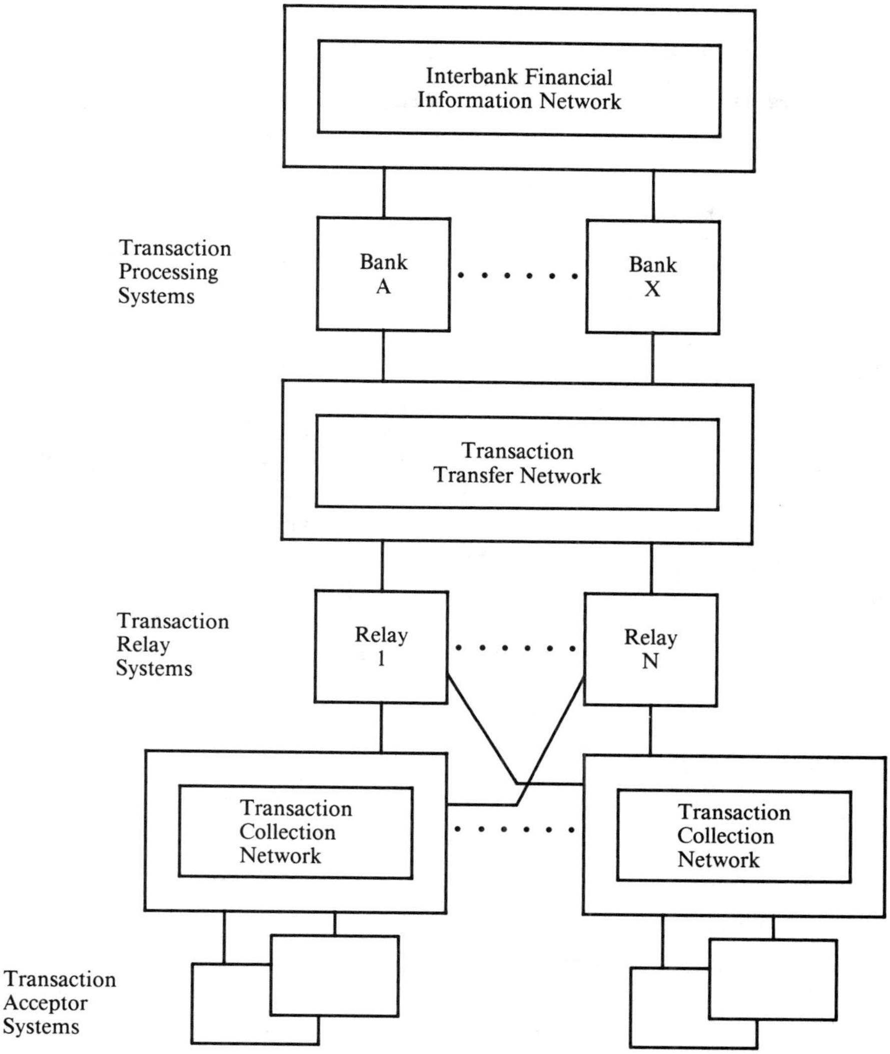

Figure 2.1 A stage 6 network for banking.

- It is a set of internationally accepted, openly developed *standards* that meet the needs of stages 5 and 6.
- It is a set of *products* that implement and conform to the standards.

OSI is the result of more than ten years of discussion, debate, and documentation in national and international standards committees. Millions of pages have been consumed in preparing the material and millions of man-hours of effort were contributed. Critics have questioned whether the results to date have lived up to the intentions and expectations, whether OSI standards will ever be finished, and whether the standards development process is efficient enough for ongoing development and maintenance of OSI.

The term *Open Systems Interconnection* has been adopted as the overall name for the set of standards for communications among computers that has been endorsed by the ISO and the CCITT. Each of the three words, *open, systems,* and *interconnection,* is significant and has special meaning in the world of OSI standards.

Formally speaking, anything qualifies as a *system* so long as it forms an "autonomous whole capable of performing information processing and/or information transfer." This is a small restriction: A system can be a single microprocessor (in a microcircuit card or an intelligent toaster, for example), or it can be a complete data processing installation. Needless to say, there will in practice be some lower limit to the size and capabilities of machines that can participate in providing OSI communications services.

Open can be applied as a qualifier when accepted nonproprietary standards (from the ISO, CCITT, or International Electrotechnical Commission [IEC]; see section 2.4) are used. This means that any system must be able to create, transmit, receive, and act upon OSI messages (as defined by the standards) in order to qualify as an open system. Although the term "open" originally applied only to OSI communications standards, it has recently become popular to apply it to other areas as well (Unix-based portable operating systems and text communication and graphics standards are examples). The principle of "openness" is gradually expanding to include the use of standards in all areas of information processing.

The *interconnection* of systems using OSI standards involves four major types of activity:

- The movement of digitized data over physical transmission media in a reliable manner
- The organization and control of the paths between those open systems that are the sources and destinations of information
- The exchange of commands and data to manage the cooperation of the systems and the user applications that desire to interwork to achieve a specified purpose
- The provision of a variety of services and facilities that directly support the user applications.

For convenience, we refer to the set of user-visible services that OSI products implement as the *OSI Communication Service.* It is these services that supply, to a business application, a rich variety of functions and features to assist in the task of distributed processing and information management. The OSI Communication Service can be viewed as providing "value-added" telecommunications.

The primary purpose of all OSI standards is to specify *protocols* that realize the services that have been defined at each of the layers of the OSI architecture (see Chapter 3). These protocols, working together, produce the OSI Communication Service. They can be compared (loosely) to the procedures we all follow when using the telephone (one person speaks at a time, we both speak English, I dial the number, etc.).

2.3 IS OSI REALLY VIABLE AND VALUABLE?

There is no longer any doubt that OSI will take its place in the telecommunications engineer's toolkit—too many public commitments have been made and too many products exist for it simply to fade away. The lingering question, of course, is the degree to which OSI will become pervasive. Although the "wired world" may still be a dream, OSI has the potential to make it realizable.

Much has been said and written about the Information Revolution, the so-called Third Wave, and the changes that society will face. Computers and communications will be the basic tools of this new era. Clearly, many opportunities for profit will be available for those who are ready. On the other hand, many companies will survive only if they can keep up with the times, and the times will certainly change faster than ever before. OSI provides a stable basis for placing these rapid changes into context, for evaluating the benefits of alternative solutions, and for protecting previous investments.

It can be claimed that there is virtually no business or personal activity that is not, in some way, dependent on communications. Computer and communication system "literacy" has become essential if people are to understand and exploit the capabilities of the tools they use. The OSI Reference Model provides a common framework for providing this knowledge. One only has to look at how the telephone has changed the face of business in the twentieth century to realize the potential impact of a worldwide "information-phone" service. Who could survive without knowing how to use a telephone these days?

Many users have recognized the value of promoting their requirements to manufacturers, carriers, and the standardization bodies so that industry-wide agreements can be reached that are relevant and practical. Any serious commitment to the use of electronic business data makes it necessary to be familiar with and plan for new developments in communications. OSI standards provide the ability to evolve and change without completely starting over every time the "technology yardstick" moves forward.

The interconnection of real systems involves cooperation among computing and communication resources that may have been produced by different manufacturers, use different technologies, be subject to different laws and regulations, be distributed geographically, and be influenced by different political constraints. Even though achieving fully interconnected systems in such a complex environment is difficult, it is becoming an increasingly important requirement and is one of the reasons that OSI was created.

OSI's most significant contribution to the advancement of communications technology is its nonproprietary orientation. OSI does not belong to any single organization or country that could profit by withholding access to information or limiting availability. OSI standards constitute international "treaties" that are destined to pave the way for global systems connectivity and to eliminate today's computing Tower of Babel.

Even though the focus of communications developments for many organizations continues to be the conversion to a uniform architecture, others have started to manage their use of communications from a global perspective. Some of the reasons for progressing to stage 5 (Network Resource Administration; see Table 2.2) and beyond, using OSI as a basis, include:

1. Business requirements
   a. The characteristics of the information to be transferred, the quality of the transmission media, and the needs of the communicating parties must all be considered when designing a communication system. A sound foundation, like that provided by OSI, improves the effectiveness of planning and development tasks. The generic services available using OSI minimize the need for custom development and reduce the investment in unique, one-off solutions.
   b. Tremendous growth in interenterprise (company-to-client) communications will occur over the next decade. Electronic Data Interchange (EDI) using OSI is expected to eliminate much routine paperwork (invoices, purchase orders, and so on). Since one company, no matter how large, cannot dictate how the rest of the world should build systems, open standards become the lowest common denominator.
   c. The demand for instantaneous information will result in a telephone-like proliferation of computer systems. Since information that is available but not accessible is a lost opportunity and a wasted asset, communications is critical to the successful adoption of distributed computing.
   d. Other business benefits of OSI include:
      - Reduced procurement costs
      - End system independence
      - Increased freedom to change and expand
      - Multinational, multiadministration consistency
2. Technical opportunities
   a. New technologies generally add functionality, improve the quality of a service, or reduce costs. The ability to deploy new services rapidly, to incorporate improvements without making existing investments obsolete or disrupting operations is especially important for a growing, evolving business.

b. Technical decisions have effectively become business decisions. A general objective is to reduce complexity, to eliminate the need for special purpose developments or resources, and to make maximum use of a small number of components. OSI masks much of the process of communicating from the end user and provides a suite of common services for use as "building blocks."

c. OSI has become the enabling technology for distributed systems. It will become a "distributed operating system" that allows information and computing resources to be shared without having to consider geographical implications.

d. OSI was conceived with the intent to accommodate various technologies. This was essential if no single vendor was to achieve any significant competitive advantage, but it has also ensured extensibility, flexibility, and tailorability.

e. The use of standards, by their stabilizing influence, can help to minimize the financial and technological exposure of users who are investing heavily in hardware and software for computing. OSI provides a stable base on which users can build applications and to which manufacturers and service providers can reference implemented products.

f. Properly designed protocol standards facilitate interoperation of various hardware, software, and network types. This allows equipment and services to be acquired more competitively. The commonality of this equipment is maintained across national borders, which improves the ability to assemble international networks with little or no national variation.

Given the move toward OSI-based stage 5 and 6 communication systems, what are the major user requirements for the 1990s? The following provides a brief summary of major trends for the larger communications users:

1. *Functionality:* Networks are becoming much larger and more complex. Many new functions are required for the management and protection of network resources, for the establishment of network operating systems, and for the support of distributed processing. Uniform services must be available from a wide range of systems. Ideally, the presence of networks should be invisible to the user.

2. *Integration:* The stage 4 introduction of proprietary architectures has led to multiple independent networks. These are complex sets of hardware and software that require significant development and operations expertise. The creation of a "network utility" would eliminate these differences. Integration of the old with the new is an obvious requirement.

3. *Management:* The most important requirement, perhaps, is network management. Communication systems, having become essential to the corpo-

ration, can no longer be treated as technical toys. Good management is essential if the communications resource is to be used to the corporation's best advantage. In this respect there is no longer any difference between voice, data, text, or image communications.

4. *Capacity:* Increased size means increased load and consequently increased use of resources. Unless efficiency can be increased, this translates directly into higher costs and more problems. A communication system requires both media and processing capacity. OSI increases the amount of processing associated with the network but improves the utilization of the media and decreases the need for specific programming for each application.

5. *Size:* Networks are getting bigger. For instance, integrated office systems could result in "one workstation per person" for many enterprises. Another example, in banking, is the move from terminals only in branches to automated banking machines, point-of-sale devices, and home banking, leading to a tenfold increase in device population. The direction is towards more dynamic systems configurations: Not all workstations will be owned by the company, processing will be carried out at the most appropriate location (which could change from day to day), and operations will need to be nonstop.

2.4 HOW DO OSI STANDARDS GET PRODUCED?

OSI is very definitely a product of the "standards industry," which makes creating OSI an arcane and mysterious process to most people. Knowing how OSI standardization works can help in understanding its strengths and weaknesses. The following section provides an overview of the organizations and procedures involved. It should be noted that what is described is the current situation; there have been several reorganizations over the past ten years and more are bound to occur.

2.4.1 The Organization of OSI Development Work

The ISO and the IEC recently joined together to advance standards in the area of information technology. They established a Joint Technical Committee (called JTC1) to guide the work, including that related to OSI. Three subcommittees have particular relevance to OSI: SC6 (Telecommunications and Information Exchange Between Systems), SC18 (Text and Office Systems), and SC21 (Information Retrieval Transfer and Management for OSI). Figure 2.2 provides a more detailed organizational structure for committees involved in OSI development. The key point is that all of this work is performed on a voluntary basis.

The CCITT has also been fully involved in the development of OSI. It is a branch of the International Telecommunications Union, a United Nations Treaty organization whose members include most of the world's telecommunications service suppliers. The CCITT and ISO have closely aligned their

JTC1

- SC1: Vocabulary
- SC2: Character Sets and Information Coding
- SC6: Telecommunications and Information Exchange Between Systems
  - WG1: Data Link Layer
  - WG2: Network Layer
  - WG3: Physical Layer
  - WG4: Transport Layer
- SC7: Software Development and System Documentation
- SC11: Flexible Magnetic Media for Digital Data Interchange
- SC13: Interconnection of Equipment
- SC14: Representation of Data Elements
- SC15: Labels and File Structure
- SC17: Identification and Credit Cards
- SC18: Text and Office Systems
  - WG1: User Requirements and Management Support
  - WG3: Document Architecture
  - WG4: Procedures for Text Interchange
  - WG5: Content Architectures
  - WG8: Text Description and Processing Languages
  - WG9: User-System Interface and Symbols
- SC20: Data Cryptographic Techniques
- SC21: Information Retrieval Transfer and Management for Open Systems Interconnection
  - WG1: OSI Architecture
  - WG3: Database
  - WG4: OSI Management
  - WG5: Specific Application Services
  - WG6: OSI Session, Presentation and Common Application Services
  - WG7: Open Distributed Processing
- SC22: Languages
- SC23: Optical Digital Disks
- SC24: Computer Graphics
- SC47B: Microprocessor Systems
- SC83: Information Technology Equipment

Figure 2.2 ISO/IEC JTC1 committee structure. SC = Subcommittee; WG = Working Group.

efforts so that the set of ISO standards and CCITT Recommendations that have been produced are essentially identical.

Many countries have national standards organizations that mirror, to a greater or lesser extent, the international committees (ANSI in the United States, the Standards Council of Canada in Canada, BSI in the United Kingdom, and AFNOR in France are well-known examples). Other players include regional organizations like the European Computer Manufacturers Association (ECMA), professional organizations like the Institute of Electrical and Electronic Engineers (IEEE), and industry organizations like the Society for Worldwide Interbank Financial Telecommunications (SWIFT).

It has been said that standards committees are inefficient, often ineffective, and typically populated with "pretend experts." It is claimed that a small number of experts working together could do a better job in much less time at much less cost. What gets forgotten is the need for global acceptance of the results: Standards are as much "treaties" as specifications. So far, no alternative to the ISO/IEC approach has been found that simultaneously satisfies everyone's needs, maintains an open and public process, produces better results, and improves development efficiency.

2.4.2 The OSI Standardization Process

In 1977 the ISO, after several years of review, approved a New Work Item to develop a framework and set of standards for interconnection of computers of different types, technologies, and architectures. This event marked the beginning of the OSI movement, although few people realized at the time just how much would be accomplished over the next decade or where it would actually lead.

Not surprisingly, the "vision" of OSI originated in the ISO Data Communications Subcommittee (which at the time was designated TC97/SC6). Telecommunications engineers had been used to the idea of common standards (the telephone system has used standards for many years, for example) and packet switching (in the form of CCITT Recommendation X.25–1976) had just been completed. OSI was arguably the first real step forward in common standards for the data processing industry. The standards organization has evolved to the point where OSI work is split into SC6 (Telecommunications and Interchange Between Systems) and SC21 (Information Retrieval Transfer and Management for OSI).

Although production of a standard varies between the ISO and the CCITT, the ISO process is most relevant to understanding how OSI has grown and evolved. (This is illustrated in Figure 2.3.) ISO operates on the basis of a consensus among members of the relevant Technical Committee (TC), Subcommittee (SC), and Working Group (WG). New work is introduced by national bodies or through existing committees, and is voted on at the TC level. Approved work is assigned to an SC that will in turn assign it to an existing WG, or may set up a new WG, to perform the detailed study and development work. Work proceeds in these experts committees until a "stable" technical agreement is reached. The SC then votes on the standard as a Draft Proposal; the TC votes on it as a Draft International Standard; and finally the ISO Council approves the final International Standard. This process usually takes three to five years to run its course and has often been criticized as slow and ponderous. It does, however, ensure that a very wide audience has had an opportunity to agree (or disagree) with the results.

The CCITT, on the other hand, operates by unanimous approval and works in four-year cycles, during which existing standards, called Recommendations, are enhanced or modified and new ones are developed.

Many consortia and organizations have been formed to support and promote OSI implementation. These include the Corporation for Open Systems (COS) in the United States, the Canadian Interest Group on Open Systems (CIGOS) in Canada, and a variety of others. Their general purpose is to promote the use of OSI standards, to act as a focal point for new require-

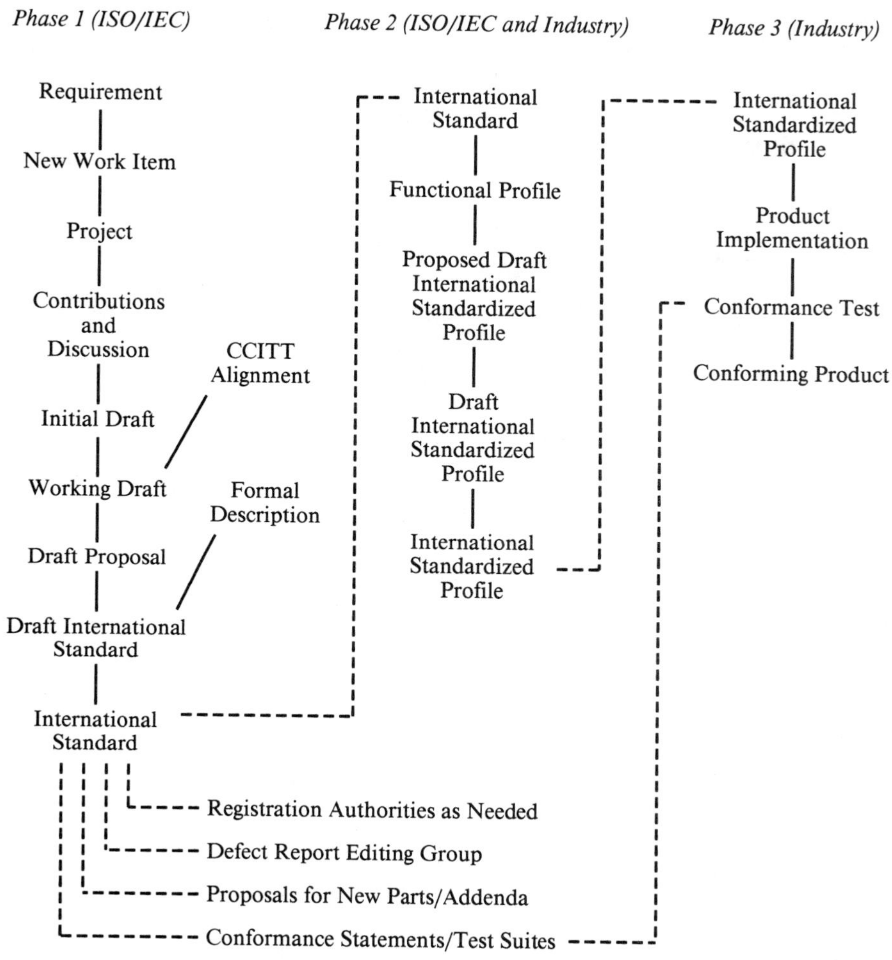

Figure 2.3 OSI standards development life cycle.

ments, and generally to provide support through functional profiles and conformance test capabilities.

Needless to say, all of this involves a tremendous cost in terms of people, paper, and travel. The whole process has been criticized as being overly cumbersome, but it has stood the test of time and is continuously being tuned to meet members' needs. In fact, the ISO has proved to be an excellent example of international cooperation and understanding. There are more than 10,000 ISO standards in some 200 different areas.

PART I

CONCEPTS AND ARCHITECTURE FOR OSI

CHAPTER 3

THE BASIC REFERENCE MODEL

A set of technical terms and concepts are the foundation for the OSI layered architecture. Agreement on this set of basic concepts, achieved in the early 1980s, was one of the first milestones in the quest for the OSI "wired world." A knowledge of this vocabulary and an appreciation of the concepts is a prerequisite for any detailed study of OSI services and protocols.

The primary references for this chapter are ISO 7498-1 (which is equivalent to CCITT Recommendation X.200–1984), the addendum for connectionless data transfer, the errata sheet, the register of interpretations, and the technical report covering service conventions (TR 8509). The more recently approved parts of ISO 7498 covering Naming and Addressing, Management, and Security are the subject of Chapter 4. Readers who are fully familiar with these references may wish to proceed directly to Chapter 5.

> Note: Major standards will be highlighted at the beginning of the chapter in which they are explained. A more complete list of standards, with formal ISO titles, is included in Appendix II. Complete consistency among all the standards has yet to be achieved and, in some cases, definitions are expanding to reflect more recent agreements. Some minor variations in terms from those of the references will occur in this book.

Our first definition is of the term *information processing system* (IPS). An IPS is considered to be any combination of hardware, software, and physical media that performs applications on behalf of its users. In general an IPS may be centralized or distributed, large or small, embedded or standalone, fixed or portable—whatever is needed—so long as it includes one or more applications.

3.1 MODELS, SERVICES, AND PROTOCOLS

Four levels of description are used in OSI standards: The reference model, specific models, service descriptions, and protocol specifications. Descriptions can be informal (normal English language) or formal (using formal description techniques; see Chapter 12).

Since an International Standard can be viewed as a specialized form of treaty, the different levels of description are a way to achieve stepwise development of this treaty. Discussions and agreements naturally proceed from the global to the specific—from models to service requirements to detailed protocols in the case of OSI. This progression is mirrored in the contents of the resulting standards. It is important at each level not to overspecify the standard; otherwise, consensus will be difficult to reach in a reasonable time and implementations are likely to be overly constrained.

3.1.1 Reference Models

A *reference model* defines a vision—a strategic outline—for a major area of standardization, such as communications, databases, and distributed processing. It specifies, in general terms, the scope of the standardization effort and describes the basic structures and mechanisms that will be used in all related standards.

The fundamental purpose of a reference model is to reduce the degrees of freedom given to standards developers. As the most basic level of agreement, a reference model should make clear most of the concepts and structures that will be needed to ensure the success of further developments.

In the Reference Model of Open Systems Interconnection (or OSI Reference Model for short) one of the most basic concepts is the hierarchical layering of functions. The OSI Reference Model defines precisely seven layers and outlines the structure that each layer must follow. It is an "abstract" model, which means that it is intended as a descriptive tool, not an implementation specification or a physical configuration.

Initially, the OSI Reference Model was intended solely to guide and direct protocol developers. It was the first level of "treaty making" and served to minimize the chances of gross misinterpretations due to language or experience differences. As a side benefit, it helped to promote editorial and technical consistency among the various projects. Over time, however, it has become clear that reference models serve other purposes as well. For example, the OSI Reference Model has become an invaluable tool for training and education. It also provides a convenient, neutral basis for comparing the functionality of proprietary communication systems.

Reference models for systems, despite the esoteric-sounding name, are not unique to computer technology and can, in fact, be found in many areas. In most cases they are intuitive and so obvious as not to need explicit definition. Most of us, for instance, have an intuitive sense of the purpose, capabilities, and limits of the postal system; formal documentation of its purpose and function is seldom needed (although there is a growing desire among users for specifications of the quality of service!). The driving force for reference models is complexity: On-demand interaction among arbitrary computer applications in widely diverse computing environments has proved to be a very complex topic for which the benefits of a more rigorous design approach based on an explicit reference model are evident.

OSI was an early example of the application of abstract modeling to standards development. Its success with OSI has led to applications in other areas, including distributed processing, graphics, and databases (see Chapter 14).

It should be remembered, again, that a model is *not* real hardware and software; it does not specify an implementation or force a certain design direction. There is not, nor can there be, any formal conformance to a model. Suppliers who claim to conform to the OSI Reference Model (instead of the particular OSI protocols) are either misinformed or trying to confuse their customers.

3.1.2 Specific Models

Whereas a reference model defines a broad area for development of standards, a *specific model* provides further detail for a more limited area of standardization (such as a layer or a major function). A specific model is also a "high-level" description that is not implementable and has no conformance. A specific model is a further application of "stepwise decomposition" to the development of standards.

Examples of specific models that will be described in more detail later in this book include the internal organization of the Network Layer, the Application Layer structure, the virtual filestore for file transfer, the directory model, the message handling model, and the transaction processing model.

3.1.3 Service Definitions

The concept of a *service* is also fundamental to the world of OSI. Services are defined at multiple levels of detail, ranging from the overall service provided by OSI to the individual "service primitives," which are the smallest defined division of the service of a layer (that is, an "atomic service"). A view of the OSI model that highlights the hierarchical and recursive nature of OSI services is illustrated in Figure 3.1.

A *service provider* is the subsystem formed by a layer and all layers below it. The services of the service provider are always provided only to users in the layer directly above, resulting in a strict hierarchical layering. These services are precisely defined and accessible only through the service boundary between the adjacent layers. Thus, even though one layer is independent of another's internal operations, there is necessarily a heavy dependency on access to the services of the next lower layer.

Standards have been developed that provide a "service definition" for the services provided by each OSI layer. These can be thought of as an informal contract between the people developing the protocols for one layer and those who make use of them to support protocols for the layer above.

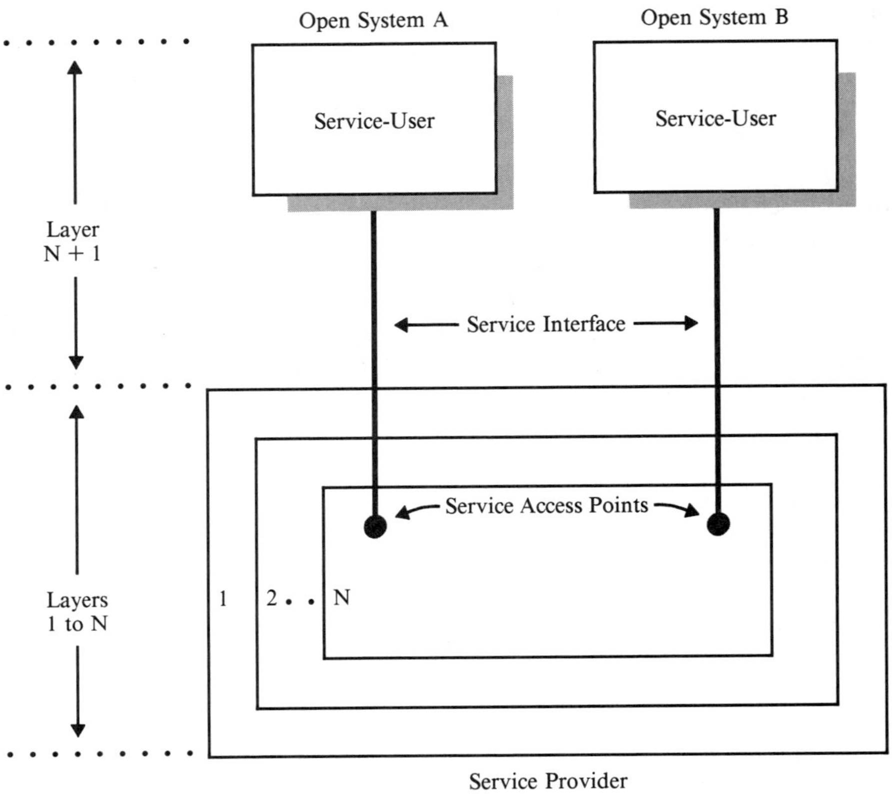

Figure 3.1 OSI service relationships.

Much discussion occurred during the early days of OSI as to whether there should be conformance tests for service definitions. It was agreed that there should not, because this would inhibit the freedom of the manufacturers and would require that the service be externally observable. This agreement notwithstanding, service definitions have proven to be very useful as the source of requirements for product developers.

3.1.4 Protocol Specifications

The goal of OSI standardization is to define unambiguously the "rules and regulations"—protocols—that govern interconnection and interworking among systems that must work together to realize a distributed system.

Protocols are complex multipart messages that are passed between the systems using physical media (copper wire, coaxial cable, fiber optics, and so on). The procedures for sending these messages, the format and meaning of each message (and combinations of messages), and the specification of the actions to be taken as a result are included in the protocol specification.

OSI protocols are, by definition, contained within a layer. Protocols are the aspects of OSI that are "visible" outside a system in the real world and are therefore subject to being tested for conformance (see Chapter 13). Figure 3.2 illustrates the peer-to-peer nature of OSI protocols.

3.2 A DEFINITION FOR OSI

Open Systems Interconnection, along with the acronym OSI, refers to the ISO standard approach to providing distribution transparency in an IPS. More simply, OSI standards permit the orderly, efficient, secure interchange of information among application programs executing in "real systems" that are cooperating to complete some user-specified activity.

"OSI" refers either to the standards themselves or to their use in products that are "open" for communications.

OSI standards include one reference model, a variety of specific models, service definitions and protocol specifications for all layers, common support applications, formal description techniques, a syntax notation, and conform-

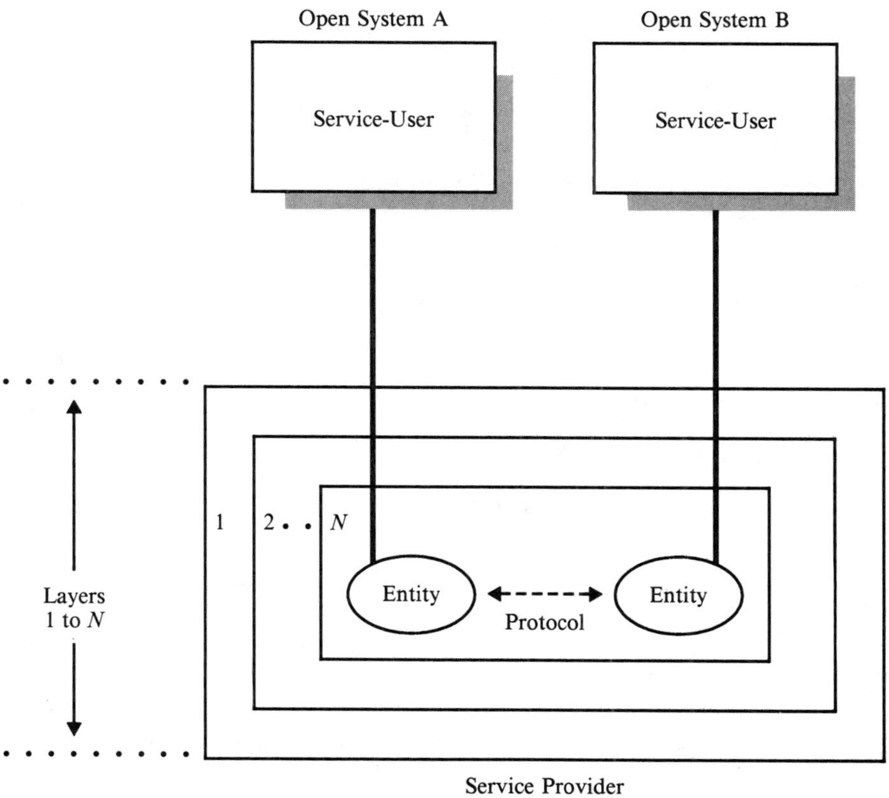

Figure 3.2 OSI protocol relationships.

ance test procedures. Recently, international standardized profiles have been added to this list (see Chapter 12).

A real system can be defined as follows:

> A set of one or more computers, the associated software, peripherals, terminals, human operators, physical processes, information transfer means, etc., that form an autonomous whole capable of performing information processing and/or information transfer. (ISO 7498–1984)

Again, the distinction between an open system, which is a component of the OSI abstract model, and a real open system, which implements and makes use of the OSI protocols, should be kept in mind. The OSI Reference Model is an abstract model that places no physical or logical constraints on the implementation, operation, or management of a real open system (except, of course, that it must use OSI protocols). The terms *system* and *real system* are used interchangeably in this book.

The implementation and use of OSI standards facilitates the exchange of information within an IPS. This is achieved when applications within the systems make use of OSI services. The information exchanged provides for control of the protocols, for OSI support services, and for information that is meaningful only to the user applications.

3.3 THE OSI ENVIRONMENT

The OSI Environment (OSIE) is where OSI happens. The OSIE is the name given to those resources in an IPS that participate in providing OSI services. It also refers to the abstract modeling representation of these resources (our preferred definition). Furthermore, it may even be used in the general sense as a name for all such resources in all open systems.

The OSIE consists of open systems and physical media. For all practical purposes, four assumptions can be made about the OSIE:

- At least two open systems exist.
- The open systems need to communicate.
- The open systems represent real systems that are able to process OSI protocols.
- Physical media exist that provide acceptable links between the real systems.

Resources in an IPS that are not used for OSI are said to be in the Local Systems Environment (LSE) (see Figure 3.3). Thus, OSI is more than a conceptual architecture but less than the complete business system.

Within the OSIE two classes of open system have been defined:

- End open systems are the source or destination of user information.
- Intermediate open systems serve as relays between separate physical media.

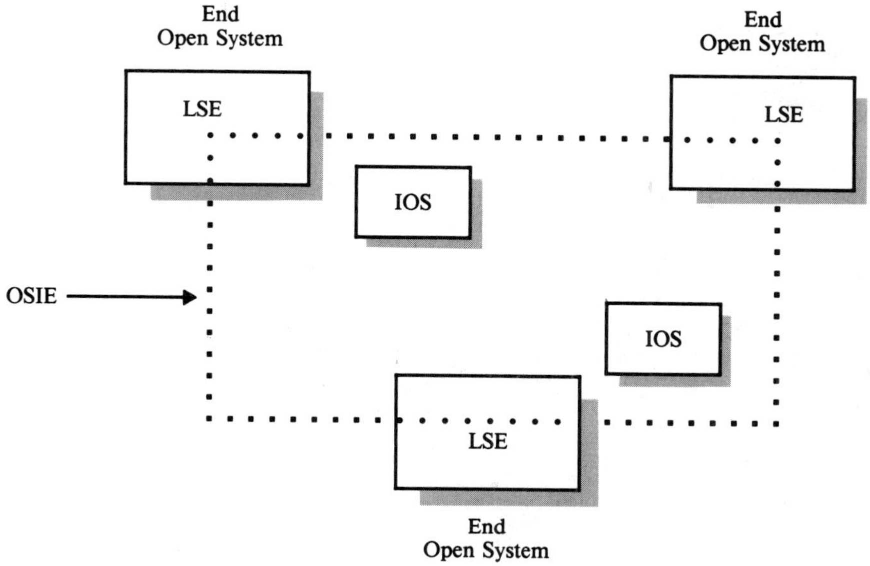

Figure 3.3 The OSI Environment. IOS = Intermediate Open System; LSE = Local System Environment.

Figure 3.4 illustrates how these basic elements of OSI are related from a distributed point of view. Again, it must be emphasized that this diagram is a modeling view that could be mapped into a wide variety of real system configurations. Additionally, it is a snapshot of interconnection "instances"; the situation in any real system will, at any given point in time, involve many active associations among many applications. Any real system that has the appropriate resources may perform the role of end open system or intermediate open system or both.

OSI is concerned only with those aspects of a system's overall operation that require information to be transferred to or received from other systems. Certain information must be known (or be accessible) for OSI communications to be meaningful.

In the description of OSI, the following concepts and terms are treated as givens:

- An *application* is a set of (possibly) distributed tasks that satisfy some real-world information processing requirement.
- An *application-process* is a subset of an application that resides in a single real open system.
- An *application-entity* is that part of an application-process that is concerned with interconnection (and is therefore the part that is visible in the OSIE).
- An *end open system* is an open system that contains application-processes.
- An *intermediate open system* provides routing and relaying functions (but does not contain application-processes).

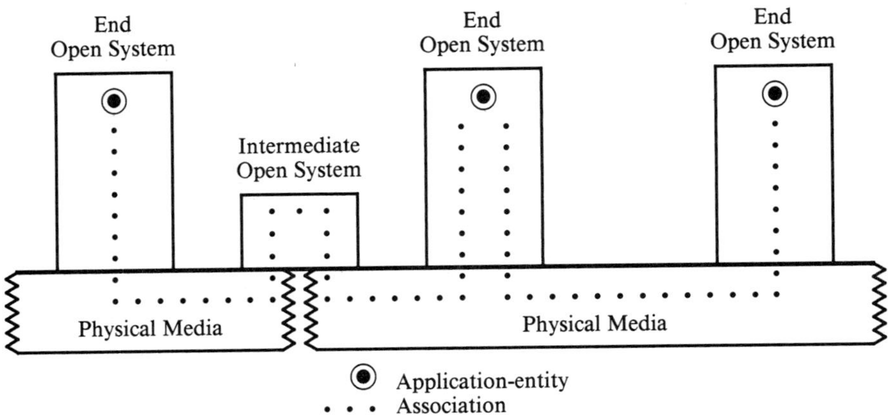

Figure 3.4 Basic elements of OSI.

- The *physical media* represent the actual telecommunications links between real open systems.
- An *association* represents the "partnership" between application-entities that need to communicate.
- *Names and addresses* exist that identify and locate resources in the OSIE (See Chapter 4).

It should always be remembered that there are two perspectives of things in OSI: the real view and the abstract view. In the real world physical circuits are connected to hardware that supports the execution of software programs. At any given instant of time some of these components will be operational and some will not; some will be communicating and some will not; some will be distributed and some will not. Only that which could be observed by "tapping into a physical circuit" (if that were possible) is of concern to OSI; everything else is simply the abstractions for describing OSI functionality.

3.4 CHOOSING THE SEVEN LAYERS

As would be expected, choosing the layers and naming them was not an easy task. The principle of layering was accepted from the beginning and has unquestionably stood the test of time. As an engineering approach, layering makes a lot of sense and provides a number of benefits. Layering can be used to make sure that all the standards work together, since the requirements of the layer above and the services available from below can be rigorously defined. Duplication of function (as happens when dissimilar systems are "lashed" together, using gateways) can be simplified or eliminated altogether. Since new technologies need not affect the interfaces, functions internal to a layer can change without disrupting the other layers. Finally, layering accommodates major political "borders," such as those between telecommunications suppliers and computer manufacturers.

The OSI Reference Model uses the concept of layering to "divide and conquer" the problem of systems interconnection. From a historical perspective this is no surprise: Modular software design was accepted practice by 1978, when work on OSI formally started. IBM's Systems Network Architecture, which was first announced in 1974, was described in layered terms. A practical motivation for layering of OSI protocols was simply to allow standards development projects to proceed in parallel.

One of the most important principles of OSI is the hierarchical ordering of the layers. Layer (N) can interact only with Layer (N+1) above and layer (N−1) below. While this may seem restrictive, it has not led to any insurmountable difficulties so far.

The OSI Reference Model defines basic concepts and structuring principles for the layers. These provide a common reference point for developers and permit much easier coordination across layers, while allowing refinements where necessary (such as in the Network and Application Layers). There is no requirement that actual implementations use the structure or even be layered, although there may be valid reasons for doing so in any given real system.

In developing the OSI Reference Model it was determined that seven layers of functionality are necessary and sufficient for open communications among application-entities. Three layers are needed to provide relay services. Figure 3.5 identifies each layer and indicates its relative position. Each of the layers will be discussed in more detail in Part II.

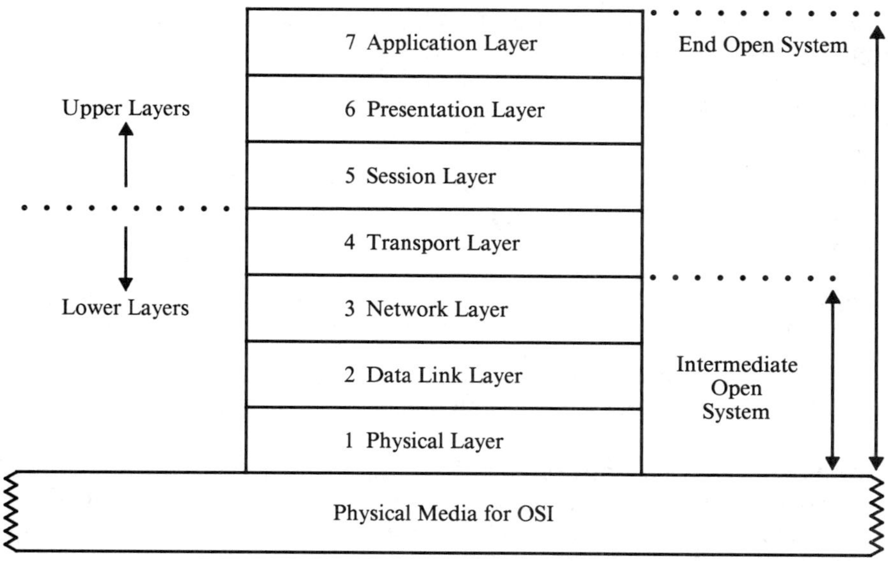

Figure 3.5 The OSI seven layer model.

A rationale for the choices made might proceed as follows:

1. There is clearly a need for an interface to the various physical media (a Physical Layer).
2. It was expected that packet switching (i.e., CCITT Recommendation X.25), which had been standardized by CCITT in 1976, would be an important part of OSI (hence, the Data Link and Network Layers);
3. The Transport Layer, the lowest end-to-end layer, serves to separate the responsibilities of the computer from those of the common carrier networks (and it guarantees whatever quality of service is required).
4. It was assumed that applications would require rules for "talking" to each other, and that these could be separately defined for common use (leading to the Session Layer).
5. Coding transformation functions were needed to ensure multivendor operation (since the ASCII and EBCDIC codings are well entrenched), and the ability to negotiate different codes became essential (leading to the Presentation Layer).
6. Finally, everything else was relegated to the Application Layer, which was called the boundary between OSI and the application.

Cooperation among open systems involves a broad range of information processing activities:

- *Interprocess communication* is concerned with the exchange of information and the synchronization of activity among applications.
- *Data representation* includes all aspects of the creation and maintenance of data descriptions and data transformations for reformatting the data exchanged between systems.
- *Data storage* concerns storage media, file systems and database systems for managing and providing access to data stored on the media.
- *Process and resource management* concerns the means by which applications are declared, initiated, and controlled and the means by which they acquire OSI resources.
- *Integrity and security* concern information processing constraints that have to be preserved during the operation of the systems.
- *Program support* concerns the definition, compilation, linking, testing, storage, transfer, and access to the programs executed in real open systems.

Providing communications support for these requirements clearly required various modes of communications, so it was known at an early stage that OSI would involve many standards with a variety of options. As we shall see, this has turned out to be a valid prediction.

Figure 3.5 illustrates an important subdivision of the OSI layers: the lower layers (Physical, Data Link, Network, and Transport); and the upper layers (Session, Presentation, and Application). The Transport/Session boundary marks the separation between those layers concerned with moving data and those concerned with interworking among application-processes.

In our telephone system example there is a similar separation of functions performed by the human (such as using the same language and not both talking at the same time) and those of the telephone network (such as setting up a call); the telephone set acts as the boundary between the two.

3.5 THE STRUCTURE OF A LAYER

One of the ways that the OSI Reference Model has been beneficial is its definition of concepts and structure for the layers. The elements of the layer structure (using the Transport Layer as an example) are illustrated in Figure 3.6. Some readers will observe that this layer structure does not seem to apply at the top, where there is no service user, and at the bottom, where there is no service provider. These boundary conditions will be discussed in Part II.

3.5.1 The Entity

The focal point of a layer is the entity, which is the representation in the OSI Reference Model of the "things at the end of a protocol." Entities exist within each open system. A single entity cannot be spread across more than one open system or layer, thus layer and system independence are preserved.

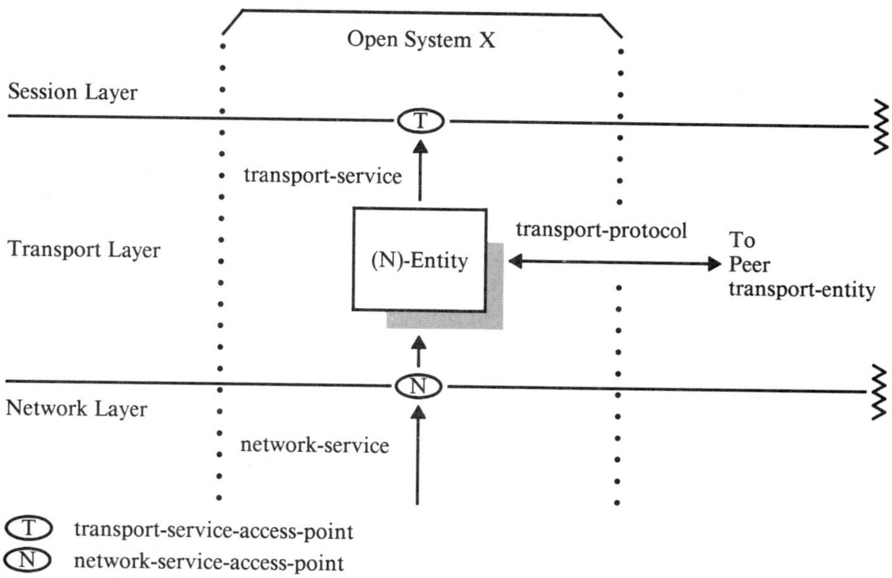

Figure 3.6 The structure of a layer (using the Transport Layer as as example).

An entity has two important aspects: types and invocations. An entity-type is a class of entities described in terms of a set of capabilities defined for the layer. A layer can be defined as the set of entities of a certain type (e.g., entity-type = transport). An entity-invocation is a specific utilization of all or part of the capabilities of a given entity.

As an example of this concept, the "telephone" is a device type, while the red telephone on your desk is an invocation of that type. OSI entities correspond in an undefined, implementation-dependent fashion to software in a real system that generates and responds to the protocol interactions of the layer.

An (N)-function is a part of the activity of an (N)-entity. An (N)-directory and (N)-address-mapping are examples of such functions.

Independence of layers is achieved by constraining protocol interactions to be strictly between entities (called peer-entities) in the same layer. Formally defined interfaces to the layer directly above and directly below ensure that changes in one layer do not affect adjacent layers.

3.5.2 The Service Primitive

An (N)-service is a capability of the (N)-layer that is provided to the (N+1)-layer. The (N)-layer creates these services using the services of the layer below if necessary. An entity in a layer may provide its services to one or more entities in the layer above (in the same open system) and may use the services of one or more entities located in the layer below.

A service consists of a number of elements of service called service primitives. Services can be of two types (confirmed or unconfirmed), depending upon whether or not the destination provides a reply to the sender's message. Four types of service primitive have been defined: request, indicate, response, confirm. These are illustrated in Figure 3.7.

3.5.3 The Service-Access-Point

(N)-services are made available at an (N)-service-access-point, usually abbreviated as (N)-SAP (transport-service-access-point, or TSAP, in the case of the Transport Layer). A SAP is the conceptual point of interaction between two layers within an open system. Relationships between entities in adjacent layers can be one-to-one or one-to-many (Figure 3.8). The SAP is an abstract modeling concept and is not meant to be a real physical location.

A SAP is a fixed reference point in the OSIE; its main purpose is to be an addressable point to which entities can be associated or "attached." Although the concepts of identifiers were included in the basic OSI Reference Model, the whole area of naming and addressing is now the subject of more detailed treatment in a refinement to the basic model. This topic will be reviewed in detail in Chapter 4.

Figure 3.8 illustrates how the SAP acts as the "point of attachment" for entities in two layers. The basic rule for a SAP is that it can be attached to only one entity in the layer above and one entity in the layer below at any

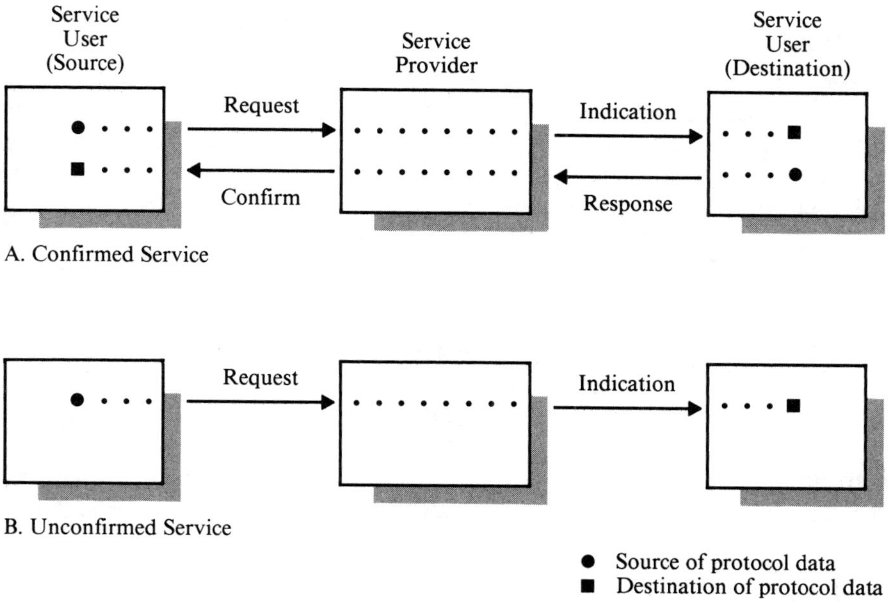

Figure 3.7 Types of service primitive.

given point in time. A SAP may be detached from its entities and reattached to the same or different entities.

3.5.4 The Protocol

In OSI terminology an (N)-protocol is defined as "a set of rules and formats (semantic and syntactic) which determines the communication behaviour of (N)-entities in the performance of (N)-functions." More than one protocol may be defined for a layer and used by an entity. Meaningful communica-

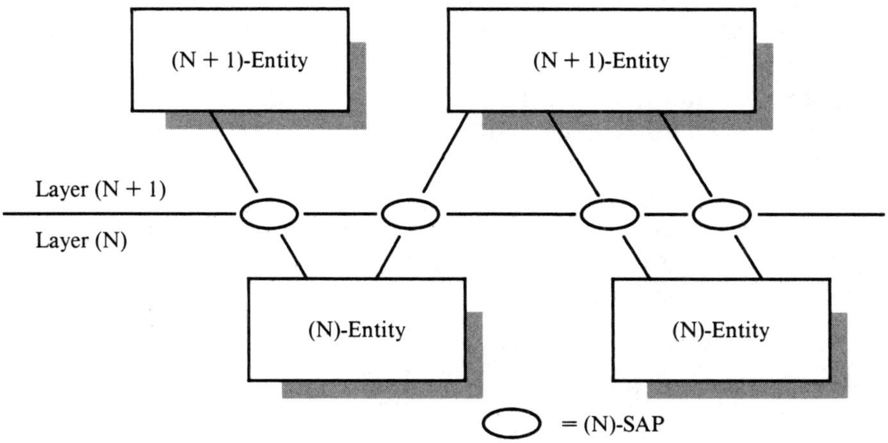

Figure 3.8 Entity relationships.

tion, however, requires that peer-entities agree on a single protocol to use for a particular instance of communication.

The characteristics of a protocol are determined by the functions it supports. In general, however, all protocols are used to transfer "user-data" on behalf of the entities in the layer above (the service users). OSI protocols typically operate between two entities. It is possible, however, to have protocols that operate with more than two entities.

3.6 UNITS OF DATA IN OSI

OSI provides the service of transferring data in such a way that the user need not be concerned with restrictions on the amount or form of the data that is to be transferred. This section describes the various transformations that can be performed on the data handled by OSI.

In the OSI world, data are described as flowing between peer-entities and between entities attached to a SAP. Needless to say, in the real world all data are actually transferred over the physical media as streams of bits.

3.6.1 General Concepts

Data in the OSIE consist of "data-units." There are two distinct views of these data:

1. *Interface-data-units:* Data passed between adjacent layers of an open system, in a single interaction across a SAP, are called interface-data-units (IDUs).

IDU	=	Interface-Control-Information (ICI)	Interface-data (Optional)

Interface-data are the data required to be transferred on behalf of the service user. Interface-control-information (ICI) is data that must be exchanged between adjacent entities to coordinate their joint operation.

A service-data-unit (SDU) is an amount of interface-data whose identity is preserved during a transfer between peer-entities. An SDU is deemed to be "expedited" if the layer ensures that it is never delivered after any subsequent SDU or expedited SDU. Expedited data may be used for signaling and interrupt purposes.

It should be noted that interchanges between adjacent layer entities, since they are local to a given open system, are not subject to standardization. Hence, the unit of data of primary concern to OSI is the SDU.

2. *Protocol-data-units:* Service-data-units are mapped onto one or more protocol-data-units (PDUs) for transfer between open systems.

PDU	=	Protocol-Control-Information (PCI)	User-Data (Optional)

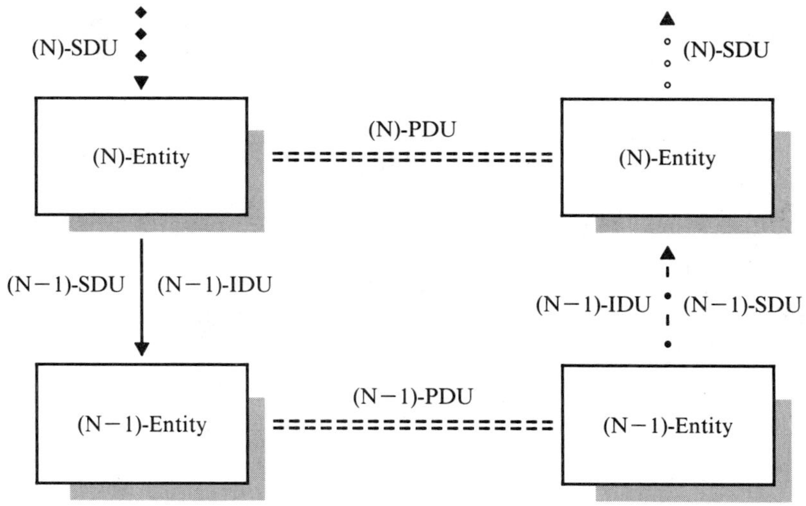

Figure 3.9 Data-unit relationships.

User-data are data that are to be transferred on behalf of the service users. Protocol-control-information is information that is passed between the communicating peer-entities to coordinate their joint operation. Note that the OSI model does not specify the positional relationships among user-data and control-information.

Figure 3.9 illustrates the relationships among data-units. Different symbols (◆ ● ○) have been used to indicate that data-unit sizes at different layers and locations can be different. In particular, an (N)-PDU may not necessarily be mapped on a one-to-one basis into an (N−1)-SDU.

3.6.2 Segmenting, Blocking, and Concatenation

Data-units in different layers may not be of compatible sizes for a variety of reasons (such as resource limitations). The OSI Reference Model defines various ways to map data-units into different sizes.

The following functions are defined for use when necessary:

1. *Segmenting/reassembling:* Segmenting is the division of SDUs into smaller pieces at the source entity in order to fit them into smaller-size PDUs. Reassembling at the destination entity is needed so that the SDU can be preserved.

$$1 \text{ (N)-SDU} \rightarrow 2 \text{ or more (N)-PDUs}$$

   PCI may be needed to allow reassembling of the segments at the destination.

2. *Blocking/deblocking:* Blocking is the joining of SDUs at the source entity in order to fill up larger-size PDUs. Deblocking at the destination entity is needed to reverse the operation.

   2 or more (N)-SDUs → 1 (N)-PDU

   PCI may be needed to allow deblocking of the SDUs at the destination.

3. *Concatenation/separation:* Concatenation is the mapping of multiple (N)-PDUs into an (N−1)-SDU. Separation identifies multiple (N)-PDUs contained in an (N−1)-SDU.

   2 or more (N)-PDUs → 1 (N−1)-SDU

3.7 OSI LAYER OPERATION

OSI layer operation involves the activation, operation, management and deactivation of entities. The purpose of an entity is to perform functions in such a way as to meet the service requirements of its users. An entity can seldom satisfy its users without the assistance and cooperation of other entities in the same layer. Entities enlist the help of other entities through the activation and operation of a protocol.

Normally, all layer operations are harmonized so that the overall OSI communication service can be provided.

To make use of the services, a calling application-process must first decide to communicate (for some business reason). Then it must decide which application-process it wants to communicate with, and must provide a name for it, perhaps obtained by querying a directory. Next, an association between the application-processes is requested. A negotiation of options and parameters occurs. After all of this is completed, the original goal of the user may be carried out. The whole structure may be released at the completion of the business activity. The similarities between this process and the steps in the telephone example are easily recognized.

3.7.1 The Process of Communicating

The process of communicating includes the transfer of user-data, the control of supporting operations that are performed, interpreting and acting according to the rules of the protocols, and the management of the resources needed to perform the tasks. OSI communications can occur only when there is a protocol actively operating between peer-entities in each of the seven layers.

The existence of a protocol operating between peer-entities in a layer defines an implicit relationship between them. Two specific types of protocol relationship, however, have been explicitly defined for OSI:

- *Connection-mode* involves an explicit setup and release of a "connection" as the logical transfer channel between the entities.

- *Connectionless-mode* involves the transfer of independent units of data without explicitly setting up a connection.

The service definition for a layer states what is being provided, not how it is accomplished. There are two ways to provide paths between end systems:

- *Direct association* between the two end open systems
- *Relaying* through an intermediate open system in which the entities route the data either immediately or in a store-and-forward fashion

Communication has two basic forms:

- *One-directional* transfer from the source system to the destination system
- *Two-directional* transfer between the systems

3.7.2 Connection-mode Operation

In connection-mode operation, the "connection" serves as an explicit relationship between communicating entities. An entity may have, simultaneously, one or more connections with other entities, with any given entity, and with itself. In more formal terms, an (N)-connection is an association established by the (N)-layer between two or more (N+1)-entities for the purpose of transferring data.

Connections are said to terminate at connection-endpoints, which are modeled as existing within SAPs. Although connections can, in theory, have multiple connection-endpoints (i.e., have more than two terminations), little progress has occurred in developing standards to accomplish this.

Figure 3.10 illustrates the concept of a connection and how it relates to layer entities.

Dynamic establishment and termination of connections allows many of the characteristics of the "invocation" of communication to be negotiated. It also allows resources to be allocated to a given user and reserved his use. The penalty, of course, is that these resources may not be used effectively if the transfer rates are low compared to the capacity of the connection.

In connection-mode operation, there are always three phases of protocol operation: connection establishment, data transfer, and connection release.

The first action, when communication is needed, is to set up a connection. An (N)-connection is created by referencing, either explicitly or implicitly, an address for the source and an address for each of the destinations (see Chapter 4). Entities may have multiple active connections, so there must be a way for an (N+1)-entity to identify one from another. This is accomplished through the use of connection-endpoint-identifiers (CEIs).

Establishment of an (N)-connection requires the ability to transfer data at the (N−1)-layer (and subsequently at all layers below), and both entities must be ready to execute the connection establishment protocol exchange. A connection may be released in an orderly or disruptive fashion. Release of a connection does not necessarily result in the release of lower layer connec-

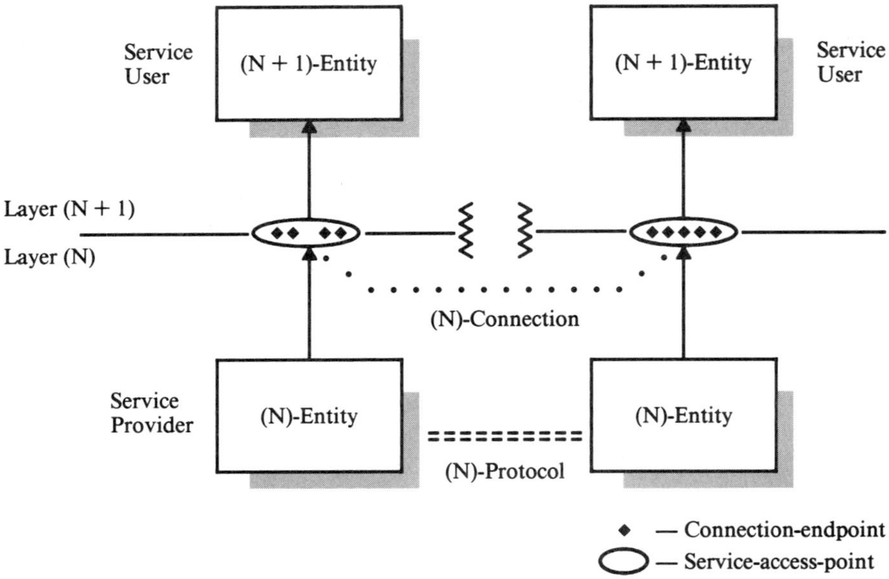

Figure 3.10 The connection.

tions. Orderly release may be immediate or delayed, according to whether data in transit are to be delivered prior to release.

User-data can be transferred as part of the connection establishment and release protocol exchanges. In this way the establishment/release functions for various layers can be combined together into a single request (see Section 3.7.3).

A connection provided by the (N)-layer makes use of lower layer services to effect the data transfer. An (N)-connection is mapped onto an (N−1)-connection in one of three ways:

- One-to-one
- Multiplexed (many-to-one)
- Split (one-to-many)

Multiplexing and splitting each involve a number of associated functions that may not be needed for one-to-one connection mapping. For instance, multiplexing requires the identification of the (N)-connection for each (N)-PDU to avoid mixing PDUs from various connections. Flow control is needed on each multiplexed connection.

3.7.3 Connection Establishment Through the Seven Layers

At first glance, the independence of layers and the potential need to establish connections at each layer would suggest that a large number of interactions are needed for "setting up" a full stack of OSI protocols. However, three methods for connection establishment across all seven layers have been identified:

- Layer-by-layer connection establishment
- Global connection establishment
- Half-global connection establishment

In the layer-by-layer approach, when the end user decides to communicate, it requests a connection with another user (called an application-association; see Chapter 7). This is turned into requests at each lower layer, resulting in establishment of connections from bottom up. As each layer is activated, it is able to transfer the connection establishment message for the next layer above as part of its user-data. In the best case, seven two-way exchanges are used to establish communication between application-processes. The results would be a long establishment delay. In the worst case, when negotiation would be required, the overheads could be much greater.

In the global approach, all connection requests are "bundled" into a single message by making use of the ability to add user-data to connection request messages. In the best case, this leads to only one round trip of messages.

In the half-global approach, all requests from the source system are bundled but the responses are transmitted layer by layer.

3.7.4 Connectionless-mode Operations

Connectionless-mode data transfer involves the transmission of a single unit of data from a source entity to one or more destination entities without establishing a connection. In contrast to connection-mode transfer, an instance of the use of a connectionless-mode service does not have a clearly distinguishable lifetime. In addition it has the following fundamental characteristics:

- It requires only a prearranged relationship between the peer-entities in the layer. This determines the characteristics of the data to be transmitted, and no dynamic agreement is involved in an instance of the use of the service.
- All the information required to deliver a unit of data—destination address, quality of service, options, etc.—is presented to the layer providing the connectionless-mode service, together with the data, in a single service access that is unrelated to any other access.

Each layer supports a single service, namely UNIT-DATA, which permits the transfer of a unit of data between peer entities.

In general, a connectionless-mode service does not guarantee that units of data will not be lost, corrupted, or delivered out of sequence. However, it is possible architecturally to incorporate segmentation, sequencing, acknowledgment, and error-handling functions within layers to lessen the probability that undesirable events will occur.

CHAPTER 4

REFINEMENTS TO THE BASIC OSI MODEL

The Basic Reference Model of OSI (Part 1 of ISO 7498) defined essential concepts and structures that were needed to start developing the layer service definitions and protocol specifications. It was well recognized at the time, however, that the development of an architecture is an iterative process and that not all aspects of the OSI architecture could be, or even needed to be, "cast in concrete" right at the beginning.

Three areas have subsequently received significant attention and have progressed to the point of becoming new parts of ISO 7498. These are Naming and Addressing, Management, and Security. Figure 4.1 attempts to place these parts of OSI into the context of the model and shows that each of these parts has an impact on all of the OSI layers.

4.1 OSI NAMING AND ADDRESSING

OSI communications would not be feasible if there were no means for open systems to identify and locate each other. The OSI Reference Model depends upon the ability of entities to interact and assumes that these entities can form relationships when required.

As an example of the need for names (identifiers) and addresses (locators), consider the telephone system example. In the telephone application, the calling and called parties have names but individual "applications" do not. The calling party usually knows the name of the called party but must obtain the correct telephone number, having been given it already or by using a directory. This telephone number is simply a name for the local loop where the called party is nominally located (extension telephones are not distinguished). The telephone can also be said to contain addressing information

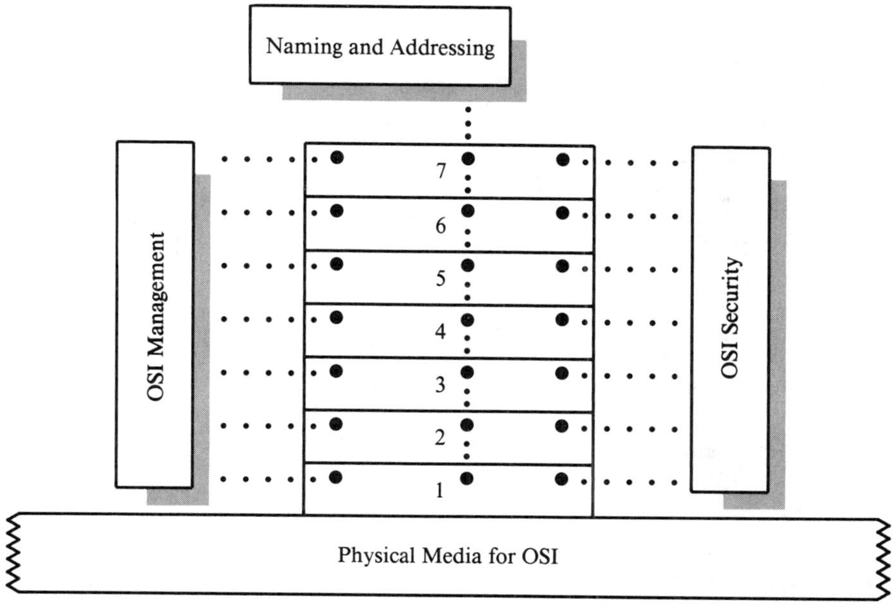

Figure 4.1 Refinements to the OSI Model.

given the geographic significance of the numbering scheme. Imagine what would happen if there were no telephone numbers, no telephone books, and no operators in the telephone system!

A name is a "linguistic construct" expressed in some language, used to identify an object. OSI names can be of two types:

- *Primitive names* identify just one object. Primitive names are assigned by a naming-authority (which is simply a source of names).
- *Descriptive names* consist of a set of assertions expressed in a formally defined language. Descriptive names may be complete (i.e., identify a single object) or incomplete (i.e., identify a set of objects). Primitive names may be a component of a descriptive name.

There are three classes of OSI name:

- *Titles* are names given to objects to identify them unambiguously. A title is descriptive in nature only; it does not identify the physical location of an entity. A title may be used to identify a system, an application-process, an application-process-type, an (N)-entity, or an (N)-entity-type.
- *Identifiers* are names given to objects where the purpose of the name is to discriminate only among occurrences of the object. Identifiers may identify an (N)-association, an application-process-invocation, or an (N)-entity-invocation.

- *Addresses* are names used to identify a set of one or more SAPs that are unique within the OSIE.

An OSI "global title" is an entity identifier that is unique within the whole of the OSIE. It has two parts:

Global Title	=	Title-Domain-Name	Local-Title

where

Title-domain = a subset of all OSI names (e.g., a layer)
Local-title = entity identifier unique within a title-domain

4.1.1 System Names

A *system-title* is a layer-independent primitive name.

4.1.2 Entity and SAP Names

Table 4.1 lists the various names associated with the entities of a layer. Service-access-points define conceptual (not geographic) locations within the OSIE. An (N)-address is the name of a set of SAPs in an open system, while an (N)-SAP-address uniquely identifies a single SAP. All SAPs identified by the same address are associated with entities of the same type at the next-higher layer.

Entities are "attached" to SAPs when they are participating in OSI communication activities. Thus, an (N)-SAP-address identifies an (N)-service-user (i.e., an (N + 1)-entity) by specifying the location where it can be accessed. Figure 4.2 illustrates entity names and addresses. Although it is the (N)-entity that is being addressed, the result of communication to an address is communication with an (N)-entity-invocation.

An (N)-selector is that part of the addressing information that is used to identify a SAP or set of SAPs in an end open system. Selectors can be used once the end system is unambiguously identified (by its Network Layer address) and hence are used above the Network Layer only.

Table 4.1 Entity Naming

Object	Identified by	Conditions
(N)-entity-type	(N)-entity-type-title	
(N)-entity	(N)-entity-title	
(N)-entity-invocation	(N)-entity-invocation-identifier	Unambiguous within the scope of the entity
Set of (N)-SAPs	(N)-address	
Single (N)-SAP	(N)-SAP-address	
SAP or set of SAPs	(N)-selector	Scope is one system

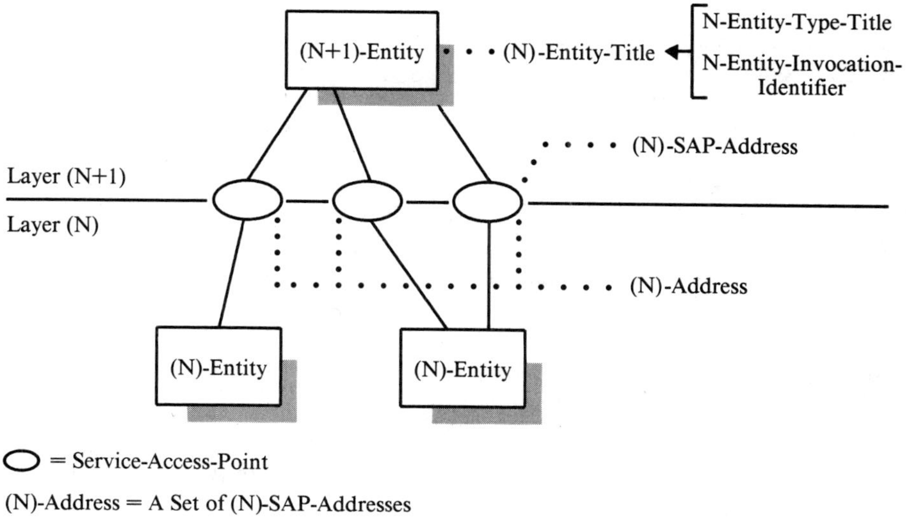

Figure 4.2 Entity names and addresses.

(N)-directory-functions process (N)- and (N − 1)-addresses, (N)-entity-titles and (N)-protocol-addressing-information to provide mappings among these items.

An (N)-address-mapping function relates (N)- and (N − 1)-addresses for a given (N)-entity. When an (N)-address is mapped onto only one (N − 1)-address, the mapping is a hierarchical construction. If the mapping is not one-to-one, the mapping must be accomplished through tables of correspondences.

A routing function translates the (N)-address of an (N + 1)-entity into a path or route by which the destination (N + 1)-entity may be reached.

4.1.3 Connection and Protocol Names

Table 4.2 lists the various names associated with the associations, connections, and protocols of a layer.

In order to provide their services, entities in a layer must cooperate. This cooperative relationship is modeled as an (N)-association between two (N)-entity-invocations (which, in real systems, equates to the information about the status and purpose of the interactions that must be maintained and shared).

(N)-associations can be supported by one or more (N − 1)-connections or can make use of an (N − 1)-connectionless service. The lifetime of an association may exceed that of its supporting connections. The association:connection binding may be 1 : 1 or 1 : many.

Connections terminate at connection-endpoints, which are located at a SAP in an open system and are identified by connection-endpoint-identifiers (CEIs). When a connection has been established, each entity is provided with a CEI that is unique within its scope. The CEI is a local identifier that serves

Table 4.2 OSI Connection Naming

Object	Identified by	Conditions
(N)-association	(N)-association-identifier	Unique within the scope of its (N)-entity-invocation
(N)-connection	(N)-connection-identifier	
(N)-connection-endpoint	(N)-connection-endpoint-identifier	

as a way of distinguishing among the connections used by that entity. It consists of two parts:

(N)-CEI	=	(N)-Address	(N)-Connection-Endpoint-Suffix

The service provider may also supply a service-connection-identifier that uniquely specifies the connection within the scope of the correspondent (N + 1)-entities.

Figure 4.3 illustrates how associations, connections, connection-endpoints, CEIs, and service-connection-identifiers relate.

4.1.4 Naming and Addressing in Specific Layers

For an application-entity, its application-entity-title at any instant in time is bound to a single presentation-address that identifies the set of PSAPs to

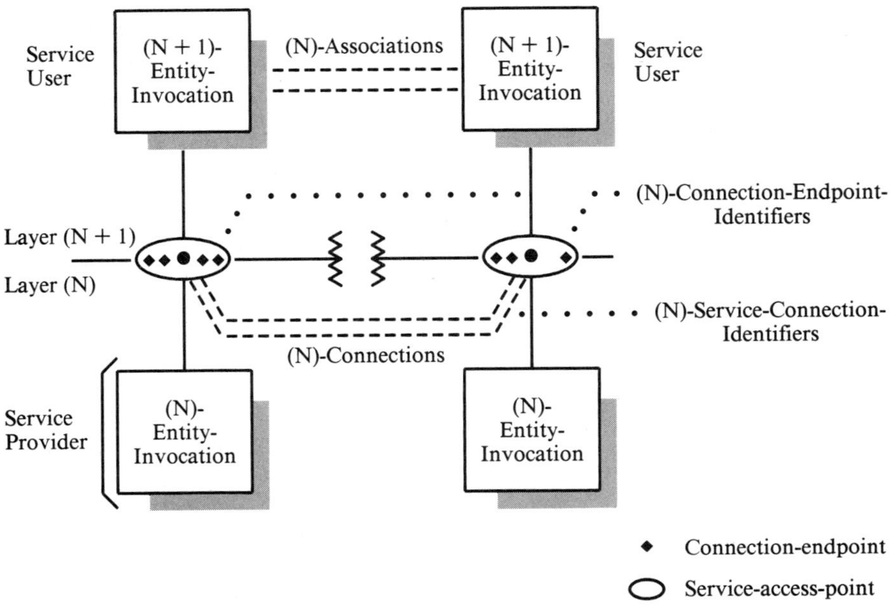

Figure 4.3 Connection identifiers.

which the application-entity is attached. This binding is recorded in the Application Title Directory Service, which provides for title-to-address mapping.

In the OSIE, Network Layer addressing normally is used to identify end open systems. Therefore, an "addressing authority" is needed to allocate unique Network Layer addresses throughout the entire OSIE. For layers above the Network Layer, addresses are under the control of local system management. An address in this case is typically hierarchical in nature, represented by a network-address plus one or more selectors that identify a set of SAPs uniquely within a layer of that system. In the case of a session-address, it would consist of a network-address plus a transport-selector and a session-selector. A presentation-address would add a presentation-selector to identify a set of PSAPs uniquely among all the sets of PSAPs associated with the presentation-entity identified by the session-address. For example, the process of establishing an application-association may proceed as follows:

1. The user supplies the title of the remote application-entity with which an association is desired.
2. The presentation-address associated with that application-entity is obtained by submitting the application-entity-title to an Application Title Directory Service, which provides a mapping from title to presentation-address.
3. Another directory function, located in the Network Layer, provides the mapping between the destination network-address and the routing information that is required to select a sequence of relay entities forming a path to the destination network-address.
4. The entire presentation-address is not conveyed in the protocol-control-information of the Presentation Layer. Instead, it is decomposed in the initiating open system into its constituent parts:

   - Presentation-selector
   - Session-selector
   - Transport-selector
   - One or more network-addresses

   These are conveyed as the protocol-address-information that is part of the protocol-control-information of the Presentation, Session, Transport, and Network Layers, respectively. At the recipient open system, they are composed again into

   - A network-address
   - The pair (network-address, transport-selector) = transport-address
   - The pair (transport-address, session-selector) = session-address
   - The pair (session-address, presentation-selector) = presentation-address

to refer to, respectively:

- A transport-entity
- A session-entity
- A presentation-entity
- An application-entity

If it is necessary to confirm that the required application-entity is still attached to the PSAP(s) identified by the presentation-address, then the application-entity-title can be passed as protocol-control-information.

A name singles out a particular object from among a collection of objects. A name must certainly be unambiguous, that is, denote just one object. However, a name need not be unique, that is, be the only name that unambiguously denotes the object.

The requirement for unambiguity of names implies some authority with control over the allocation of names. The ISO has proposed a hierarchical naming convention such that different naming authorities would have responsibility for naming "domains," corresponding to different levels in the naming hierarchy. The most likely naming domains are countries, with further subdivisions inside a country. Other domains, such as technical committees within the ISO, could also be envisaged. Every local system manager will be a naming authority for the naming domain consisting of SAP-address selectors within a given end system.

4.2 OSI MANAGEMENT

Within the OSIE, planning, organizing, supervising, and controlling the communications resources is a critical function. OSI Management can be thought of as a specialized information processing system whose purpose is to collect information from and initiate operations on OSI resources.

The resources that are visible to OSI Management are called managed objects. A managed object can be characterized by the attributes it possesses, the management operations that can be performed on it, and the notifications it may issue. The set of managed objects in a system, together with their attributes, constitutes that system's Management Information Base (MIB).

There exist three levels of management for OSI resources: systems management, (N)-layer management, and (N)-layer operation.

Systems management provides mechanisms for monitoring, controlling, and coordinating all OSI managed objects. It provides the ability to manage OSI managed objects relating to single or multiple layers. Systems management is the only means by which OSI management of multiple layers is accomplished. Systems management communication is effected by using application-protocols between system management application-entities.

Layer management provides mechanisms for the monitoring, control, and coordination of those managed objects used to accomplish communication activities within a layer. Layer management can affect multiple instances of communication. Layer management entities communicate with one another to support management control of managed objects used for communication activities between their respective open systems. Layer management communication is effected through systems management protocols or through layer management protocols, or both.

An (N)-layer operation provides the mechanisms for the monitoring and control of a single instance of communication. Only a single instance of communication within a single layer can be affected through this type of OSI Management.

The following areas of management have been defined within the scope of OSI Management:

1. *Configuration and Name Management:* control and monitoring of managed objects to provide for continuous operation of OSI services
2. *Performance Management:* control and assessment of the performance of communication activities
3. *Fault Management:* detection, isolation, and correction of faults
4. *Security Management:* security for OSI Management and managed objects
5. *Accounting Management:* tracking and reporting usage of the communication resources and providing costing-charging information.

Within each of these specific management functional areas, there will need to be one or more standards that define specific functions. Satisfying the overall requirements for management services will involve combining sets of functions into an application. Clearly, systems management standards are closely interrelated.

Data exchanges may provide monitoring information or may result in the exercise of control. Data exchanges between the MIB and administrative agents occur entirely within the local system. The format of these data is outside the scope of OSI Management standardization. However, both the abstract syntax and the semantics of information in the MIB are defined so that they can be represented in OSI protocol exchanges.

Management Information Services (MIS) are conceived of as a set of application services and associated Managing Processes (MPs) and Agent Processes (APs) that are used to exchange management information and management control sequences. There are number of functional areas supported by MIS; each is described below.

4.2.1 Configuration Management

Configuration management is the set of facilities that exercise control over, identify, collect information from, and provide information to OSI managed objects for the purpose of assisting in providing for continuous operation of interconnection services. Configuration management provides facilities to

- Set the open system parameters
- Initialize and close down OSI managed objects

- Collect information concerning the open system state both on a routine basis and in recognition of a significant change of state
- Provide specified information to open systems upon request

Distribution of OSI names and any information concerning the relationship between named OSI managed objects or an inquiry of such information, may be assisted by the appropriate utilization of the OSI Directory Service (see Section 11.5).

4.2.2 Fault Management

Fault management is the set of facilities that enable the detection, isolation, and correction of abnormal operation of the OSIE. Faults cause open systems to fail to meet their operational objectives; they may be persistent or transient. They manifest themselves as errors in the operation of an open system. Error detection provides the mechanism for recognizing faults. Fault management provides facilities to

- Maintain and examine error logs
- Accept and act upon error detection notifications
- Trace faults
- Carry out sequences of tests
- Correct faults

4.2.3 Accounting Management

Accounting management is the set of facilities that enable charges to be set for the use of resources and costs to be identified for the use of those resources. It provides facilities to

- Inform users of costs incurred or resources consumed
- Enable accounting limits for use of OSI resources to be set
- Enable costs to be combined, where multiple OSI resources are invoked to achieve a given communication objective.

4.2.4 Security Management

Security management provides the facilities for managing OSI security. Management support is provided for

- Authorization facilities
- Access controls
- Encryption and key management

- Authentication
- Maintenance and examination of security logs

4.2.5 Performance Management

Performance management provides the set of facilities needed to evaluate the behavior of OSI managed objects and the effectiveness of communication activities. The performance management facilities include

- Gathering statistical data, e.g., for the purpose of analyzing trends
- Maintaining and examining logs of system state histories

4.3 OSI SECURITY

The objective of OSI is to permit the interconnection of heterogeneous computer systems so that meaningful communication between applications can be achieved. At various times, security controls must be established in order to protect the information that is exchanged between the applications. Such controls should make the cost of illegally obtaining or modifying data greater than the potential value of obtaining or modifying the data.

In ISO 7498-2 an architectural framework for the provision of security features for OSI has been developed. Work is underway to incorporate these features into the OSI layer protocols.

Security services that can optionally be provided within the framework of the OSI Reference Model include the following:

1. Services that provide for the authentication of a communicating peer-entity and the source of data:

    - *Peer-entity Authentication:* This service is provided at the establishment of a connection or at times during the data transfer phase. It confirms the identities of one or more of the entities connected and provides confidence that an entity is not attempting a masquerade or an unauthorized replay of a previous connection establishment.
    - *Data Origin Authentication:* This service, when provided by the (N)-layer, provides corroboration to the (N + 1)-layer that the source of the data is the claimed peer (N + 1)-entity. It applies to single connectionless data-units only.

2. Services that provide protection against unauthorized use of the resources accessible via OSI. Protection may be applied to various types of access to a resource (e.g., the use of a communications resource, the reading, writing, or the deletion of an information resource; the execution of a processing resource), or to all accesses to a resource.

The following services provide for the protection of data from unauthorized disclosure:

- *Connection Confidentiality:* This service provides confidentiality of all user-data on a connection.
- *Connectionless Confidentiality:* This service provides confidentiality of user-data in a single connectionless service-data-unit.
- *Selective Field Confidentiality:* This service provides confidentiality of selected fields within the user-data on a connection or in a single connectionless service-data-unit.
- *Traffic Flow Confidentiality:* This service provides for the protection of the information that might be derived from observation of traffic flows.

3. Services that counter active threats:

- *Connection Integrity with Recovery:* This service provides for the integrity of all user-data on a connection and detects any modification, insertion, deletion, or replay of any data within an entire service-data-unit sequence (with recovery attempted).
- *Connection Integrity Without Recovery:* As above, but without recovery.
- *Selective Field Connection Integrity:* This service provides for the integrity of selected fields within the user-data on a connection and takes the form of determination of whether the selected fields have been modified, inserted, deleted, or replayed.
- *Connectionless Integrity:* This service provides for the integrity of a single connectionless service-data-unit and may take the form of determination of whether a received service-data-unit has been modified. Additionally, a limited form of detection of insertion or replay may be provided.
- *Selective Field Connectionless Integrity:* This service provides for the integrity of selected fields within a single connectionless service-data-unit and takes the form of determination of whether the selected fields have been modified.

4. Services that provide nonrepudiation assurance:

- *Nonrepudiation with Proof of Origin:* The recipient of data is provided with proof of the data's origin, which protects against any attempt by the sender to falsely deny sending the data or its contents.
- *Nonrepudiation with Proof of Delivery:* The sender of data is provided with proof of the data's delivery, which protects against any subsequent attempt by the recipient to falsely deny receiving the data or its contents.

A variety of mechanisms have been identified to provide the capabilities described above. These include

Table 4.3 Matrix of Security Services and Layers

Layer Service	1	2	3	4	5	6	7*
Peer-entity Authentication	—	—	Y	Y	—	—	Y
Data Origin Authentication	—	—	Y	Y	—	—	Y
Access Control	—	—	Y	Y	—	—	Y
Connection Confidentiality	Y	Y	Y	Y	—	Y	Y
Connectionless Confidentiality	—	Y	Y	Y	—	Y	Y
Selective Field Confidentiality	—	—	—	—	—	Y	Y
Traffic Flow Confidentiality	Y	—	Y	—	—	—	Y
Connection Integrity (recovery)	—	—	—	Y	—	—	Y
Connection Integrity (no recovery)	—	—	Y	Y	—	—	Y
Selective Field Connection Integrity	—	—	—	—	—	—	Y
Connectionless Integrity	—	—	Y	Y	—	—	Y
Selective Field Connectionless Integrity	—	—	—	—	—	—	Y
Nonrepudiation (origin)	—	—	—	—	—	—	Y
Nonrepudiation (delivery)	—	—	—	—	—	—	Y

Legend:
Y = Yes, service should be provided in the standards for this layer as a provider option
N = Not provided
*It should be noted, with respect to layer 7, that the application may itself provide security services

- Encipherment
- Digital signature mechanisms
- Access control mechanisms (e.g., closed user groups)
- Authentication exchange mechanisms (e.g., exchange of passwords)
- Data integrity mechanisms (e.g., use of redundancy checks)
- Traffic padding (e.g., sending spurious data to disguise the length and number of transmitted protocol-data-units)
- Routing control (e.g., selecting only secure communication paths)
- Notarization (e.g., use of a trusted third party as a relay)
- Ensuring trusted functionality of software and hardware
- Incorporation of event detection and handling procedures (e.g., local and remote reporting of unusual events)
- Provision for audit trails (e.g., logging all events)
- Incorporation of security recovery (e.g., actions taken after reporting of real or suspected breaches in security)

Security services may be provided by different layers, according to circumstance. Table 4.3 (from ISO 7498-2) indicates the layers of the Reference

Model in which particular security services can be provided. The table makes no attempt to indicate that entries are of equal weight or importance; on the contrary, there is considerable gradation of scale within the table entries. Note that although few security services are provided by the Presentation Layer, this layer contains a number of security mechanisms that support the provision of security services by the Application Layer.

PART II

SERVICES AND PROTOCOLS FOR OSI

CHAPTER 5

LOWER LAYER CONCEPTS AND SERVICES

In Chapter 3 the seven layers of the OSI Reference Model were introduced and two major categories were identified: The upper layers (Application, Presentation, and Session) and the lower layers (Transport, Network, Data Link, and Physical). The lower layers of the OSI Reference Model are responsible for distributing data among the open systems (more precisely, among the session-entities that are the transport-service-users).

The lower layers are closely aligned with the "real networks" of the telecommunications world. There is a considerable amount of technical detail involved in specifying how a given "real network" provides the OSI network-service. Since an examination of all possible networking protocols, technologies, and interconnection strategies is beyond the scope of this book, the focus of this chapter is on concepts and services only. Many excellent references discuss local area networks and packet switching and provide a level of detail that is not possible in this introductory text. The Transport Layer, which forms the border between the lower and upper layers, will be considered in detail.

The goal of the lower layers is not only to move data between systems but also to perform a variety of functions that shield the application from the specific characteristics and configurations of the physical media. Lower layer protocols are generally dictated by the specific requirements of the physical media. This chapter first introduces the basic concepts of the lower layers, using the "telephone application" example. The services and protocol of the Transport Layer are then discussed in some detail, and a brief description of Physical, Data Link, and Network Layer concepts is provided.

5.1 THE TELEPHONE SYSTEM EXAMPLE

Although the telephone network is usually thought of as being the telephone set and wires provided by the telephone company, the "telephone application" actually involves both the network and the people doing the talking. The telephone handset can be viewed as the interface between the two parts. The telephone network supplies "network services," while the people perform functions that are analogous to the Transport and higher layers. This can be illustrated as shown in Figure 5.1.

A number of resources must be available for a telephone call to occur. There must be a local loop (physical media) from the person to the telephone exchange, connections among the telephone exchanges (both local and long distance), and switches to route the call through the network. Needless to say, a calling party and called party are required (both to determine the telephone number to call, and to do the talking).

All parts of the telephone network may belong to the same supplier (e.g., a local call through a PBX in an office) or there may be complex combinations, such as would occur for an international call. The telephone sets, which must

OSI Layers	Telephone System Functions
7 Application	Choice of language (e.g., lawyer terms)
6 Presentation	Choice of speech (e.g., English)
5 Session	Two-way alternate speech control
4 Transport	End-to-end telephone call
3 Network	Telephone handsets, local loops, PBX, Centrex, voice channels, switching centers, country gateways, and so on
2 Data Link	
1 Physical	

Figure 5.1 Telephone application analogy.

be connected to the local distribution service, may use different technologies (tone versus pulse, mechanical versus electronic, etc.).

The wiring of the telephone is analogous to the OSI physical media and Physical Layer.

The telephone network has no direct equivalent of the framing and error correction of the OSI Data Link Layer. Perhaps this is a legacy of the old age of the telephone network (the telephone system was initially built using analogue networks for which digital techniques, such as error correction, could not be applied), but it is also due to the excellent ability of people to interpret meaning despite the loss of some words. Voice communications among people generally provides sufficient built-in redundancy that people can compensate for problems in the telephone network. This could be viewed as providing error correction in the Transport and Application Layers.

There are many, many millions of telephones in the world, most of which can now interconnect automatically (i.e., without operator intervention). A universal dialing plan and the ability to distribute management functionality to various national administrations was a prerequisite.

Dialing a telephone number is analogous to activating the addressing and routing functions of the OSI Network Layer and serves to establish a path through the physical media and relay systems. The interconnection of national telephone networks across country borders equates to the linking of various OSI subnetworks.

For the telephone application, functions of the Transport Layer and above are performed by the people who are talking. The people do not have to worry about the actual physical facilities that are used during their call; in fact, the caller usually has no knowledge of the internal network details. The Transport Layer, being the first end-to-end connection, can be compared to saying "Hello, I'm . . ." as a way to ensure the desired person has answered.

Many variations of this example are possible. For instance, a secretary may answer a telephone for several people. Calls can be redirected, conferencing can be established, voice mail can be included, abbreviated dialing may be provided within an organization, and so on.

5.2 THE TRANSPORT LAYER (LAYER 4)

The Transport Layer has overall responsibility for achieving the transparent transfer of data between session-entities in the end open systems. The Transport Layer makes use of and complements the capabilities of the Physical, Data Link, and Network Layers to provide a firm, consistent service to the Session Layer. A major goal of the Transport Layer is to hide the details of how to achieve reliable and cost-effective movement of data among the session-entities.

The Transport Layer acts as a boundary between the distribution services and the interworking aspects of OSI and thereby decouples the changes in telecommunications and computer technologies while preserving the "marriage" between the two. The Transport Layer also strives to make the best possible use of the resources available to it to achieve the level of service requested by the user at the lowest possible cost. This is accomplished by selecting only those functions that are needed to enhance the capabilities of the Network Layer to the required service level.

In the standards development process two Transport Layer standards were published by ISO in 1986. These are the Connection Oriented Transport Service Specification (ISO 8072) and the Connection Oriented Transport Protocol Specification (ISO 8073). The main body of this section deals with these two standards. As with other OSI standards these were also issued as CCITT recommendations, X.214 and X.224 respectively. Additional specifications have been developed for provision of a connectionless-mode transport-service over a connection-mode or connectionless-mode network-service. These, together with various addenda, are described briefly toward the end of this section.

5.2.1 Services of the Transport Layer

In a connection-mode operation there are three phases of activity: connection establishment, data transfer, and connection release.

5.2.1.1 Connection Establishment

The service primitives for connection establishment are as shown in Table 5.1. Connection establishment is accomplished in the following manner. A transport-service-user issues what is called a T-CONNECT request. This is passed to the remote transport-entity implied by the address parameter of the T-CONNECT request. The remote transport-entity will then pass a T-CONNECT indication containing the parameters of the original request up to the ad-

Table 5.1 Transport Layer Service Primitives

Phase	Service	Primitives
Connection establishment	Connection establishment	T-CONNECT request T-CONNECT indication T-CONNECT response T-CONNECT confirm
Connection-mode data transfer	Normal data transfer	T-DATA request T-DATA indication
	Expedited data transfer	T-EXPEDITED-DATA request T-EXPEDITED-DATA indication
Connection release	Connection release	T-DISCONNECT request T-DISCONNECT indication
Connectionless-mode data transfer	Data Transfer	T-UNITDATA request T-UNITDATA indication

dressed transport-service-user. The transport-service-user may decide to accept or reject the transport-connection.

Reasons for not accepting a connection request may include an inability to meet the minimum acceptable quality of service (QOS) specified in the request and insufficient local resources. If the connection is to be rejected, a T-DISCONNECT request is sent back.

If the connection is to be accepted, a T-CONNECT confirm is returned. Once the T-CONNECT confirm has been sent, the sender considers the connection to be established and in the data transfer phase. The connection initiator does not consider itself to be in the data transfer phase until it receives the T-CONNECT confirm.

The initiator may optionally request the use of the T-EXPEDITED-DATA service via a parameter setting in the T-CONNECT request. The receiving user may accept or reject the use of T-EXPEDITED-DATA service via a parameter setting in the T-CONNECT confirm. When available, the T-EXPEDITED-DATA service is always bidirectional.

5.2.1.2 T-DATA Transfer

Data are transferred by one user sending a T-DATA request primitive, which is passed by the Transport Layer to the remote user as a T-DATA indication. Receipt is not confirmed. The amount of data that may be transferred with a single T-DATA request primitive can be unlimited. Real implementations will, of course, require a finite limit. For example, a file would not likely be transferred as a whole. In such a case the Transport Layer must determine the optimum size of protocol-data-units to accomplish the data transfer within bounds of the quality of service requested, e.g., with respect to delays and error rate.

For expedited data a limit of 16 octets is placed on the amount of data that may be transferred in a single T-EXPEDITED-DATA request. It may overtake previously submitted T-DATA requests but cannot itself be overtaken by subsequent T-DATA requests.

A transport-connection must go through the establishment phase before it can proceed to the data transfer phase. During the time of connection establishment, negotiations and decisions are made within the Transport Layer with respect to QOS requirements. If connection establishment is rejected or fails for some reason, or if the data transfer phase is complete, the connection release phase begins.

The data transfer phase permits two-way simultaneous transfer of data transparently. This is subject to flow control operation so that the receiving transport-service-user can control the rate at which data is sent over the connection. Provision is also made for expedited data transfer to permit the transfer of separate expedited units of data when agreed upon by both ends of a connection. Expedited data are not subject to normal flow control and can overtake data already sent.

The transport-connection can be released by either end of the connection or when the transport-entity is unable to maintain the connection or the required QOS any longer. Release of the transport-connection is unconditional and therefore possibly destructive to data in transit at time of release. It is a responsibility of the Session Layer to ensure that all data have been successfully transferred before initiating transport-connection release.

Service primitives of the Transport Layer each have two forms:

- *Requests* issued by the service-user to initiate an action by the Transport Layer
- *Indications* passed by the Transport Layer up to the service-user to indicate that a request has been made by the remote service-user.

Names for service primitives adhere to the following convention:

- Capital letters are used.
- The first one or two letters represent the layer or the application.
- The layer or application identifier is separated from the service identifier by a hyphen.
- A descriptive name is given for the service.
- A service primitive is formed by appending the primitive name (not capitalized) to the service name.

5.2.1.3 Connection Release

The connection release phase is permitted at any time, regardless of the current status of the transport-connection. A request for release cannot be denied, and there is no guarantee of delivery of any transport-service-user data once the release phase is entered.

The release phase can be entered by one of the transport-service-users issuing a T-DISCONNECT request. This is passed to the remote service-user as a T-DISCONNECT indication. A connection can also be released by one of the transport-entities causing a T-DISCONNECT indication to be passed to both transport-service-users.

5.2.1.4 Quality of Service

QOS is defined in terms of a number of parameters that the transport-service-user can employ to specify the requirements placed on a connection. The definitions are summarized as follows:

- *Transport Connection Establishment Delay:* This is the maximum acceptable delay between the T-CONNECT request and the corresponding T-CONNECT confirm primitives. This parameter would influence the choice of subnetwork over which a connection is to be established.

- *Transport-Connection Establishment Failure Probability:* This is also affected by the choice of subnetwork and is used in specifying the required connection setup reliability.
- *Throughput:* This is defined for each direction of transmission and will be a major factor influencing the choice of subnetwork, such as wide-band, satellite, leased line and PSTN. It is defined in terms of "maximum" and "average" throughput. These are based on the maximum and average expected rates at which the transport-service provider can continuously accept and deliver transport-service-data-units.
- *Transit Delay:* This is specified for each direction of transmission independently. The same comments apply as for throughput.
- *Residual Error Rate:* This parameter can affect the choice of subnetwork and protocol class. It enables the transport-service-user to specify the acceptable rate of undetected errors from the transport-service.
- *Transfer Failure Probability:* A transfer failure is defined to be any data transfer that is not accomplished with better than the minimum acceptable QOS in terms of throughput, delay, or errors. This parameter can affect choice of subnetwork or protocol class.
- *Transport Connection Release Delay:* This parameter, which is used to specify the maximum acceptable delay between a T-DISCONNECT request initiated by a transport-service-user and the successful disconnect, can affect the choice of timers in some protocol classes.
- *Transport Connection Release Failure Probability:* The same comments apply as for Establishment Failure Probability.
- *Transport Connection Protection:* This parameter allows the user to indicate security requirements with respect to prevention of unauthorized monitoring or manipulation of transport-service-user-data.
- *Transport Connection Priority:* This parameter is concerned with the relationship between transport-connections. It permits specification of relative priority between them with respect to losing the required QOS or the connection during periods of overload conditions. To be effective both end systems should operate a priority management scheme with appropriate values signaled between them.
- *Resilience of the Transport-Connection:* This parameter relates to the probability that a transport-connection may be lost, unknown to the user. Notification of loss may be of major importance in certain applications such as alarm systems. Timer values and selection of protocol classes are of significance in specification of this parameter.

5.2.1.5 Connectionless-Mode Operation

This transport-service provides for the transfer of data between transport-service-users on a connectionless-mode basis. This means that there are no connection establishment or connection release functions. Only two primitives are defined for the connectionless-mode service: T-UNITDATA request and T-UNITDATA indication.

Since there is no connection establishment phase, it is not possible to negotiate QOS options. In fact, by definition, many of these are not relevant to this mode of operation. Those that are relevant are:

- Transit Delay
- Protection
- Residual Error Probability

The simplicity of the connectionless-mode service means that few primitives need to be defined. Storage capacity for connection-related information is not required, nor are mechanisms needed for setup and release of connections. This comes at the price of limited service-data-unit sizes, complete addressing information required for each invocation of a T-UNITDATA request primitive, and weak confirmation of received data.

5.2.2 The Transport-protocol

The transport-protocol must satisfy requirements that vary with respect to both the quality of the underlying network-service and the nature of the user application. In cases where the underlying network-service already meets the requirements of the application, little or no enhancement is required from the Transport Layer. Where the quality of the underlying network-service is inadequate to meet the application requirements, the Transport Layer must provide the necessary enhancement. Consequently the transport-protocol has been designed in a modular way using the concept of classes of protocol.

5.2.2.1 Transport Layer Functions

The Transport Layer functions are aimed at enhancement of QOS, including aspects relating to cost optimization. Depending on the type and quality of network available, the transport-protocol can be quite complex. As the underlying network-service increases in quality, so the Transport Layer requirements become less complex. Three types of network-service are identified for the purposes of OSI standardization:

- *Type A:* Network-connections with an acceptable residual error rate (for example, not signaled by disconnect or reset) and an acceptable rate of signaled errors.
- *Type B:* Network-connections with an acceptable residual error rate (for example not signaled by disconnect or reset) but an unacceptable rate of signaled errors.

- *Type C:* Network-connections with an unacceptable residual error rate.

The principal functions provided by the Transport Layer to enhance these network types to achieve the required transport-service are:

- *Assignment to a Network-connection:* This function assigns each transport-connection to one or more network-connections. The initiator may assign the transport-connection to an existing network-connection one which it has control or to a new network-connection that it creates for this purpose.

- *Transport-Protocol-Data-Unit (TPDU) Transfer:* The TPDU transfer function is used in all protocol classes to convey TPDUs in user fields of network-service primitives.

- *Segmenting and Reassembling:* This function permits the subdivision of large blocks of user-data, passed in a single service primitive, into blocks of suitable size for transmission via the network-service. Each block is sent in a separate TPDU and reassembled before being passed up to the remote transport-service-user.

- *Connection Establishment:* This is accomplished by mutual agreement and involves an exchange of TPDUs. During the exchange, the choice of protocol class and options to be used is negotiated.

- *Connection Refusal:* This function permits a transport-service-user to decline a T-CONNECT request TPDU. There could be such a refusal because a connection is not desired at that time or because it is not possible to support a connection.

- *Normal Release:* The release function is used to terminate a transport-connection. There are two variants of this function: implicit and explicit. When the implicit variant is used, the lifetime of the transport-connection is directly correlated with the network-connection lifetime. In the explicit variant case the release procedure enables the transport-connection to be released independently of the underlying network-connection.

- *Association of TPDUs with Transport-Connections:* This function enables interpretation of a received network-service-data-unit (NSDU) as TPDU(s) and, if possible, association of each such TPDU with a transport-connection.

- *TPDU Numbering:* This function, used in some of the protocol classes, enables recovery, flow control, and resequencing functions to be used.

- *Expedited Data Transfer:* This function provides the protocol mechanism to support the expedited-data primitive of the transport-service. It is an implementation matter, whether expedited TPDUs can bypass queues of normal data and normal data flow control.

- *Reassignment After Failure:* This provides for a procedure in some of the protocol classes to recover from a failure of the network-connection to which it was assigned.
- *Retention Until Acknowledgment of TPDUs:* This function is used to enable and minimize retransmission after possible loss of TPDUs.
- *Resynchronization:* This function is used to restore the transport-connection to normal after a reset or during reassignment after a failure.
- *Multiplexing and Demultiplexing:* These functions permit more than one transport-connection to be carried over a single network-connection at the same time. It has cost reduction implications, since it can minimize the number of network-connections needed to meet an application's required QOS.
- *Checksum:* This function checks for corruption of TPDUs by the network-service provider.
- *Frozen Reference:* This function prevents reuse of the unique reference number identifying a connection, after the connection has been released, for a period long enough for there to be no TPDUs in existence belonging to the connection.
- *Retransmission on Time-Out:* This function copes with unsignaled loss of TPDUs by the network-service provider. A timer is set, running when data are transmitted, and if no acknowledgment has been received before expiry, the data must be retransmitted.
- *Resequencing:* In cases where the network-service cannot be assumed to preserve the sequence of transmitted data, this function is invoked to properly resequence the misordered data.
- *Inactivity Control:* This function copes with unsignaled termination of a network-connection.
- *Treatment of Protocol Errors:* This function deals with invalid TPDUs.
- *Splitting and Recombining:* This function is used in cases where multiple network-connections are used by a transport-connection for purposes such as resilience against network failure or to increase throughput.

5.2.2.2 Classes of Transport-protocol

The transport-protocol has been divided into five classes. These provide increasing functionality, permitting selection of the minimum additional functionality needed to bridge between the network-service and the service required by a transport-service-user. A summary of the functions of transport-protocol classes is given in Table 5.2.

Table 5.2 Summary of Functions of Transport-protocol Classes.

Protocol mechanism	Class 0	1	2	3	4
Assignment to network-connection	■	■	■	■	■
TPDU transfer	■	■	■	■	■
Segmenting and reassembling	■	■	■	■	■
Concatenation and separation		■	■	■	■
Connection establishment	■	■	■	■	■
Connection refusal	■	■	■	■	■
Normal release					
Implicit	■				
Explicit		■	■	■	■
Error release	■		■		
Association of TPDUs with Transport-connection	■	■	■	■	■
Data Transfer TPDU numbering					
Normal		■	■	■	■
Extended			■	■	■
Expedited data transfer					
Network normal		■	■	■	■
Network expedited		■			
Reassignment after failure		■		■	■
Retention until acknowledgment of TPDUs					
confirmation receipt		■			
Acknowledgment				■	■
Resynchronization		■		■	■
Multiplexing and demultiplexing			■	■	■
Explicit flow control					
With				■	■
Without	■	■	■		
Checksum					
Use of					■
Nonuse of	■	■	■	■	■
Frozen references		■		■	■
Retransmission on timeout					■
Resequencing					■
Inactivity control					■
Treatment of protocol errors	■	■	■	■	■
Splitting and recombining					■

Class 0: Simple Class. This class provides the simplest type of transport-connection. It provides only the facilities needed for connection establishment with negotiation, data transfer with segmenting, and protocol error reporting. Class 0 contains no facilities for multiplexing, disconnection, flow control, error detection, error recovery, or expedited data transfer. For Class 0 the

standard maximum TPDU length is 128 octets. Optional maximum TPDU sizes are restricted to 256, 512, 1024, and 2048 octets.

Class 1: Basic Error Recovery Class. This class provides the ability to recover after a failure signaled by the network-service, in addition to the functionality of class 0. It is particularly suited for use when the supporting network-connection can be depended upon to signal errors. The use of Network Receipt Confirmation, which is an option in this class, to acknowledge and release from retention data TPDUs can result in considerable savings in networks such as public packet networks (due to savings in the number of NSDUs transmitted).

Class 2: Multiplexing Class. This class provides transport-connections with or without flow control. It is the class to be used when multiplexing is required and the QOS of the underlying network-connection is suitable for the application using this transport-connection.

If the network-connection resets or disconnects, the transport-connection is terminated without a transport release operation and the transport-service-user is informed.

When explicit flow control is used a credit mechanism is defined which allows the receiver to inform the sender of the exact amount of data he is willing to receive and whether expedited data transfer is available.

Class 3: Error Recovery and Multiplexing Class. This class provides the functionality of class 2 and also the ability to recover after a failure signaled by the Network Layer, without involving the user of the transport-service. It essentially masks errors indicated by the network-service. Class 3 is suitable when multiplexing is required and the expected frequency of network-signaled errors is too high for the application.

Class 4: Error Detection and Recovery Class. This class provides the functionality of class 3 and also the ability to detect and recover from lost, duplicated, or out-of-sequence TPDUs, without involving the transport-service-user. Class 4 detects signaled and unsignaled network-service failures and recovers from these by using time-out mechanisms. It uses checksum methods to detect and recover from damaged TPDUs. Since it also permits the transport-connection to use multiple network-connections, there results increased resilience to network-service failures and increased throughput capability.

5.2.2.3 Conformance

It became clear as OSI protocol standards were evolving that the specification of options and classes could present a real barrier to interoperability. Implementation experience showed that even a simple protocol specified in natural language was open to various interpretations. The transport-protocol, with its five classes, clearly needed a statement of requirements for conforming implementations. This is stated in the standard at an overview level, which is described in the following section. The detailed specification for conforming implementations will appear in an as yet incomplete test suite specification (in early 1989). (See also Chapter 13 on conformance testing). For transport-protocol conformance:

- A system shall implement class 0 or class 2 or both.
- If the system implements class 3 or class 4, it shall also implement class 2.
- If the system implements class 1, it shall also implement class 0.

TPDU sizes of 128 octets are always implemented, other sizes being optional. An implementation must also state which options are included.

It should be noted that the transport-protocol was one of the first OSI protocols to be designed. It is the only protocol that incorporates the concept of classes. While this seemed like a good idea at the time, in the final analysis it gives rise to two groups of mutually incompatible implementations: those supporting class 0 and those supporting class 2. Some bodies have recommended that implementations for their requirements should include both class 0 and class 2.

5.2.2.4 Network-Connection Management Subprotocol

An addendum has been added to the transport-protocol, called the Network-Connection Management Subprotocol (NCMS). This is contained in Addendum 1 and identified as ISO 8073/DAD 1. The procedures defined are optional extensions that permit improved management of the use of the network-services by the Transport Layer. For classes 2, 3, and 4, where multiplexing is defined, the NCMS permits full sharing of a network-connection by many transport-connections. It also takes care of cases where simultaneous connections are being set up between peer transport-entities, which would otherwise result in the inefficiencies of maintaining and operating separate connections.

When the NCMS is to be used, this is signaled by the Use of Network-connection TPDU (UN TPDU) and the Network-Connection Management TPDU (NCM TPDU) in the N-CONNECT request. Otherwise the standard protocol features apply. In addition, the feature of the NCMS that allows for the transport-entities at each end of a network-connection to have assignment rights is signaled in the N-CONNECT request by means of the NCM TPDU. Provision is also made for determining which end of the connection, the initiator or responder, is the "owner".

5.3 THE NETWORK LAYER (LAYER 3)

The purpose of the Network Layer is to provide services that enable open systems anywhere to exchange data without concern for the types of subnetwork, i.e., real network, to which the systems are attached or the means used to achieve the physical interconnection. The Network Layer also provides functions for routing and relaying among subnetworks, thereby making it unnecessary for the upper layers to know about the actual paths between the systems. End open systems can assume that arbitrarily complex combinations of real networks can be assembled and that data transfer can be achieved between any endpoints.

The Network Layer provides its users with a uniform network-service regardless of potentially wide variation in the underlying subnetwork technologies, configurations, and administrative organizations.

There has always been a danger of confusion between the use of "network" in the OSI Reference Model (when referring to the Network Layer) and its use in normal English to refer to real circuits (as in banking network, airline network, etc.). The latter, in OSI terminology, is called a "subnetwork." Any particular subnetwork may or may not support the OSI network-service. In the longer term, however, it is expected that most subnetworks will evolve so that they do. The CCITT X.25 Recommendation for packet-switched networks, for example, does not meet all the needs of the network-service in the 1980 version, but it does with the 1984 version.

5.3.1 Internal Organization of the Network Layer

There is no doubt that the Network Layer is one of the more important OSI layers. It is also one of the more complex layers. In fact, it has been found that it is necessary (or at least very desirable) to develop a specific model for the Network Layer, and this has been called the Internal Organization of the Network Layer (IONL). The purposes of this model are to act as a framework for Network Layer standards development and to encourage subnetwork designs that fully support the OSI network-service.

The IONL was designed to accommodate a variety of networking technologies, to incorporate several approaches to network operation, and to permit arbitrarily complex configurations of subnetworks. The model is a "bridge" between the world of real subnetworks and the OSI abstract representations.

The Network Layer also has the distinction of being the "border" between the communications carriers (who typically provide layers 1 to 3) and the computer manufacturers (the suppliers of the Transport Layer and above).

The IONL defines an "interworking unit" as a real system that performs Network Layer relay functions (that is, it forwards data); a relay system is its OSI equivalent. A real subnetwork is a set of equipment and physical media that provide data transmission services; a subnetwork is its abstract representation in OSI. Real subnetworks and end systems may or may not include interworking units. An intermediate system can be either a subnetwork or a relay system.

Open systems can communicate in many ways. Several relatively straightforward configurations are illustrated in Figure 5.2.

Every real subnetwork provides some set of services to its users. These services may be connection-mode or connectionless-mode and may or may not include all of the OSI network-service features. The Network Layer performs functions that enhance the real subnetwork to the level of the

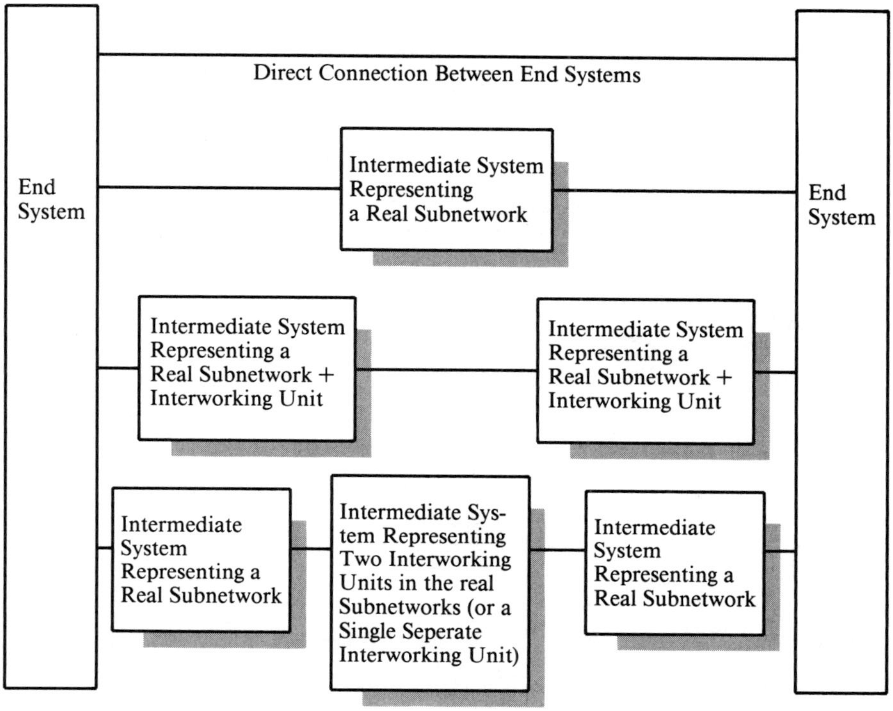

Figure 5.2 Examples of interconnection of end systems.

network-service. For complex subnetwork configurations, there may be a need for different enhancements for each subnetwork or for combinations of subnetworks.

Three distinct roles have been defined for network-protocols:

1. The Subnetwork Independent Convergence (SNIC) role constructs the OSI network-service over a well-defined set of underlying capabilities that need not be based on the characteristics of any particular subnetwork-service.
2. The Subnetwork Dependent Convergence (SNDC) role is used over a subnetwork access protocol (SNAcP) to provide the capabilities assumed by the subnetwork independent convergence protocol (SNICP) or to provide the network-service directly.
3. The Subnetwork Access (SNAc) role contributes to the provision of a subnetwork service specific to the subnetwork involved.

In addition to adopting the above roles, the network-protocol must provide relaying functions that enable a network-entity to forward information received from one peer entity to another and routing functions that determine the most appropriate route between network-addresses.

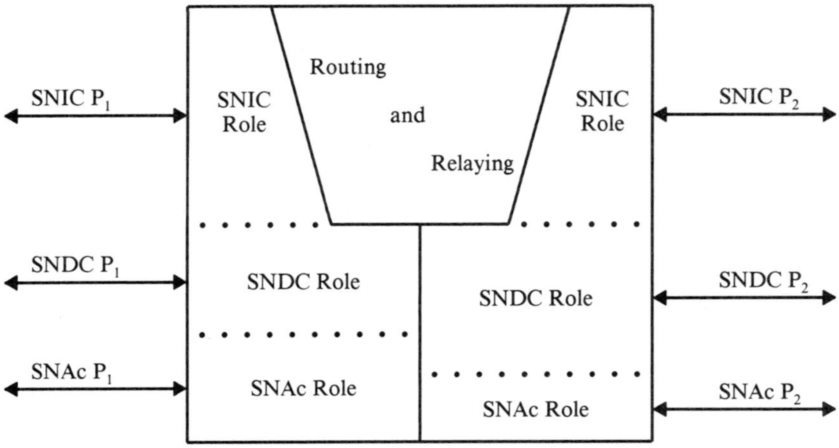

Figure 5.3 Network Layer protocol roles. (P_x= protocol type x).

Figure 5.3 illustrates the network-protocol roles.

Three approaches to the application of the IONL to subnetwork-connection have been defined:

- Interconnection of subnetworks that each support the network-service directly
- Hop-by-hop harmonization over individual subnetworks
- Use of an internetworking protocol over more than one subnetwork

These approaches can be applied to each phase of connection-mode operation independently. A wide variety of interconnection scenarios are possible but will not be discussed in detail here.

5.3.2 Services of the Network Layer

The service definition of the Network Layer closely resembles that of the Transport Layer. Connection-mode operation has the same three phases of activity: connection establishment, data transfer, and connection release. Connectionless-mode operation involves a simple transfer of independent units of data without using a connection. A comparison of Tables 5.1 and 5.3 will show that the only difference in service primitives is the change of a *T* to an *N*.

The network-service provides for the following:

- *Independence from underlying transmission media:* Users need not worry about how the subnetworks are used; network differences other than QOS are hidden.

Table 5.3 Network Layer Service Primitives

Phase	Service	Service Primitives
Connection establishment	Connection establishment	N-CONNECT request N-CONNECT indication N-CONNECT response N-CONNECT confirm
Connection-mode data transfer	Normal data transfer	N-DATA request N-DATA indication
	Expedited data transfer*	N-EXPEDITED-DATA request N-EXPEDITED-DATA indication
Connection release	Connection release	N-DISCONNECT request N-DISCONNECT indication
Connectionless-mode data transfer	Data transfer	N-UNITDATA request N-UNITDATA indication

*A provider-option service, not always available

- *End-to-end data transfer:* Transfer of data between end open systems through intermediate systems is provided as necessary.
- *Transparency of transferred information:* Octet-aligned user-data and control-information are transferred transparently, with no need to interpret or examine the data being transferred.
- *QOS selection:* Network-service-users are provided the means to request and to agree to the QOS that is acceptable for the transfer of data.
- *Network-service-user addressing:* A system of addressing that allows users to refer unambiguously to one another is provided.

The Network Layer may perform multiplexing, error control, and flow control when it is desirable to optimize resources.

The QOS provided by the Network Layer directly impacts on the Transport Layer. The QOS is negotiated between the transport-entities and the network-service provider at the time of establishment of a network-connection. While this QOS may vary from one network-connection to another it will be agreed for a given network-connection and will be the same at both network-connection-endpoints.

For connectionless-mode operations the QOS is agreed to between the sender and the network-service provider.

The QOS parameters that are passed in the service primitives are equivalent to those of the Transport Layer, with the addition of a parameter for maximum acceptable network-connection cost.

As was noted in Section 5.2, three categories of network-connection have been defined on the basis of the level of QOS that can be assumed:

	Residual Error Rate	*Rate of Signaled Errors*
Type A	Acceptable	Acceptable
Type B	Acceptable	Unacceptable
Type C	Unacceptable	Unacceptable

5.3.3 Network Layer Addressing

The Network Layer must take an address provided by its service-user and convert it into the addresses of the real subnetworks that it uses to perform the data transfer. In order to minimize confusion over which addresses are being discussed, the following distinctions are made:

1. *Subnetwork-address* (also called subnetwork point of attachment address):
   - The point at which a real subnetwork connects to a real end system, real subnetwork, or interworking unit
   - Corresponds, for example, to "DTE address" in a public data network and represents the implementation-dependent address of a particular network
2. *NSAP-address* (also called network-service-access-point-address):
   - Refers to an NSAP, the point at which the network-service is made available to its users in the OSI environment
   - NSAP-addresses are included as parameters in the network-service primitives
3. *Network-protocol-address-information* (NPAI):
   - An address carried in the network-protocol that relates to NSAP addressing information but is defined precisely by the specific network-protocol.

The set of all NSAP-addresses (the NSAP-address space) is called the global network addressing domain. For many practical reasons, the NSAP-address space is divided into subsets called network addressing domains (same term, minus the word *global*), which are defined as being under the control of an "addressing authority." These subsets may be further decomposed to form a strict hierarchy of domains. The addressing authority, which is defined as that which ensures uniqueness of NSAP-addresses within its span of control (i.e., its domain), takes responsibility for setting rules for further decomposition or for assigning unique NSAP-addresses.

An example of how this works may be seen in the telephone system with its numbers. Part of the telephone number identifies the country, part is an area code, part is a smaller area (an exchange), and part is the unique number assigned to a telephone (and which identifies the registered owner of that telephone). The major advantage of providing for domains is the ability to delegate the job of assigning addresses as much as is needed to minimize bureaucracy.

It is important to recognize that there is no relationship between NSAP-addresses and subnetwork-addresses (or anything else, for that matter), as far as the *user* is concerned. Hence, the NSAP-address does not explicitly or implicitly provide any routing information to users. It is natural, however, to attempt to create NSAP-address assignment rules that facilitate their processing and use by the network-service provider to create routes and to perform relaying functions.

The NSAP-address consists of two basic parts (see Figure 5.4):

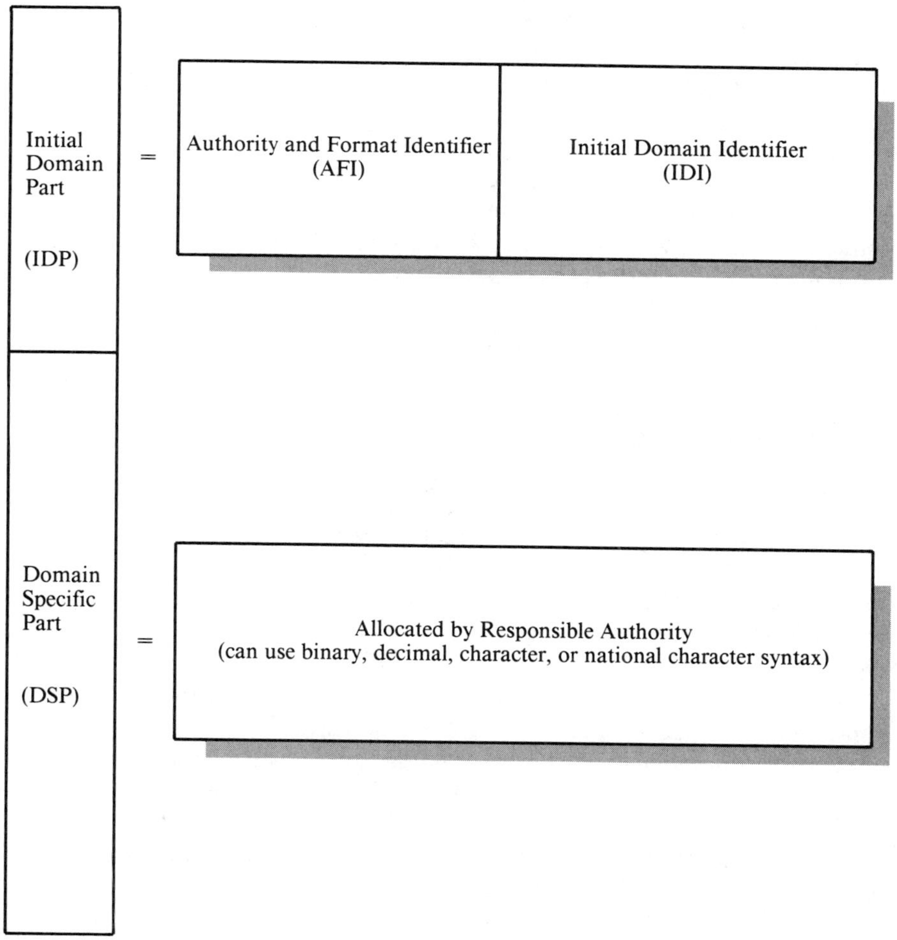

Figure 5.4 NSAP-address format.

- *Initial Domain Part* (IDP), which includes an authority and format identifier (AFI) and an initial domain identifier (IDI)
- *Domain Specific Part* (DSP), the format and contents of which are determined by the addressing authority

The AFI has three functions. It specifies the format of the IDI, identifies the addressing authority responsible for allocating the IDI, and indicates the syntax (not the encoding) of the DSP. The AFI consists of two decimal digits (i.e., a number from 0 to 99). The IDI specifies the addressing domain and the addressing authority responsible for allocating the values of the DSP for that domain. A number of formats for the IDI have been assigned, including (for example) a public switched telephone network number of up to 12 digits (allocated according to CCITT Recommendation E.163, commencing with the telephone network country code). The DSP is the part that is allocated for each NSAP-address by the responsible addressing authority. It can be expressed in binary octets, decimal digits or characters and is of variable length.

The actual length of the NSAP-address will vary according to the formats, syntax, and encodings used. Using the preferred encodings suggested in the ISO documents, the maximum length is 20 octets (with binary encoding) and 40 digits (with decimal encoding).

There may be some question as to whether NSAP-addresses should be expressed in a form that is easily read by humans. While this is possible using national character sets, it should be remembered that the NSAP-address is not an application-title and is not expected to need the same degree of human-readable, user-friendly naming and addressing capability that might be expected for the Application Layer.

5.3.4 Routing and Relaying Functions

The ability to pass data-units over arbitrary concatenations of interworking units and subnetworks involves being able to set up the required resources, establish routes that meet the specified QOS, and relay the data-units through intermediate points on the route. Hence, the functions of relaying and routing are critical to the Network Layer being able to perform its assigned role in OSI.

Routing should be able to operate effectively in a variety of environments, which makes routing a relatively difficult problem. For example, local area networks, campus/factory networks, public and private data networks, circuit-switched networks, and so on must all be able to participate as OSI subnetworks.

Relaying is concerned primarily with the actual transformation and manipulation of network-protocol-data-units (NPDUs) as they transit relay open systems.

Routing is concerned with the maintenance and selection of paths through the subnetworks and relay systems. It involves the following four different, but interrelated, aspects:

- *Routing Information Bases* (RIB), which include all information required to accomplish routing, such as next-hop routing tables, lists of neighbors, path quality characteristics, and network maps
- *Information collection*, which involves accepting and using information received from the local environment and other systems (such as operator directives, directory updates, and status information)
- *Information distribution*, which involves sending relevant information to other systems
- *Route calculation and maintenance*, which is the internal processing done by systems in the performance of routing activities

Routing is provided by a combination of Network Layer protocols and Application Layer protocols. Although it is both necessary and desirable that some routing functions be performed at the Network Layer, the transfer of such things as routing tables and routing parameters will require the full capabilities of OSI System management protocols.

Routing must be able to operate both globally and in domains, much like NSAP-addresses, although the domains are likely to be different. A "routing domain" is defined as a set of intermediate systems that use a common routing procedure.

The global routing framework can be decomposed into three categories:

- *Single subnetwork routing*, for which routing exchange protocols are used to interconnect end systems and intermediate systems on a subnetwork
- *Intra-administrative domain routing*, which is concerned with communication among intermediate systems that are managed and controlled by a single administrative authority
- *Interadministrative domain routing*, which is concerned with managing and controlling the exchange of information between intermediate systems where significantly more formal cooperation is necessary (such as between different organizations)

5.3.5 Network/Transport Protocol Interworking Issues

The goal of OSI, as has been stated previously, is to enable the interconnection of systems independently of the specific technologies, modes of operation, or administrative arrangements used. One threat to achieving this is the definition of both connection-mode and connectionless-mode communications as part of OSI itself. The problem arises when systems conforming to the connection-mode network-service (CONS) must interwork with those implementing the connectionless-mode network-service (CLNS). Three specific cases of interest are:

1. CLNS ⟷ CONS
   end end
   system system

   This case arises when two end systems using different network-service modes wish to interconnect.

2. CLNS ⟷ CLNS ⟷ CONS ⟷ CLNS ⟷ CLNS
   end subnetwork subnetwork subnetwork end
   system system

   This case might, for example, represent two local area networks interconnected by a public data network (such as a X.25 based network).

3. CONS ⟷ CONS ⟷ CLNS ⟷ CONS ⟷ CONS
   end subnetwork subnetwork subnetwork end
   system system

   This case is the opposite of the previous case, i.e., two wide area networks interconnected by a local area network.

Reconciling CONS/CLNS interconnections involves the use of an interworking unit that provides for the appropriate conversions. Although the following two solutions have been developed, there is yet to emerge a full consensus in this area:

- The *Transport Layer approach*, which places an interworking function in the Transport Layer of an interworking unit
- The *Network Layer approach*, which places an interworking function in the Network Layer of an interworking unit

Each of these approaches has its strengths and weaknesses (and its followers). Some of the considerations are:

- Both violate the basic OSI model, although the introduction of Transport Layer relays is the more serious change.
- The Network Layer approach would involve some changes to transport-protocol usage.
- The Transport Layer approach cannot support end-to-end encryption of the transport-protocol.
- Certain restrictions on paths are required for both.

The final answer to this problem has not yet been determined, but in any case there will be some important consequences for the lower layers.

5.4 THE DATA LINK LAYER (LAYER 2)

The Data Link Layer satisfies the requirement to connect the nodes of a real network and enable the error-free exchange of data. It therefore contains the functions necessary for the establishment, maintenance, and release of data-link-connections that are built upon physical-connections. The definition of the data-link-service is contained in ISO 8886. A number of protocol standards relate to this layer, catering to the various real networking environments, including those designed for local area networks packet and circuit-switching networks, the telephone network, and the integrated services digital network (ISDN).

Unlike the requirements for the Network Layer and above, the Data Link Layer provides a service that has only hop-by-hop, as opposed to end-to-end, significance. Consequently, Data Link Layer protocol standards such as CCITT Recommendation X.25 (LAP B), Q.921 (LAP D) or ISO 8802 (Logical Link Control), represent different protocols that provide the data-link-service appropriate to the Network Layer.

5.4.1 Data-Link-Service Overview

The data-link-service provides for

- Independence from the Physical Layer that may include point-to-point, multipoint, full- or half-duplex circuits
- Independence of data format, content, encoding, structure, or meaning (i.e., transparency)
- Error-free data transfer, including freedom from misordering, loss, or duplication (except in some cases of irrecoverable errors)
- QOS selection
- Addressing that has local significance only

Two distinct modes of operation have been defined: connection-mode and connectionless-mode.

In connection-mode operation, the data-link-service-user is provided with mechanisms for

- Connection establishment
- QOS negotiation
- Data transfer
- Flow control
- Connection reset
- Connection release

In connectionless-mode operation, the data-link-service-user is provided with mechanisms for the transfer of units of data.

5.4.2 Connection Establishment

Data-link-connections are established between data-link-service-access-points (DLSAPs). They are modeled as a pair of queues, one for each direction of information flow. For connection establishment a DL-CONNECT request is issued at one end. Successful connection establishment results in the receipt of a DL-CONNECT confirm primitive, after which the data transfer phase is entered and exchange of information can begin. Figure 5.5 is a state transition diagram representing possible sequences of primitives for the connection-mode operation.

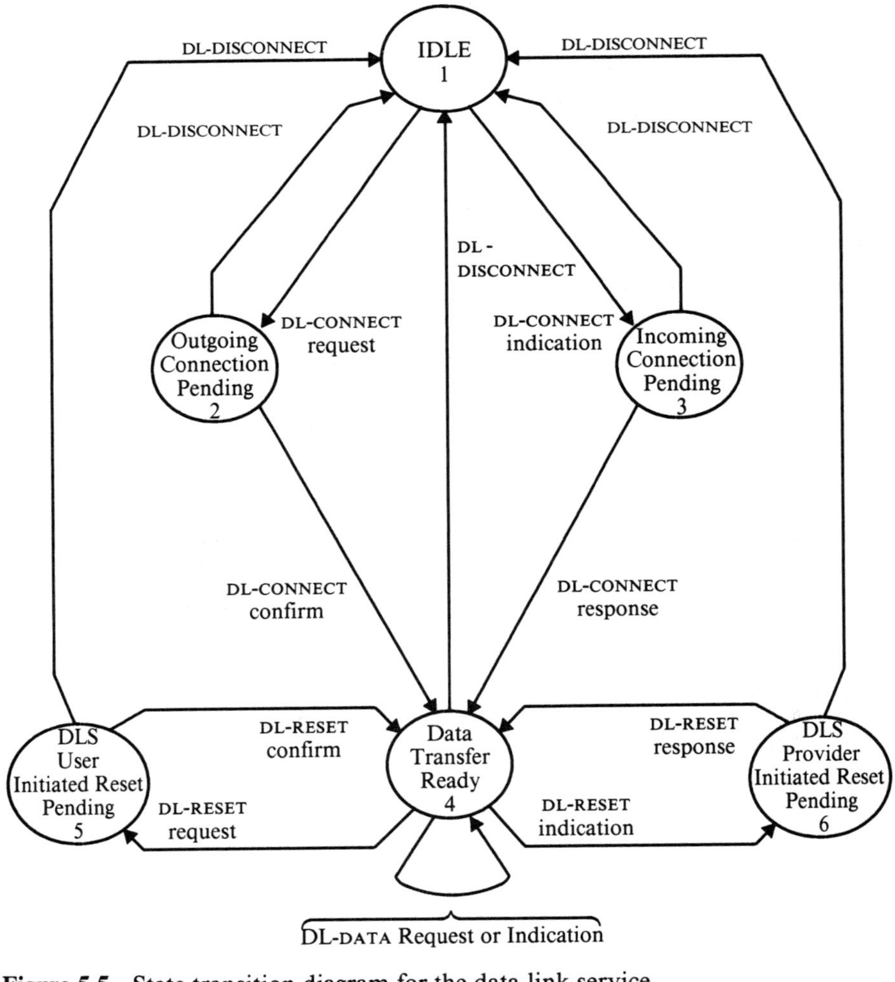

Figure 5.5 State transition diagram for the data-link-service.

5.4.3 Data Transfer

Data transfer across a data-link-connection is subject to flow control. Reset requests are defined to be destructive to all other data in transit, except in respect to connect and disconnect requests.

5.4.4 Connection Release

Data-link-connections may be released at any time by issuing a DL-DISCONNECT request. This may cause loss of data in transit and results in complete disassociation of the queues from the connection.

5.4.5 Quality of Service

The connection-mode data-link-service provides for six QOS parameters, three of which are selected during connection establishment. Once a connection is established, the agreed-upon QOS values are not changed. The three selected during connection establishment are defined as

- *Throughput* is defined as the total number of data bits successfully transferred over a data-link-connection per unit time, i.e., in the proper order and error free. This QOS parameter is specified separately for each direction of transmission.
- *Protection* is a measure of the extent to which the data-link-service provider attempts to prevent the unauthorized monitoring or manipulation of data. It is specified by a minimum and maximum characterization within the range of three protection options:

  No protection
  Passive monitoring protection
  Protection against modification, replay, addition or deletion

  Within the OSI Environment, the data being exchanged are particularly exposed during their transmission over the link. The protection features are aimed at reducing the risk of threats to privacy or security.
- *Priority* is the QOS parameter that deals with the relationship between connections. It specifies the relative importance of a data-link-connection with respect to:

  The order in which they are to have their QOS degraded
  The order in which they are to be released, if necessary

As with protection, priority is specified in terms of a minimum and a maximum within a given range.

The remaining QOS parameters are transit delay, resilience, and residual error rate.

A summary of service primitives for connection-mode layer operation is given in Table 5.4.

Table 5.4 Data Link Layer Service Primitives

Phase	Service	Primitives
Connection establishment	Connection establishment	DL-CONNECT request DL-CONNECT indication DL-CONNECT response DL-CONNECT confirm
Connection-mode data transfer	Normal data transfer	DL-DATA request DL-DATA indication
	Reset	DL-RESET request DL-RESET indication DL-RESET response DL-RESET confirm
Connection Release	Connection release	DL-DISCONNECT request DL-DISCONNECT indication
Connectionless-mode data transfer	Data transfer	DL-UNITDATA request DL-UNITDATA indication

5.4.6 Connectionless-mode Service

In the connectionless-mode data-link-service, no connection is maintained between the communicating parties. Each data-link-service-data-unit (DLSDU) is self-contained and bears no relationship to any others. A connectionless-mode DLSDU contains all the necessary information for its delivery to the target DLSAP. No guarantee of the order of the DLSDUs delivered is provided, although the integrity of each DLSDU is preserved by the data-link-service. There is also no peer-to-peer flow control.

QOS parameters are defined in the same way as for the connection-mode service, except for those, like "Resilience of a Connection," that clearly have no meaning in this context. A summary of the connectionless-mode service primitives is given in Table 5.4.

5.4.7 ISDN and the Data Link Layer

An important application of OSI Data Link Layer standards is in the Integrated Services Digital Network (ISDN). Specification of the ISDN has followed a layered structure for its access protocols. The ISDN supports a wide range of voice and nonvoice applications in the same network. There are some 78 separate I-series Recommendations dealing with ISDN in the CCITT.

The Data Link Layer specification for ISDN, called the Link Access Procedure on the D-channel (LAP D), is described in CCITT Recommendations I.440 (general aspects) and I.441 (detailed specification). LAP D uses the same principles and terminology as Recommendation X.25 (LAP B) for packet-mode terminals and ISO 3309 and 4335 (High-level Data Link Control) for frame structure and elements of procedure.

LAP D messages are transmitted in frames, delimited by flags. Flags are unique bit patterns not permitted within the information fields of messages. LAP D supports the following functions:

- One or more data-link-connections on a D-channel
- Frame delimiting, alignment, and transparency
- Sequencing
- Error detection
- Recovery from detected transmission, format, and operational errors
- Flow control

Point-to-point and broadcast data-link configurations are supported. Operation of the LAP D service may be with acknowledged or unacknowledged information frames. In the former case, no error recovery or flow control mechanisms are defined. In the latter case, error recovery based on retransmission of frames, and flow control mechanisms, are provided.

Detailed specifications for the frame structure, elements of procedure, format of fields, and procedures for the proper operation of the ISDN LAP D are contained in CCITT Recommendation I.441.

5.5 THE PHYSICAL LAYER (LAYER 1)

The purpose of the Physical Layer is to provide a bit transparent interface to the physical media for the transfer of data between open systems. The Physical Layer specifies the mechanical, electrical, functional and procedural means to activate, maintain, and deactivate physical-connections between open systems. The detailed physical-services definition is found in ISO 10022.

A physical-connection is a logical concept even though it has a direct relation to real physical media, such as twisted pairwiring, coaxial cable, or other types. There is no distinction between connection- and connectionless-mode communication. Physical-connections may span systems comprising several types of physical media in tandem.

5.5.1 Distinctions of Physical-service

The Physical Layer provides for the following types of transmission, modes of operation, and network topologies:

- Synchronous or asynchronous transmission
- Duplex, half-duplex, and simplex modes of operation
- Point-to-point and multipoint topologies

5.5.2 Physical-connection Model

Figure 5.6 shows a model of a relayed point-to-point physical-connection. The point-to-point operation is simply modeled by a pair of bit streams linking the physical-service-access-points (PhSAPs), i.e., the points at which the physical-service is available to the layer above. There is one bit stream for each direction of transmission, and bits are delivered in the same order in which they are submitted. The Physical Layer relay models the case where tandem physical media are involved in making up the physical-connection.

5.5.3 Synchronization

The physical-service provides synchronization including bit synchronization. This is a process whereby the presence and timing of signaling pulses on the physical media are determined. In the case of synchronous transmission, the presence of data bits occurs at regular clocked intervals. In asynchronous transmission, data are transmitted at irregular intervals, with each meaningful unit of information (e.g., an encoded character) containing its own synchronization information.

5.5.4 Quality of Service

A physical-connection will exhibit various qualities depending on the composition of the physical media making up the overall physical-circuit. This gives rise to the concept of QOS, which may be characterized by service availability, error rate, throughput, transit delay, and protection.

5.5.5 ISDN and the Physical Layer

CCITT Recommendation I.430 describes the Physical Layer for the ISDN User–Network Interface. It specifies the requirement for a balanced metallic

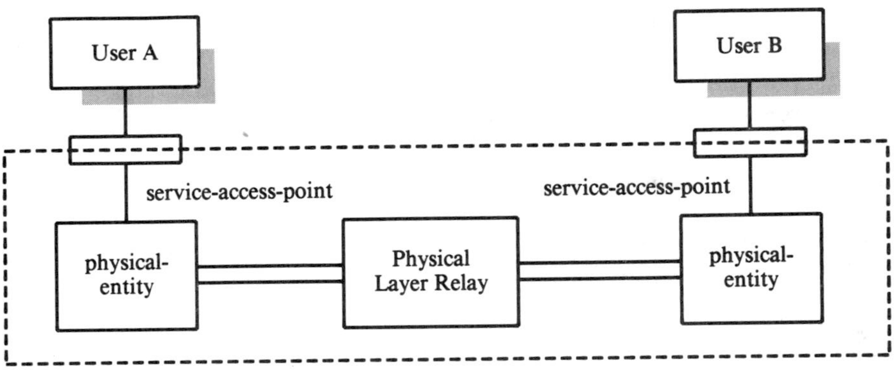

Figure 5.6 Relayed point-to-point physical-connection.

transmission medium having a capability, for each direction of transmission, of supporting 192 kbit/sec. The ISDN Physical Layer supports the requirements for

- Transmission of encoded bit streams for B-channels (64 kbit/sec) and D-channels (various bit rates), plus timing and synchronization
- Activation and deactivation of subscriber terminals and/or network terminating equipment
- Providing access to the common resource of the C-channel for terminals
- Physical Layer maintenance functions
- Indication of Physical Layer status to the higher layers

In the ISDN the basic interface structure is defined as 2B-channels + 1D-channel, where the D-channel bit rate in this case is 16 kbit/sec. A second ISDN Physical Layer recommendation, I.431, deals with electrical, format, and channel usage characteristics for the ISDN primary rates of 1544 and 2048 kbit/sec.

CHAPTER 6

AN OVERVIEW OF THE UPPER LAYERS

Whereas the lower four layers are responsible for reliable transport of information from end system to end system, the upper layers are responsible for ensuring successful interworking between end systems. By *interworking* is meant the ability to exchange meaningful information in support of a distributed processing task. All three upper layers are driven by application semantics, with the Session and Presentation Layers performing standardized functions under the control of the Application Layer. The Application Layer contains the application-specific communications functionality, which supports distributed processing.

This chapter introduces the basic concepts pertaining to the upper three layers by way of an analogy to the communications requirements of interpersonal telephone communication. A more detailed look at each of the upper layers follows in the subsequent three chapters. Chapter 7 on the Application Layer includes the layer model, a description of the protocols standardized to date, a discussion of the relationship among the upper three layers, and other aspects relevant to the Application Layer. Chapters 8 (Session Layer) and 9 (Presentation Layer) include a description of the layer model, a summary of the available services, and an explanation of the layer usage from the perspective of an application-protocol developer.

6.1 TELEPHONE SYSTEM EXAMPLE

For successful person-to-person communication via the telephone system, it is necessary but not sufficient that the telephone network itself function properly, i.e., that a line is available, that the supplied telephone number reaches the desired destination, that the target telephone is not busy and that the connection is not noisy or broken off in the course of the call.

There are a number of aspects not related to the telephone network that influence the success or failure of communication. These pertain to the nature of interpersonal communication, as described in the following.

6.1.1 Addressing

Once the call is answered, it is typically necessary to identify the called and calling parties, especially when one telephone number services many persons. This corresponds to application addressing in the OSI Environment.

6.1.2 Common Language of Communication

There is no point in calling someone on the telephone unless there is commonality of language between the callers; someone who speaks and understands only English will not be able to communicate successfully with someone who speaks and understands only Russian. The language of communication in many cases is determined by default; i.e., the calling parties speak only one language. In other cases, there may be a choice of languages available, and so negotiation of language(s) may be needed.

This situation occurs frequently in parts of Canada, where both English and French are accepted as official languages of business and government. One commonly hears a receptionist answer the telephone with a salutation that combines both English and French, e.g., "The ABC Company, *bonjour*." The message to the caller is that either language is acceptable; the caller then completes this implicit language negotiation by speaking in the selected language.

In OSI-based communication, the need for different possible syntactical representations for the same information is recognized. It is the responsibility of the Presentation Layer to negotiate the so-called transfer syntax used to interchange application information, and to perform any needed syntax conversions between local representations of this information and the interchange representation. Thus, the Presentation Layer acts as a form of language translation facility.

6.1.3 Dialogue Management

The telephone system is inherently a full-duplex channel; i.e., it permits both parties to speak at once without garbling the signal. However, it is the nature of interpersonal conversation that information is communicated most successfully when only one person is speaking at a time. Thus one of the first rules of telephone usage is that the listener waits for the speaker to finish speaking before responding. Essentially then, a telephone conversation takes on a half-duplex nature, with an implicit handover of the right to speak from one person to the other at pauses in the conversation. Of course, in many instances, the conversation deviates markedly from a rigid half-duplex discipline, particularly when the conversation is lively. It is to the credit of the human speech-processing system that it can, in many cases, successfully perform simultaneous speech generation and reception.

In a data communications environment, there is frequently a need to manage the dialogue between the communicating parties; and as computer systems are generally less tolerant of undisciplined dialogue than humans, it is normally necessary to structure the dialogue carefully. The OSI Session Layer provides the appropriate dialogue management capabilities. It allows the communicating parties to negotiate the use of full or half-duplex communication, and in the case of half-duplex communication, it provides the tools, in the form of tokens, to control the right to send data.

Now, imagine one person dictating a recipe to another person over the telephone. Both persons want to be sure that all the information is properly transferred; the recipient therefore acknowledges (e.g., via an "OK" response) each ingredient and each step of the recipe as it is listed. Failing to understand a step in the instructions, the recipient can ask the sender to backtrack and repeat that step. These two people are engaging in a form of synchronization that allows the sender to know what the recipient has successfully received (via checkpoints in the dialogue) and allows the recipient to request resynchronization to a previous checkpoint when needed.

The OSI Session Layer provides comparable synchronization capabilities that allow checkpoints to be inserted by the sender at appropriate points in an interchanged data stream. The checkpoint acknowledgments by the recipient indicate successful reception of the information. In case of difficulty, it is possible to resynchronize to a previously acknowledged checkpoint and continue the dialogue at that point.

Taking the recipe analogy one step further, consider the situation where a number of recipes are being dictated during one telephone conversation. The transfer of the set of recipes can be considered as a single activity that is subdivided into "dialogue units," each corresponding to one recipe. Each dialogue unit is self-contained; i.e., the sender does not begin a new recipe until the recipient has acknowledged reception of the current recipe, and once this acknowledgment has been sent, the recipient cannot ask to backtrack to that recipe. The Session Layer supports this form of the dialogue via major and minor synchronization points.

Should one person have to interrupt the conversation and hang up, the normal practice would be to reestablish the connection at some later time, resynchronize to an agreed point in the dialogue, e.g., start the last recipe over again from the beginning, and continue. It is not necessary to dictate again the recipes that have been transferred successfully. The Session Layer also supports resynchronization of activities across connections.

Notice that it is the sender and recipient of the recipes who decide what are the appropriate points in the dialogue for checkpoints, and it is they who interpret the semantics of such checkpoints, i.e., what reaching a certain checkpoint means to the recipient. Similarly, the OSI Session Layer simply provides general capabilities for managing a dialogue; it does not decide where checkpoints are to be inserted, nor does it associate any semantics with them. Therefore, it cannot decide when to initiate resynchronization. All this is the responsibility of the end-user application.

6.1.4 Application Context

The purpose of interpersonal telephone communication is to interchange meaningful verbal information. For the information to be meaningful, the parties to a telephone conversation must have a mutual understanding of the information that is communicated. It is pointless for someone to discuss the intricacies of a complex mathematical theorem to someone with no mathematical training; the two parties are not operating in the same context, so little or no useful interchange of information is possible. It is essential, therefore, that there be an agreed-upon context for the communication. This context determines what is meaningful to both parties; i.e., it determines the semantics of the interchanged information.

By default, the context of normal telephone conversation is the sum total of the common knowledge and experiences of the parties. Typically, however, a telephone conversation at any given time is focused on a particular topic that in effect defines a more restricted context, e.g., a particular business deal or a discussion of the weekend's sports results. In a single telephone conversation, there may be a number of contexts invoked in succession, each introduced formally ("I want to talk about the agenda for the upcoming meeting") or informally, by a casual change in conversation ("Say, it was nice to see the Giants win for a change!").

The application context not only determines the applicable semantics but may also determine the roles of the parties and the actions they can perform. For example, a call from a subscriber to a telephone information service (e.g., a 411 number in North America) has a well-defined set of rules regarding the behavior of each of the parties. The operator asks the caller for the city; the caller supplies the name of the city and the identification of the desired party; the operator responds with the telephone number if a match is found.

In OSI, all communication between application-processes is governed by application-contexts that determine the semantics of the interchanged information, identify the communications functions that are available, and specify the rules of behavior of the communicating parties. Unless, the communicating parties agree on the context of their communication, they cannot communicate effectively.

Just as a person may be capable of talking about many different topics, an application-process may support many different application-contexts.

6.1.5 Commonly Used Procedures

In most telephone conversations there are certain common procedures that serve a purpose not specific to the particular topic of conversation. Examples are the introductory procedure for identifying the called and calling parties, the "good-bye" at the end of a call, and the various ways in which a topic of conversation can be selected. Such procedures are intermixed with the application-specific exchanges in the course of a conversation.

Similarly, OSI has identified and standardized a number of procedures that can be used in a variety of applications. An example is the association control procedure for establishing an application-association and the corresponding application-context. A specific application is expected to incorporate these procedures wherever appropriate. The effect is that a specific application consists of a mixture of procedures, some of which are common to many applications, while others are specific to that particular application. More complex applications can in fact be a composite of other specific applications. OSI imposes no restrictions on the way in which application procedures are combined (they need not be hierarchically related); it demands only that such combinations be well defined.

6.1.6 Specific Application Protocols

Although there are examples in the interpersonal telephone conversation world of fairly rigid application-specific procedures (the telephone number information service described above is a case in point), these are not standardized internationally. ISO, on the other hand, has recognized a need for standardizing a number of application-specific protocols considered to be of widespread interest and importance. The four applications that have been standardized to date within ISO/IEC JTC1 are file transfer, virtual terminal, job transfer and manipulation, and message transfer (electronic mail). These are described in Chapter 10. Work is now underway on a protocol for transaction processing.

The OSI model imposes no restriction on the number and nature of application-protocols that can be developed. It is expected that within ISO, various industry-specific standards will be developed, e.g., office communications standards in ISO/IEC JTC1/SC18, banking communications standards in ISO TC68, and library communications standards in ISO TC46. OSI-compatible application-protocols can also be developed by non-ISO groups. ISO has defined a procedure whereby such protocols can be registered formally and therefore be publicly known.

CHAPTER 7

THE APPLICATION LAYER (LAYER 7)

7.1 ROLE OF THE APPLICATION LAYER

The essential purpose of OSI is to support distributed information processing. Such processing involves interworking among two or more application-processes (AP). The Application Layer acts as the window between interworking APs that permits the exchange of meaningful information.

The Application Layer contains all functions that imply communication between open systems that are not already performed by the lower layers. These include functions performed by programs as well as functions performed by human beings. The Application Layer is the only layer that directly provides services to APs and necessarily provides all OSI services directly usable by such processes.

7.2 BASIC CONCEPTS OF THE APPLICATION LAYER

The concepts described here are abstract in nature and are not intended to represent how real systems are implemented.

7.2.1 Application-Process and Application-Entity

A distributed application may be modeled as a collection of *application-processes*. An AP is an identifiable set of cooperating capabilities within a real open system that takes part in the execution of one or more information-processing tasks.

The activity of a given AP is represented by an AP-invocation. At a given time, an AP may be represented by none, one, or more than one AP-invocation. Each AP-invocation performs particular actions in order to operate on (e.g., create, modify) information related to the overall objectives of the information-processing task(s) at hand.

An AP may be viewed as operating in two environments, as shown in Figure 7.1. The Local System Environment is where local, communications-independent processing functions are performed. The OSIE is the union of all communications functionality related to the distributed application. There is only one OSIE. The Application Layer is the highest hierarchical layer within the OSIE.

There is no explicit boundary between the Local System Environment and the OSIE within a real open system; i.e., the Application Layer does not represent a programming interface to user applications. The separation between the two environments is conceptual only. Within a real open system, the part of the AP that is concerned with communications, and hence is part of the Application Layer and the OSIE, is called an *application-entity* (AE).

The OSI communications functions of an AP may be grouped into multiple sets of functions and, thus, a single AP may be represented by multiple AEs. Each AE represents one and only one AP.

An application-entity-invocation (AE-invocation) models the communications functions and state information for a particular instance of communication of an application-entity. For each of the AEs associated with one AP, a related AP-invocation may be represented at any time by none, one, or more than one AE-invocation. For any AE-invocation, there is one and only one AP-invocation. If there are two or more active AE-invocations for a specific AP-invocation, the operations of these AE-invocations may take place in any order, either serially or simultaneously, or both.

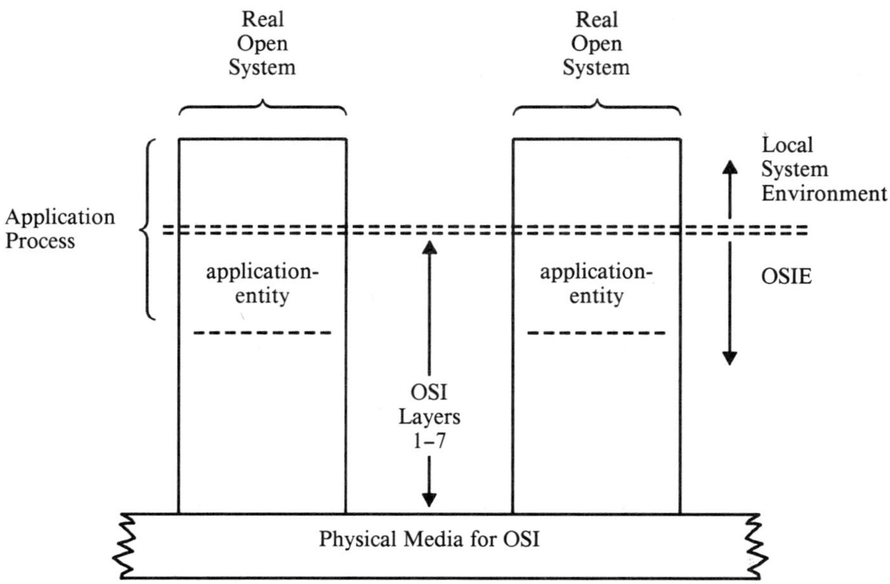

Figure 7.1 Local System and Open Systems Interconnection environments.

7.2.2 Types and Invocations

An AP represents an identifiable set of capabilities for executing an information processing task within a real open system. It is an instance of an *application-process type.* An AP type is a specification of a particular set of information processing functions that may be common to many systems. Within a real open system, there may be many concurrent executions of an AP, each termed an *AP-invocation.*

An analogy is seen in a computer program like a compiler. A compiler for a programming language corresponds to an AP type. The executable object code within a particular computer system corresponds to an AP. Note that this object code is identifiable, e.g., "cc" for a "C" language compiler. In a multiuser system, there may be several concurrent executions of that compiler; each such execution corresponds to an AP-invocation.

Similarly, an *application-entity type* is a specification of a specific set of Application Layer (i.e., communications) functions. An AE is an instance of an AE type, representing the parts of an AP involved in OSI communications. An *AE-invocation* is then the OSI communications functionality associated with an AP-invocation. For example, an AE type could represent the file transfer functionality for a particular AP type. The file transfer functionality in a particular real open system corresponds to an AE while an actual file transfer is performed by an AE-invocation.

If the type of an AP or an AE is reflected in its name, then it becomes possible to ascertain which systems are likely to be able to interwork, simply on the basis of names. This information is typically available via a directory service (see Chapter 11).

7.2.3 Application-Service-Elements

An application-service-element (ASE) is a coherent set of communications functions that provides a capability for interworking of AEs for a specific purpose. In general, an Application Layer protocol is realized by the use of the communication capabilities of a number of ASEs. These ASEs may be used sequentially or in combination.

The term *application-service-element* is used in this context to refer to a divisible part of the object that the AE represents; this is in contrast with the usage of the term *service* applied to other OSI layers, where it refers to functional interactions that can be described at the upper boundary of a layer.

The communication capabilities of an ASE are defined by the specification of a set of application-protocol-data-units (APDUs) and the procedures governing their use. This information is contained within a protocol specification.

There typically is an accompanying service definition for an ASE, which provides a user view of the communication functions of the ASE. This combination of a service definition and a protocol specification is typical for all OSI layers. The Application Layer is slightly different in that there may be many service and protocol specifications defined, as opposed to the single set defined for the Presentation, Session, and Transport Layers.

The user of one ASE may be another ASE, or it could be the *Application Layer User* (ALU), which is that function within the AP that uses the ASEs needed to accomplish the communications objectives of that AP.

Note: In ISO 7498 – 1984, the term "user element" is used to describe the ALU. However, as the user element is considered part of the AE, this creates a difficulty in the more elaborate model of the Application Layer discussed later. As a result, the term *Application Layer User* is used as an alternative in this overview. The ALU is not part of the AE. It is anticipated that the term "user element" will be removed from the Basic Reference Model.

ASEs receive service requests from each other and from the ALU. They make use of each other and of services of the Presentation Layer to perform their functions. ASEs receive indications of services performed either from other ASEs or from the Presentation Layer via the associated presentation-service-access-point (PSAP).

The ALU is the original initiator of requests to the various ASEs and the ultimate recipient of responses from the various ASEs. Each ASE has a set of rules governing its use and the use it makes of other ASEs, regardless of whether it is defined as a standard or is privately designed. It is the responsibility of the user invoking or responding to ASEs to do so in a sequence that conforms to the applicable rules.

The Application Layer differs from other layers in that its services are not provided to a higher layer; the absence of an upper layer boundary means that there is no SAP through which services are made available. ASEs are considered to be an integral part of the AE. Nevertheless, the service model used for lower layers (see Section 8.2) can still be used. The service-users are the ALUs and the service provider is the totality of all ASEs in the AEs that participate in the distributed application, in addition to all lower layers (see Figure 7.2). It should be emphasized that there is no true boundary between the ALUs and the service provider. In particular, the horizontal dashed lines in Figure 7.2 are not meant to represent a programming interface.

Figure 7.2 also illustrates the fact that some ASEs may be directly visible to the ALU, while others may not. A directly visible ASE is one whose services may be invoked directly by the ALU; other ASEs may play a supporting role in the provision of such services, but their services are invoked by the user-visible ASEs and not by the ALU. There is, however, no concept of sublayering within the Application Layer. One ASE that is not directly visible in one AE may be visible to the ALU in another AE.

7.2.4 Application-Associations

In order for meaningful interaction to be possible between AEs, a cooperative relationship must exist. Such a relationship in a connection-oriented environment is termed an *application-association* (AA). AAs are established

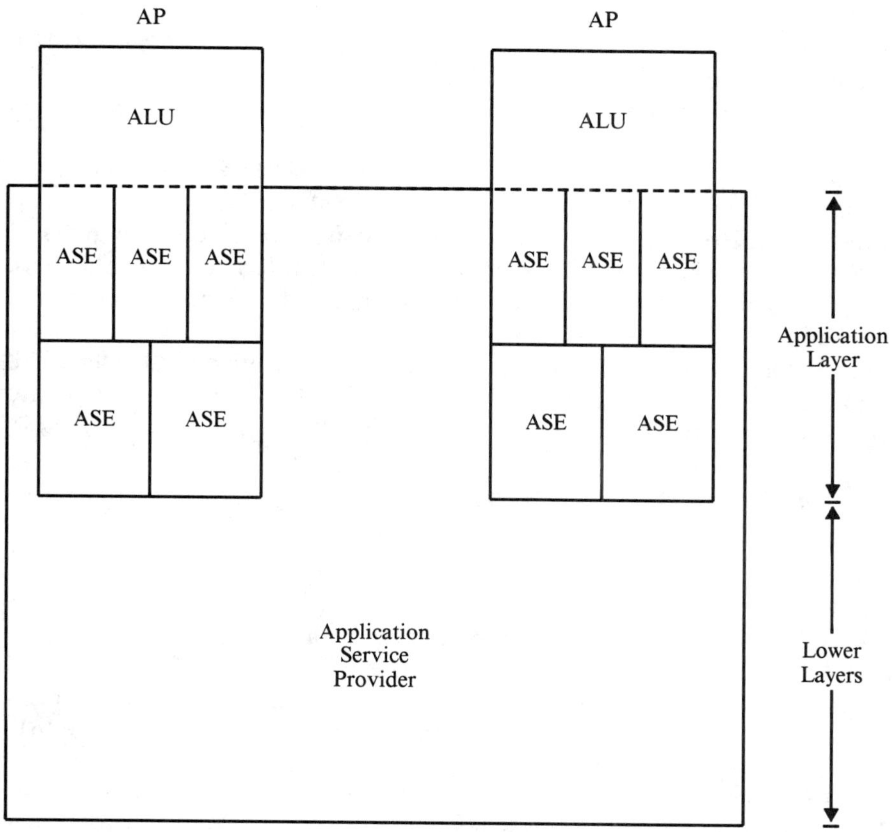

Figure 7.2 View of the application service provider.

explicitly by the exchange of application-protocol-control-information over a presentation-connection.

7.2.5 Association Control Service Elements

All connection-oriented AEs require functionality for establishing and releasing AAs. The *Association Control Service Element* (ACSE) is the ASE that exists solely for this purpose.

The process of AA establishment is initiated by the ALU or by some ASE in the initiating AE-invocation that invokes the A-ASSOCIATE service of the ACSE. This causes a P-CONNECT request to be issued across the attached PSAP. This in turn results in protocol exchanges that trigger the occurrence of a P-CONNECT indication at the requested PSAP in the receiving system. The protocol-control-information for AA establishment for the upper three layers is typically embedded into a single transport-service-data-unit.

At the receiving system, an invocation of the called AE is created by a local management function. The A-ASSOCIATE service within this AE-invocation interacts with its service-user to determine whether to accept the requested association and then issues the appropriate response over the established presentation-connection.

Only one AE is attached to a particular PSAP. Therefore, it is normally possible to reach the desired AE simply by specifying the correct presentation-address. However, it is possible that the desired AE is no longer attached to the specified PSAP (e.g., if a particular end system has been reconfigured). To verify that the correct AE is being accessed, the title of the destination AE can be provided during AA establishment.

Given that the AE-title is correct, the target AP is unambiguously identified. This is because an AE is associated with a single AP. The following titles are fixed relative to the AE:

- AP-type title (optional)
- AP title
- AE-type title (optional)

All of the services of the Presentation Layer are available to the ASEs at the PSAP to which the AE is attached. Each presentation-connection is identified by its presentation-connection-endpoint-identifier (PCEI). This identifier distinguishes a presentation-connection from all other connections at that PSAP. Since a single presentation-connection supports a single AA, there is a one-to-one mapping between a PCEI and the AE-invocation that is the source or sink for each presentation-service-data-unit for that connection crossing the conceptual interface at the PSAP.

In addition to the AE title, it is possible to pass the following identifiers as part of the application-protocol-control-information exchanged to establish an AA:

- AE-invocation identifier
- AP-invocation identifier
- AA identifier

This information may be helpful to identify a particular AE-invocation and AA when multiple AE-invocations and multiple AAs are active at a particular PSAP.

An AE-invocation has the entire set of ASEs of the AE available for its use; however, it may choose to make use of only a subset in specific situations. Such subsets are identified by application-contexts.

7.2.6 Use of Services

One example of an AE with multiple ASEs is shown in Figure 7.3. The ALU interacts with ASE1, which in turn interacts with other ASEs and uses the

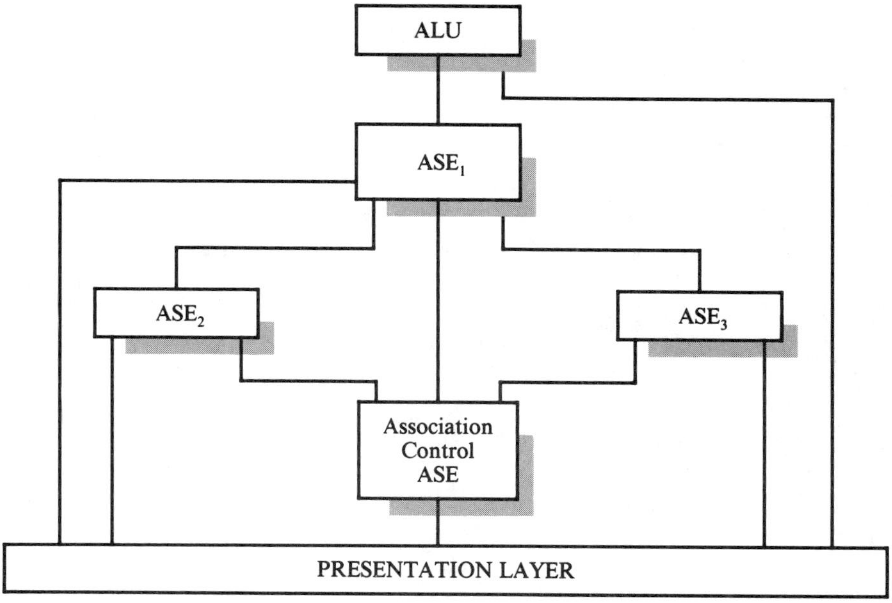

Figure 7.3 Possible interactions involving ASEs, the ALU, and the Presentation Layer.

presentation-service. This example illustrates possible interactions involving ASEs, the ALU, and the Presentation Layer. Many other configurations for an AE can be identified.

7.2.7 Application-Context

Exchanges of information on an AA must follow a set of mutually understood rules if the communication activity is to proceed successfully. This set of rules is called the application-context.

The set of rules in an application-context will always include a list of a set of ASEs (by reference to the relevant standards). Other items that may be specified by the application-context include:

- Specifications for the logical structure of relevant information
- Inter-ASE dependencies and coordination rules
- Additional rules related to selection, use, concatenation, and sequencing of PDUs
- Designation of and rules for the use of application functions, such as the directory
- Rules for changing rules
- Rules for mapping APCI from ASEs onto the presentation-service and/or other ASEs
- Rules concerning information that outlasts an association

The communications behavior of an AE when using an AA is constrained to be compatible with a generic behavior defined by the application-context in use. An application-context may prescribe several active ASEs whose services may be invoked asynchronously or in parallel on a single AA. The ASEs themselves and the definition of their use in an application-context must ensure cooperative use of the presentation-service.

An application-context is not in general associated with a single AE. Its definition may exist quite apart from the definition of any particular AE, and the context may be incorporated into widely varying AEs. For example, the File Transfer Access and Management (FTAM) standard defines a particular file transfer context that may be used in a wide variety of distributed processing applications, each with different AE characteristics.

In the case of simple applications, a single application-context may be associated with an AE. For example, for an AE that performs only file transfers, the single FTAM application-context may be sufficient. On the other hand, if an AE supports both remote terminal access and file transfer, then two application-contexts might be appropriate.

An AA has only one application-context, although the rules defined by it may change during the lifetime of the corresponding AA.

An ASE may be referred to by more than one application-context.

7.2.8 The Single Association Object

The AA between two AE-invocations is modeled as a relationship between *Single Association Objects* (SAOs), each of which exists within their AE-invocations. The SAO is a proper subset of the functionality of the AE. SAO is simply a name for the collection of objects in an AE related to a single AA.

Each SAO within an AE-invocation may contain the same or different functionality, depending on the application-contexts supported. Each SAO consists of an Association Control Service Element, one or more other ASEs, and a *Single Association Control Function* (SACF). The SACF is used to model the coordination of the use of the ACSE and the presentation-service. The rules governing this coordination form part of the application-context selected for a particular instance of communication. Conceptually, all service requests from the "user" of the SAO or from any ASE within the SAO to either the presentation-service, any ASE, or any local function (e.g., Directory, Security, or Management functions) pass through the SACF. The SACF acts as the arbiter that ensures consistent operation of the SAO as a whole.

It is important to realize that the SACF is only a concept. There is no requirement that an implementation of Application Layer protocols incorporate an identifiable SACF.

7.3 CONCEPTUAL MODEL OF THE APPLICATION LAYER

A basic model of the Application Layer associates a single AE with an AP, a single AE-invocation per AP-invocation, a single AA per AE-invocation, and a single application-context per AA. The most general Application Layer model allows multiplicity in all cases.

7.3.1 Multiple Application-Associations per Application-Entity-Invocation

When an AE-invocation supports multiple AAs, then a *Multiple Association Control Function* (MACF) may be required to coordinate the activities on the various associations. The MACF is part of the AE-invocation, but distinct from the SAOs. It does not generate any application-protocol-control-information, so is not considered to be an ASE. If there is a need for two or more MACFs in separate open systems to coordinate their activities, then any necessary application-protocol-control-information is generated by an ASE within one or more of the SAOs that form part of the AE-invocation.

The rules of coordination that pertain to a particular SAO may form part of the definition of the application-context associated with that SAO.

A MACF provides the mapping between the services seen by the ALU and those provided by the individual SAOs. This mapping need not be one-to-one. For example, a single transaction processing service request may be mapped by the MACF to multiple transaction branches, each represented by a different AA.

7.3.2 Multiple AE-Invocations per Application-Process-Invocation

Only one information exchange activity is supported by a single AA at a given time. Therefore, when an AP-invocation wishes to make use of multiple AAs, an alternative to establishing multiple AAs per AE-invocation is to establish multiple AE-invocations, each supporting one or more AAs.

Each such AE-invocation is derived from the same AE and has available the full set of ASEs associated with that AE. This is illustrated in Figure 7.4. The actual set of ASEs used on a given association is determined in the usual manner, i.e., negotiation of the application-context.

7.3.3 Multiple Application-Entities per Application-Process

The model for the Application Layer allows for multiple AEs per AP. Each AE can be of a different type, reflecting different combinations of communications functionality. Figure 7.5 illustrates the situation where AE-invocations representing two different AE types are associated with the same AP-invocation. In this case, if there is a requirement to coordinate the activities of the two AE-invocations, the MACFs of the various AE-invocations may operate together to provide an integrated coordination capability. No name has been given to this function as yet.

Each AE in an AP (and hence each AE-invocation) would have a distinct presentation-address associated with it. This is required to preserve the one-to-one mapping between the presentation-address and the AE.

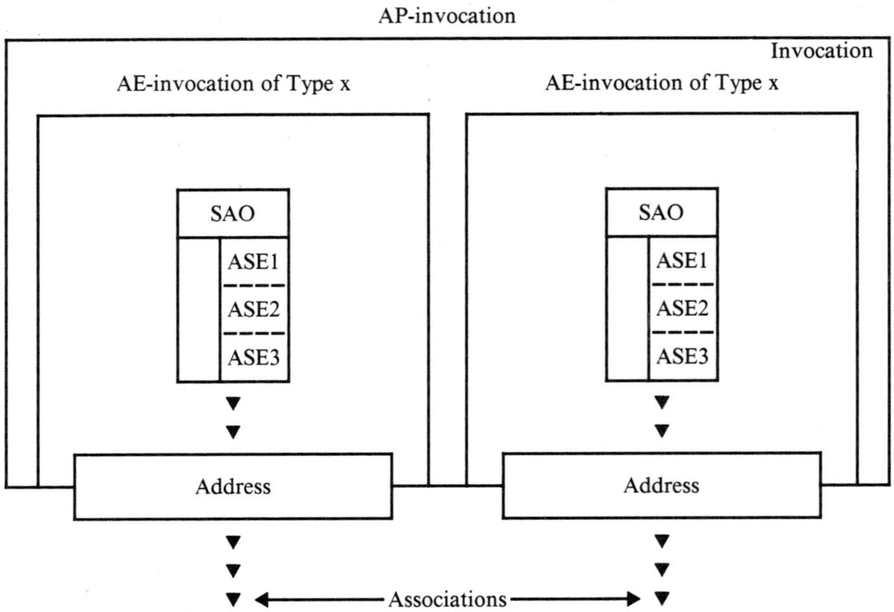

Figure 7.4 Multiple AE-invocations per AP-invocation.

7.3.4 Application-Context Versus Application-Entity

Both the application-context and the AE represent ways of selecting the functionality that is to be available on an association. An AP wishing to divide its functionality into identifiable subsets could do so in two ways:

1. Define a separate AE with its own title for each functional subset. Each subset would include at least one application-context. In this case, the desired subset is accessed by first selecting the appropriate AE-title and then the appropriate application-context, i.e., the desired set of ASEs.
2. Define a single AE with a separate application-context for each functional subset.

No specific guidelines exist for selecting between these possibilities.

7.4 MODES OF COMMUNICATION

There are three possible modes of communication between open systems: connection-mode, connectionless-mode and store-and-forward.

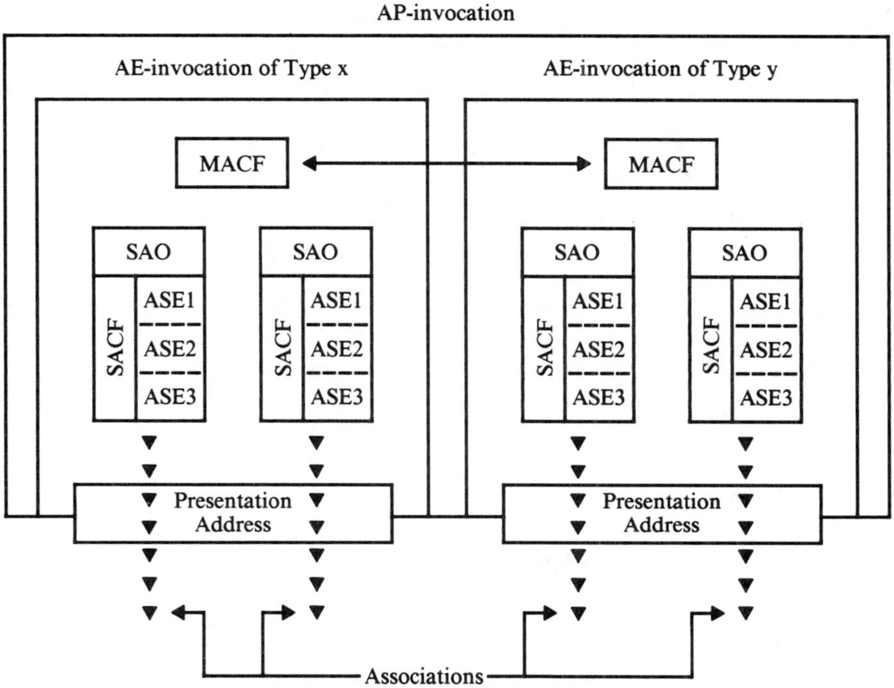

Figure 7.5 Full Application Layer Model.

Note: At this time, ISO/IEC JTC1/SC 21 is working only on the connection- and connectionless-modes of communication. Work on store-and-forward communication is being performed by CCITT SG VII and ISO/IEC JTC1/SC 18, both in the area of message handling (electronic mail).

In connection-mode communication, an AA is established explicitly each time interworking is to take place including the establishment of lower layer connections. The supporting layers 4 through 7 (at least) must also be connection-mode. In situations where supporting connections already exist at one or more layers, only those connections not already in place need to be established.

In connectionless-mode communication, there is no concept of a connection between AEs. This mode is intended for the transfer of independent units of information, each of which is self-contained. The communications channel is potentially unreliable, with the possibility that units of information will be lost, corrupted, or received out of sequence. Architecturally, it is possible to include sequencing and error detection capabilities within individual layers, but at present, no connectionless-mode protocols include such functions. This mode of communication is appropriate when transmission efficiency is of paramount concern and when transmission unreliability is either unimportant or known to be acceptably low. An example of its use is for the remote acquisition of data samples that are to be averaged over time. It is also applicable for sending single units of information to multiple destinations, particularly when the underlying communications medium supports broadcasting.

In store-and-forward communication, no end-to-end connections are established, but connections are established with intermediate systems that perform Application Layer relaying. This is illustrated in Figure 7.6. In effect, this is a mixture of connection-mode and connectionless-mode. The highest level application-protocol is connectionless on an end-to-end basis while a lower-level application protocol and all lower layers are typically connection-mode on a hop-by-hop basis.

Thus, transmission reliability equal to connection-mode communication is possible for each hop; however, the relay systems are potential failure points. This form of communication can be used when response-time requirements are low or when an end system is not always available; in this case, the data can be sent to the final relay system for retrieval by the target system at its convenience.

Two implications of this mode of communication are that the amount of data that can be interchanged in one message is usually restricted due to limited buffer capacity in the intermediate systems, and there is no longer a one-to-one relationship between an AA and traffic flow. Whereas in a connection-mode environment related traffic between AEs can be identified by a CEI (which identifies the AA), in a store-and-forward environment there is no end-to-end connection. An additional mechanism, such as a transaction or message identifier, is needed to identify related messages, e.g., responses to requests.

7.5 OTHER APPLICATION LAYER CONCEPTS

7.5.1 Relationship to Implementations

The architecture described in this overview is conceptual in nature and in no way constrains implementations. In the OSI world, implementations are constrained only to the extent that implementations of protocols must conform to the conformance clauses stated in the corresponding standards. These

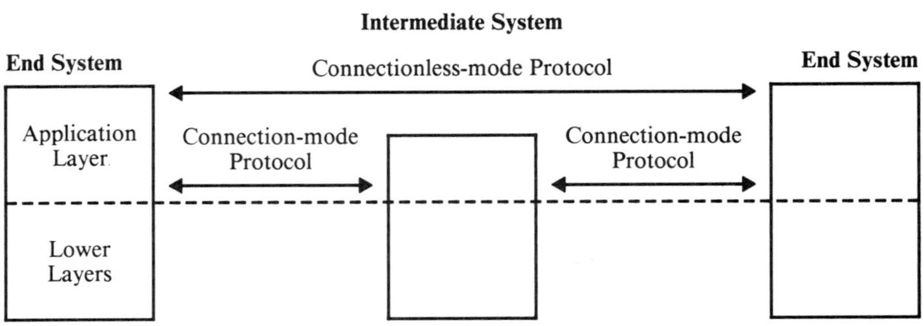

Figure 7.6 A store-and-forward environment.

conformance clauses specify only the externally visible behavior to which an implementation must adhere, and then only in terms of syntax and sequencing of protocol-data-units (PDUs). There is no conformance to service definition standards. This leaves the implementor considerable freedom.

In practice, service definition standards serve as a useful interface specification for layer implementations. With these standards, it becomes possible to develop bindings for commonly used computer programming languages. A binding in this case is a mapping of a sequence of one or more service primitives into a language-specific procedure or function specification. The availability of such mappings in turn encourages the development of OSI software libraries. Although not yet standardized, language bindings for OSI services, if they become widely accepted and available, can help transform the OSI software from "special purpose" and therefore expensive to "utilitarian" and therefore inexpensive.

Note: At the present time, such bindings have not been developed in ISO but are produced by the implementors themselves for each systems environment.

7.5.2 Relationship Between Association, Connection, and Context

An AA is a cooperative relationship between two AE-invocations that is formed by the exchange of mutually understandable application-protocol-control-information (APCI). There is a one-to-one mapping between an AA and a presentation-connection, and similarly between a presentation-connection and a session-connection.

The establishment of a presentation-connection is the first step in the process of establishing an AA. It permits identification of the cooperating AEs by their presentation-addresses. The second step is the exchange of A-ASSOCIATE PDUs, which serve to identify the AEs by title and to identify the application-context that applies to the association.

The application-context in turn identifies the set of ASEs that are potentially available during the association, as well as the rules for their use. It acts as the frame of reference for successful interworking between the AEs.

7.5.3 Embedding of Protocol-Data-Units

At any layer, the PDUs exchanged between peer entities have two components: PCI relating to the operation of the protocol and user-data supplied by the service-user. These user-data are not meaningful to the peer entities using the protocol and are delivered intact to the recipient service-user.

This fundamental concept of embedding for connection establishment is illustrated in Figure 7.7. In this example, a user wishes to transfer a file using the FTAM ASE. The first step is to initialize the FTAM protocol. This results in the generation of FTAM PCI, which is supplied as user-data to an A-ASSOCIATE request issued to the Association Control ASE. ACSE adds its own PCI to form an A-ASSOCIATE PDU. This PDU in turn becomes the user-data of a P-CONNECT request. The resulting Presentation PDU then becomes the user-

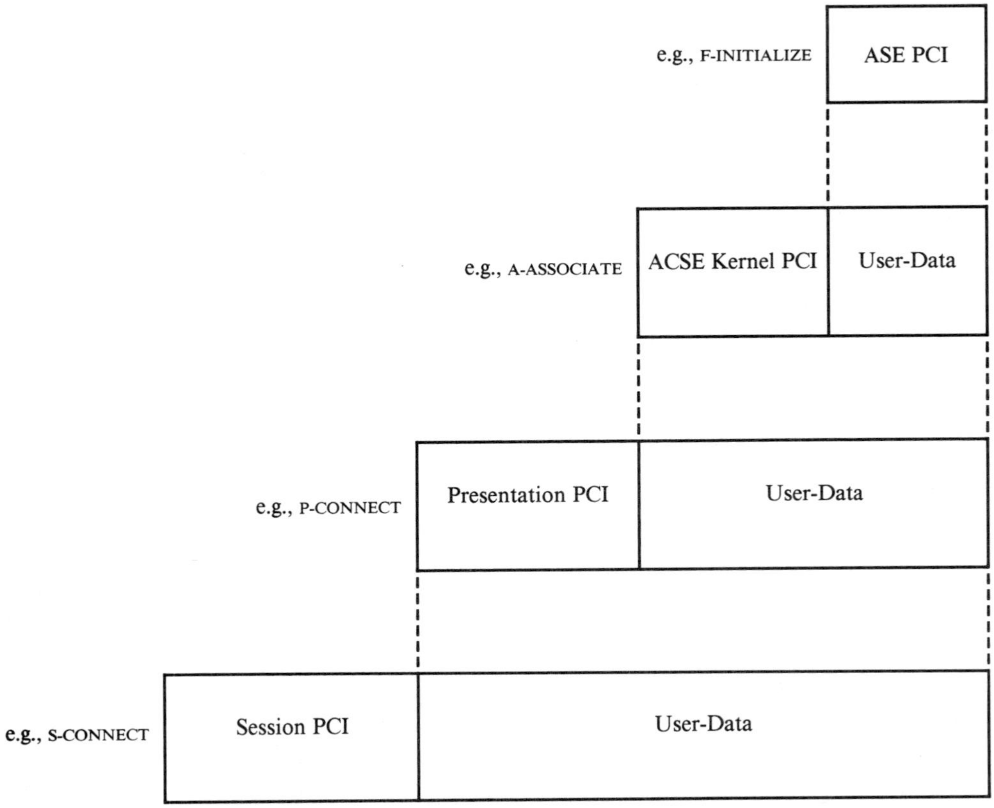

Figure 7.7 Embedding of PDUs.

data of an S-CONNECT request. The resulting S-CONNECT PDU is sent as the user-data of a T-DATA request after a transport-connection has been established.

The example above illustrates the case where the AA and the presentation- and session-connections are all established at the same time. In this situation, the failure of connection establishment in any layer causes failure in all of the upper three layers.

It is not necessary that the upper layers establish connections in unison. It is also possible to establish layer connections sequentially. The CONNECT PDU of one layer can be sent as user-data of a DATA PDU of the next lower layer once its connection has been established; this corresponds to the behavior of the Session Layer relative to transport-connection establishment. At present, however, all upper layer standards use the technique of embedding.

7.5.4 Quality of Service (QOS)

In the OSIE it is possible for an end user to specify requirements for the QOS it needs for communication. In a connection-mode environment, these requirements are stated at the time of connection establishment and, if accepted

Table 7.1 Summary of Session QOS Parameters

(a) Performance Related Parameters	
Speed	Session-Connection Establishment Delay Session-Connection Release Delay Throughput Transit Delay
Accuracy/Reliability	Session-Connection Establishment Failure Probability Session-Connection Release Failure Probability Residual Error Rate Session-Connection Resilience Transfer Failure Probability
(b) Other Parameters	
	Extended Control Session-Connection Protection Session-Connection Priority Optimized Dialogue Transfer

by the service provider, are expected to be maintained throughout the lifetime of the connection: A service provider that knows it is unable to satisfy these requirements would refuse the request for a connection. In a connectionless or store-and-forward environment, QOS is specified each time a service-data-unit is to be transferred. While it is the end user who must ultimately determine personal QOS requirements, all the upper layers typically will be involved in satisfying them with the support of the Transport and Network Layers.

At present, QOS parameters are defined in the most detail for the Session Layer. The Session Layer supports some non-performance-related QOS parameters that deal with a variety of issues:

1. The *Protection parameter* states requirements for protection measures, such as those discussed under Security.
2. The *Priority parameter* specifies the relative importance of a session-connection in case QOS must be degraded or resources must be reclaimed.
3. The *Extended Control parameter* allows session-service-users to make use of the resynchronize, abort, activity interrupt, and activity discard services when normal data flow is congested. This is useful if the expedited data functional unit is not available.
4. The *Optimized Dialogue parameter* permits concatenated transfer of certain session-service requests to improve transmission efficiency.

Table 7.1 lists all the available Session Layer QOS parameters. These parameters are visible to the ALU through the services of ACSE.

Examples of QOS issues that may be dealt with in the Application Layer include PDU grouping, as in FTAM, and maximum service-data-unit size.

CHAPTER 8

THE PRESENTATION LAYER (LAYER 6)

8.1 ROLE OF THE PRESENTATION LAYER

The Presentation Layer provides for the representation of information that AEs communicate between themselves. The Presentation Layer is concerned only with the syntax, i.e., the representation of the data, and not with its semantics, i.e., their meaning to the Application Layer.

8.2 SERVICE MODEL OF THE PRESENTATION LAYER

The external, abstract view of the Presentation Layer is of a service provider that interacts with service-users (SUs) at service-access-points (SAPs), as shown in Figure 8.1. SAPs are conceptually at the upper layer boundary; hence, the SUs are located in the Application Layer.

The presentation-service is in practice provided by presentation-entities (PEs) making use of the services available from the Session Layer through session-SAPs. A PE is the embodiment of the presentation-protocol functionality within an open system. Figure 8.2 is equivalent to Figure 8.1 but provides more detail. Each of the possible mappings between SUs and PEs is illustrated. As can be seen from this diagram, each SAP defines a one-to-one relationship between a PE and an SU, although a PE or an SU may be associated with more than one SAP. For a given connection, the services of the Application Layer can invoke Presentation Layer Services only through the SAP that was selected at connection establishment time. Note that the PEs act as users of the session-service.

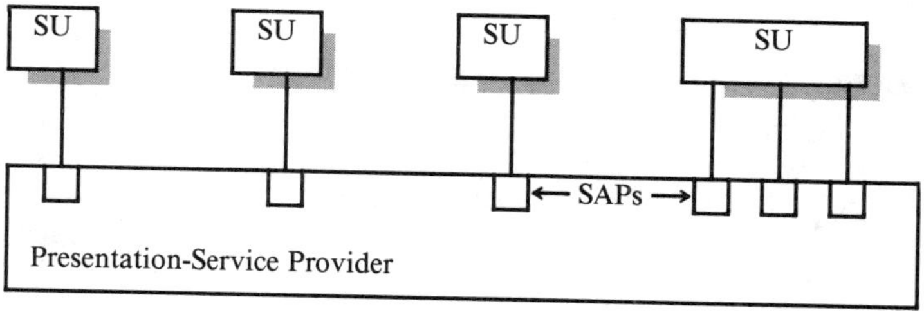

Figure 8.1 Model of presentation-service. (SU = service-user, SAP = Service access point)

8.3 ABSTRACT SYNTAX, TRANSFER SYNTAX, AND PRESENTATION-CONTEXT

The central function of the Presentation Layer is syntax transformation. The concepts of abstract syntax, transfer syntax, and presentation-context are key to the understanding of this function.

Formally, an *abstract syntax* is defined as the aspects of the rules used in the formal specification of data that are independent of the encoding technique used to represent the data. Informally, an abstract syntax can be viewed as describing the abstract structure of data. For example, an abstract syntax could be defined in terms of a set of data-type definitions, e.g., definition of data in terms of character strings, integers, etc.

Formally, a *transfer syntax* is defined as those aspects of the rules used in the formal specification of data that are concerned with a specific representation of those data used in the transfer of data between open systems. The transfer syntax is concerned with the way data are actually represented in terms of bit patterns while in transit.

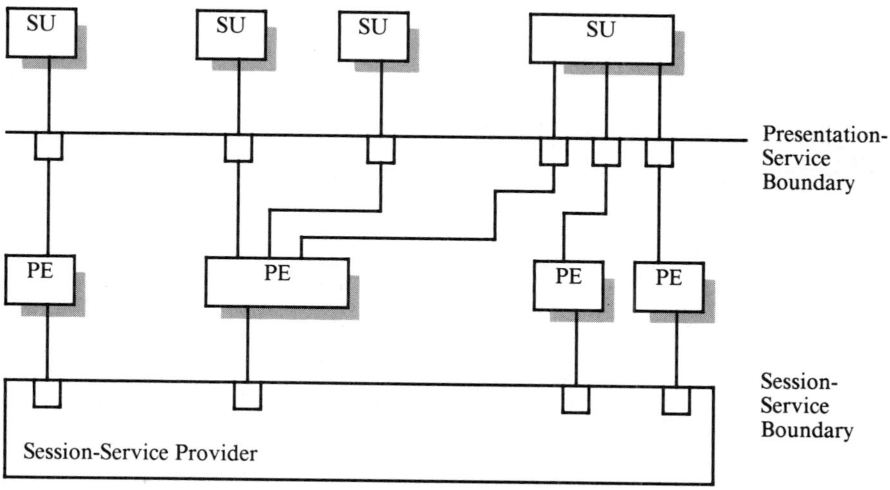

Figure 8.2 Exploded view of presentation-service provider.

For the purposes of transferring data between open systems, it is necessary to identify the abstract syntax being used and a transfer syntax that is capable of representing data values that may be generated using this abstract syntax. In general, there need not be a unique abstract/transfer syntax combination. It may be possible to support a specific abstract syntax with one or more different transfer syntaxes. Also, it may be possible to use one transfer syntax to support more than one abstract syntax.

ISO has defined a notation for specifying the abstract syntax of data. It is called Abstract Syntax Notation One (ASN.1) (ISO 8824). The purpose of ASN.1 is to provide designers of upper layer protocols with an effective technique for abstract syntax specification and to encourage a uniform approach to such specifications; however, its use is not required for OSI conformance.

Associated with ASN.1 is a set of encoding rules (ISO 8825) for generating a transfer syntax conveniently from an abstract syntax specification. For an abstract syntax specified using ASN.1, the identification of the encoding rules to be associated with it effectively specifies the transfer syntax. When this condition applies, it is sufficient for the presentation-protocol to identify the encoding rules to be used, rather than the explicit syntax specification.

ASN.1 is described further in Section 11.9.

Figure 8.3 illustrates the case where the Presentation Layer supports two transfer syntaxes for a single abstract syntax. Transfer syntax A uses character encoding for human readability, while transfer syntax B uses bit-level encoding for transmission efficiency. The Application Layer provides identification of the abstract syntax being used and supplies data items encoded in the local system syntax. A syntax transformation module in the Presentation Layer accepts this information and generates encoded data items in one of the two transfer syntaxes. The choice of transfer syntaxes is negotiated by the communicating PEs using the presentation-protocol (ISO 8823).

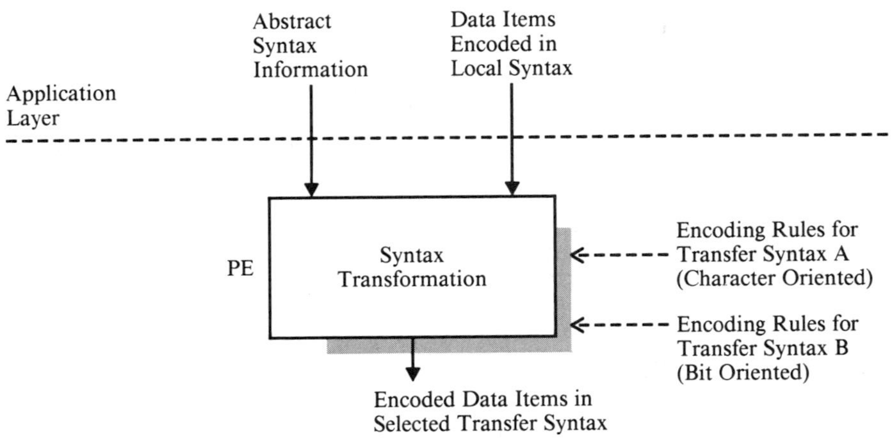

Figure 8.3 Illustration of possible mapping of an abstract syntax onto multiple transfer syntaxes.

A presentation-context is defined as a particular abstract/transfer syntax combination that can be used for the transfer of data using the presentation-service. At least one presentation-context is required to provide an application with a fully defined environment for the transfer of data. To define a presentation-context, the SU identifies an abstract syntax and the service provider attempts to identify a transfer syntax that will support the abstract syntax and also be supported by the cooperating open systems. The service provider uses a negotiation mechanism to determine a mutually acceptable transfer syntax.

For the context definition mechanism to work it is necessary that both the SUs and the service provider have knowledge of the abstract syntax to be supported by the context. The presentation-protocol assumes that abstract syntax specifications can be referred to by name. Moreover, the service provider requires knowledge of transfer syntaxes (or equivalent encoding rules) that may be associated with an abstract syntax. Again, the presentation-protocol assumes that these can be referred to by name.

In defining a presentation-context, the negotiation mechanism enables the initiator to supply a list of transfer syntaxes, any one of which may be selected by the responder. The list of offered transfer syntaxes is in a preference order, to assist the responder in making a suitable selection in cases where more than one offered syntax is supported.

8.4 RELATIONSHIP BETWEEN THE PRESENTATION AND APPLICATION LAYERS

The principal function of the Presentation Layer is to perform syntax transformation. For this to be possible, the Presentation Layer must be aware of and must understand the abstract syntax(es) used by the Application Layer on a given presentation-connection. Thus, the Application Layer is responsible for identifying the abstract syntax(es).

The use made by the Application Layer of the presentation-services (excluding directly mapped Session Layer services) is very much dependent on the variety of syntaxes that the Application Layer may need to use on a given presentation-connection.

In the simplest case, only one abstract syntax is used by the Application Layer and the local representation of that syntax corresponds to the transfer syntax. In this case, no data transformation functionality is required of the Presentation Layer; its role is reduced to connection establishment and release and acting as a conduit for session-services.

More typically, more than one abstract syntax is required for an application. Normally, one syntax would be used for Association Control, Commitment, Concurrency, and Recovery (CCR), etc. and another for each ASE that is invoked by the application. Depending on the selected abstract syntaxes, negotiation of transfer syntax may or may not be needed.

When more than one transfer syntax can be used with a given abstract syntax, the selection of transfer syntax by the Presentation Layer may be influenced by local management considerations; e.g., a requirement for lowest cost transfer would encourage the choice of a transfer syntax that provided data compression.

Hence, the functionality of the Presentation Layer for any given connection is dependent on the requirements of the Application Layer.

8.5 SERVICES OF THE PRESENTATION LAYER

In a connection-mode environment, the services of the Presentation Layer can be classified into the following areas:

1. *Connection establishment* permits the establishment of a presentation-connection and the specification and selection of a set of initial transfer syntaxes.
2. *Connection release* permits release of the presentation-connection. This release can be:
   - Orderly—all data already in transit are preserved
   - Abrupt—the presentation-connection is aborted and there may be loss of data
3. *Context management* permits the definition and deletion of presentation-contexts.
4. *Data transfer* permits five forms of data transfer:
   - Data transfer subject to token control, depending on the selected session-service
   - Data transfer with no token control
   - Expedited data transfer
   - Capability data transfer
   - Data transfer within "user-data" fields of some services, such as P-CONNECT and P-ABORT.
5. Dialogue Control permits access to Session Layer dialogue control services.

8.6 MODES OF OPERATION

The Presentation Layer supports two modes of operation: normal and X.410.

The normal mode allows all the capabilities of the Presentation Layer to be utilized, including transfer syntax negotiation and presentation-context management. This mode is the preferred one for supporting all new application-protocols.

The X.410 mode is more restrictive and exists for compatibility with CCITT Recommendation X.410 (1984), which defines a Reliable Transfer Service (RTS) used to support the 1984 Message Handling System (MHS) application-protocols. When this mode is used, no negotiation of transfer syntax and no context management are allowed. Use of this mode for applications other than MHS is discouraged.

8.7 FUNCTIONAL UNITS

The capabilities of the Presentation Layer are organized into functional units. The application designer must be aware of these functional units as they form the basis for selection of presentation-service options during connection establishment. Table 8.1 lists the functional units of the Presentation Layer and the services associated with each (functional units derived from session functional units are not listed). The functional units include:

Kernel functional unit: Supports data transfer on whatever session functional unit data services are selected. This functional unit is always available.

Context Management functional unit: Supports the definition and deletion of presentation-contexts by agreement among the two SUs and the service provider. A name is associated with each defined presentation-context, but this name has no significance beyond the current presentation-connection. This functional unit is optional, and its use must be negotiated during connection establishment.

8.8 USE OF THE PRESENTATION LAYER

8.8.1 Defined Context Set

All data interchanged over a presentation-connection must be associated with a presentation-context. For simple applications, only one presentation-context may be required; this could be a default context known to the communi-

Table 8.1 Services Associated with Each Presentation Functional Unit (Other Than Those Derived from Session Functional Units)

Functional Unit	Service(s)
Kernel (nonnegotiable)	P-CONNECT P-U-ABORT P-P-ABORT
Context Management	P-DEFINE-CONTEXT P-DELETE-CONTEXT

cating parties by prior agreement or it could be negotiated as part of presentation-connection establishment.

When more than one presentation-context must be available simultaneously, a defined context set (DCS) must be agreed to by all three parties (i.e., the presentation service provider and the two SUs).

Most applications involve the transfer of both PCI and user-data. A different abstract syntax would normally be used for each type of information. Hence, there is a need for a defined context set when the two types of information are intermingled.

The definition of presentation-contexts is normally performed during connection establishment. The addition and deletion of contexts in the course of a connection need be performed only if a particular presentation-context is not required for the entire duration of the connection. An example of such a situation is a file transfer protocol, which might require a different presentation-context for the contents of each file being transferred. In this case, the appropriate-context would be defined and deleted before and after each file transfer. The application-entity becomes responsible for these actions.

8.8.2 Resynchronization

This section explains the impact of the use of the Session resynchronization services on the Presentation Layer. See Section 9.3 for a description of the Session Layer resynchronization services.

When an application instigates resynchronization, the Presentation Layer is responsible for resetting the presentation-context. Unlike the Session Layer, the Presentation Layer tries to remember information so that it can be restored when resynchronization occurs.

When a resynchronization with restart is invoked, the DCS is restored to the one that was in force at the specified synchronization point if the synchronization point occurred within the current connection; otherwise, the DCS is set to that determined by the P-CONNECT service. An exception to this is when resynchronization occurs after a P-ACTIVITY-RESUME service, in which case the scope of synchronization points that may be specified is set to the beginning of the activity, which may not have occurred within the current presentation-connection.

When a resynchronization with set occurs, an activity discard occurs or an activity interrupt occurs, the DCS is restored to that determined at the time of the connection establishment.

When a resynchronization with abandon occurs, the user may choose to restore to the DCS associated with a previous synchronization point. Otherwise, the DCS becomes that determined during connection establishment.

If the application does not wish to maintain the DCS selected by the Presentation Layer, it must explicitly delete and add presentation-contexts using the available services of the Presentation Layer.

CHAPTER 9

THE SESSION LAYER (LAYER 5)

9.1 ROLE OF THE SESSION LAYER

The Session Layer uses the simple, reliable, full-duplex transmission service that is provided between two communicating systems by the Transport Layer. The Session Layer builds upon this transport-service and provides the Presentation Layer with a set of services for organizing and synchronizing the dialogue between two systems and for managing the exchange of data.

9.2 SERVICE MODEL OF THE SESSION LAYER

The model of the Session Layer is similar to that of the Presentation Layer. The only distinction is that the users of the Session Layer services are presentation-entities and the session-entities are users of the transport-service.

9.3 SERVICES OF THE SESSION LAYER

In a connection-mode environment, the services of the Session Layer can be classified as follows:

1. *Connection establishment* permits the establishment of a session-connection and the negotiation of parameters related to the use of the various functions.
2. *Connection release* permits release of the session-connection. This release can be:

- Orderly: all data already in transit are preserved
- Abrupt: the session-connection is aborted and there may be loss of data

3. *Normal data transfer* permits the exchange of data with usual dialogue and/or flow control.
4. *Expedited data transfer* permits the exchange of data where the exchange is not constrained by the dialogue control or flow control of normal data; in some instances, expedited data may bypass previously transmitted normal data.
5. *Token management* allows the user to request and transfer tokens that control the exclusive right to exercise certain functions. Services under token control can be invoked only when the associated token is in the possession of the user wishing to invoke the service. Tokens can be exchanged between users to pass control as needed. Four tokens are defined:

   - The data token
   - The release token
   - The synchronize-minor token
   - The major/activity token

   An example of the use of the data token is to control a dialogue in a virtual terminal environment, as described in ISO 9041.

6. *Dialogue control* permits a session to operate either in a two-way alternate style, where only one of the systems (the owner of the data token) has the right to send data at any particular time, or a two-way simultaneous style, where both systems are permitted to send data at any time. The two styles are called half-duplex and full-duplex, respectively.
7. *Synchronization* permits the placement of synchronization marks in the data flow to mark and acknowledge identifiable points. Should an error be detected, this function makes possible the resetting of the session-connection to a defined state and the agreement on a resynchronization point (mark). Each mark has an associated serial number that is unique within a given session-connection. The right to place such marks is controlled by the assignment of the major/activity token. Synchronization marks are of two types:

   - Major marks permit a clear delineation of the dialogue before and after the mark. A major mark must be confirmed by the receiver.
   - Minor marks optionally can be acknowledged by the receiver.

8. *Resynchronization* permits a "rollback" in the dialogue flow, i.e., designation of a resynchronization point, discarding of part of the data transfer, and then a restart of the data transfer as though the data after the

resynchronization point had not been previously sent. The three styles of resynchronization are:

- The first style of resynchronization is called "restart." The resynchronization point in the dialogue is identified by a serial number associated with a (preceding) mark. It is not possible to resynchronize to a point earlier than the last confirmed major synchronization point.
- A second style of resynchronization permits the present dialogue to be "abandoned" and a new serial number (i.e., one greater than any preceding serial number) to be used for the next synchronization point.
- A third style of resynchronization allows the serial number to be "set" to any value.

Any semantics attached to serial numbers and the effect of resynchronization is left entirely to the user of the Session Layer.

9. *Activity management* is an extension of the major synchronization concept. It provides the means to break a dialogue into discrete activities. Each activity can be regarded as a "separate" data transfer; however, the activity management function also has mechanisms that allow the identification of a particular activity, the transfer of data, interruption of the activity, and then resumption of the activity at a later time on the same or even on a different session-connection.
10. *Exception reporting* permits notification of unanticipated situations not covered by other services, e.g., protocol errors.
11. *Typed data* permits the transfer of transparent user-data independent of the token availability and position.
12. *Capability data* permits the transfer of a limited amount of transparent data outside an activity for special control purposes.
13. *Negotiated release* which permits one system to refuse a disconnect request and to continue in the data transfer phase.

9.4 FUNCTIONAL UNITS

The capabilities of the Session Layer are organized into functional units. The application designer must be aware of these functional units as they form the basis for selection of session-services during connection establishment.

Table 9.1 lists the functional units and the services associated with each. It also indicates which services are directly mapped through the Presentation Layer and are therefore available to the Application Layer. Note that in most cases, services are associated with only one functional unit. The principal exceptions are the token management services, which are associated with many functional units; this is a consequence of the multiplicity of tokens that are managed by the same set of services. A description of each functional unit follows.

Table 9.1 Services Associated with Each Session Functional Unit

Functional Unit	Service(s)	Directly Mapped
Kernel	Session-connection	No
(nonnegotiable)	Normal data transfer	Yes
	Orderly release	Yes
	U-Abort	No
	P-Abort	No
Negotiated release	Orderly release	Yes
	Give tokens	Yes
	Please tokens	Yes
Half-duplex	Give tokens	Yes
	Please tokens	Yes
Duplex	No additional service	
Expedited data	Expedited data transfer	Yes
Typed data	Typed data transfer	Yes
Capability data	Capability data exchange	Yes
Exchange		
Minor synchronize	Minor synchronization point	Yes
	Give tokens	Yes
	Please tokens	Yes
Major synchronize	Major synchronization point	Yes
	Give tokens	Yes
	Please tokens	Yes
Resynchronize	Resynchronize	No
Exceptions	Provider exception reporting	Yes
	User exception reporting	Yes
Activity management	Activity start	Yes
	Activity resume	Yes
	Activity interrupt	Yes
	Activity discard	Yes
	Activity end	Yes
	Give tokens	Yes
	Please tokens	Yes
	Give control	Yes

Kernel functional unit: Supports the basic session-services required to establish a session-connection, transfer normal data, and release the session-connection. This functional unit is mandatory.

Negotiated release functional unit: Supports the negotiated orderly release service, which permits the party not initiating the release to accept or reject the release attempt. Without this functional unit, release cannot be rejected. This functional unit may be useful for applications where both parties to a connection may wish to send data; should one party attempt to release a connection once it has completed sending all its data, this functional unit allows the other party to refuse the release and proceed with its data transfer. The use of negotiated release is controlled by the release token.

Half-duplex functional unit: Supports the normal transfer of data under the control of the data token. Only the owner of the data token is allowed to send normal data. As the data token can be owned by only one party at a time, this functional unit constrains the flow of normal data traffic to be in one direction. This functional unit cannot be used in conjunction with the duplex functional unit.

Duplex functional unit: Supports full-duplex transfer of normal data without token control. Therefore, transfer of normal data is possible in both directions simultaneously. This functional unit and the half-duplex functional units are mutually exclusive.

Expedited data functional unit: Supports the transfer of small quantities (1 to 14 octets) of high-priority data that are free from the token and flow control constraints of the other data transfer services.

Typed data functional unit: Supports the transfer of data regardless of the availability and assignment of the data token. This form of data transfer is still subject to normal flow control; it is particularly useful when the half-duplex functional unit is selected for the transfer of PDUs associated with presentation- and application-protocols.

Capability data functional unit: Supports the transfer of a limited amount of user data (1 to 512 octets) while not within an activity. This functional unit can be selected only in conjunction with the activity management functional unit. Its functionality is very similar to the typed data functional unit; it exists for historical reasons.

Minor synchronize functional unit: Supports the minor synchronization point service, which allows the session-service user to separate normal and typed data transmitted before a minor synchronization point from subsequent normal and typed data. Its use is controlled by the synchronize-minor token.

Major synchronize functional unit: Supports the major synchronization point service, which allows the session-service user to confine the flow of sequentially transmitted normal, typed, and expedited data in each direction within a dialogue unit. A dialogue unit is demarcated by major synchronization points and has the property that all communication within it is completely separated from all communication before and after it. The use of major synchronization is controlled by the major/activity token.

Minor synchronization points can be used within dialogue units to provide a finer degree of structuring. Figure 9.1 illustrates how a dialogue unit is structured through the use of minor and major synchronization points. Each minor synchronization point may or may not be confirmed explicitly.

Resynchronize functional unit: Supports the resynchronize service, which sets the session-connection to a defined state including reassignment of tokens and purging of all undelivered data. The principal uses of this functional unit are to recover from detected errors or to terminate a data transfer activity abruptly, without terminating the connection.

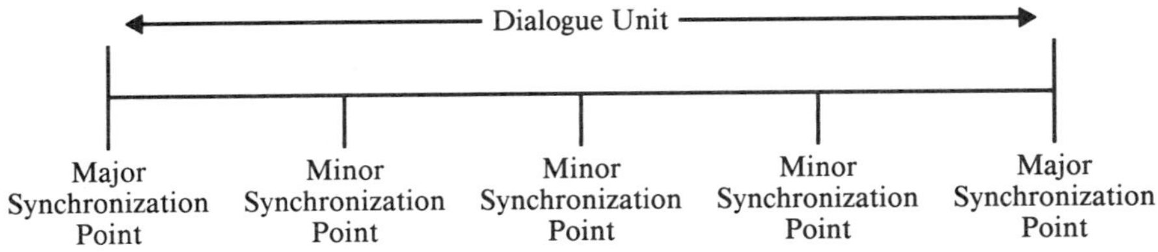

Figure 9.1 A structured dialogue unit.

Exceptions functional unit: Supports the reporting of error conditions or unanticipated situations detected by either the session-service user or session-service provider. This functional unit can only be selected in conjunction with the half-duplex functional unit; the user-initiated exception-reporting service can be used only when the data token is not available to the party wishing to report an error.

Activity management functional unit: Supports the services associated with activities. An activity is a logical piece of work that consists of one or more dialogue units, as shown in Figure 9.2. Only one activity is allowed on a session-connection at a time, but there may be several consecutive activities during a session-connection. An activity may also span more than one session-connection. An activity can be interrupted and then resumed on the same or on a subsequent session-connection. There are five services associated with activities:

- The *activity start* service is used to indicate that a new activity is entered.
- the *activity resume* service is used to indicate that a previously interrupted actity is reentered.
- the *activity interrupt* service allows an activity to be abnormally terminated, with the implication that the work so far achieved is not to be discarded and may be resumed later.
- the *activity discard* service allows an activity to be abnormally terminated, with the implication that the work so far achieved is to be discarded, not resumed.

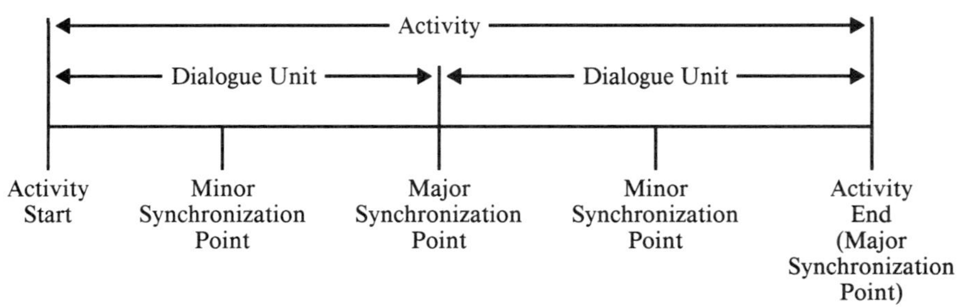

Figure 9.2 A structured activity.

- the *activity end* service is used to end an activity (and set a major synchronization point).

The use of each of the above services is controlled by the major/activity token.

9.5 USE OF THE SESSION LAYER

The use of each Session Layer functional unit has been outlined above. The discussion in this section focuses on the general philosophy of the use of session-services, particularly as it applies to synchronization, and on the restrictions that apply to the use of session-services.

9.5.1 Session Philosophy

A very important characteristic of the session-service is that it deliberately does not handle resynchronization automatically. Resynchronization is initiated only by session-service users and not by the session-service provider. The point to which resynchronization is being done is controlled by the user.

The implication of this is that the semantics of synchronization points are determined solely by the application. The application developer must decide what the effects of major and minor synchronization points are on the application and must relate them to the service elements of the application. As an example, the file transfer protocol associates a major synchronization point with the completion of a file transfer; minor synchronization points correspond to checkpoints inserted in the transferred file.

The session-service provides only the mechanisms for setting the state of a data stream to a previous state associated with a specified synchronization mark or to a completely new state. This approach permits considerable flexibility in the use of the session-services, but it places the onus on the higher layers to manage error recovery. This means that the Application Layer is responsible for determining what and when resynchronization action is to be taken and for resetting the application-context to the state associated with the specified synchronization mark.

The management of resynchronization can become more complex for the application if application-associations are built containing multiple ASEs. It is not always possible to know the various combinations of application-protocols that will be used, so it becomes impossible to document the relationship one standard may have with all other standards for the purposes of resynchronization.

The application designer must be aware of this problem and must apply the following rule to ensure consistency in the handling of resynchronization: If a process is performing a task defined by one standard, then resynchronization cannot be used to move out of that task into another task defined in another standard. For example, assume an action in JTM requires the moving of three files from one system to another. The JTM protocol may cause the generation of marks to control the state of the job movement. The FTAM protocol may also generate marks in each instance of the three file movements. If a problem occurred in the third file transfer (after two successful ones), then it would not be permitted to resynchronize out of the FTAM context to the JTM context. Instead, resynchronization would be constrained to the current FTAM context, permitting a clean end to the action as defined by the FTAM standard. Then, having moved to the JTM context, resynchronization could be used to close the JTM action, e.g., discard the successfully transferred files.

9.5.2 Restrictions

9.5.2.1 Choice of Functional Units

Only two restrictions apply to the session-service user's choice of Session Layer functional units:

1. Either the duplex- or half-duplex style of dialogue must be selected.
2. If the capability data functional unit is selected, the activity management functional unit must be selected as well.

9.5.2.2 Restart Style of Resynchronization

When major marks are used with resynchronization, the restart style of resynchronization cannot be requested to any mark that preceded the last confirmed major mark.

9.5.2.3 Activities

Nested activities are not permitted on a session-connection. Only one activity can be in progress at any one time. Use of synchronization services (e.g., major and minor synchronization) are not permitted outside activities. Those two restrictions mean that any application-protocol that uses the activity management functional unit cannot be nested with any other application-protocol requiring synchronization services. This is a significant limitation.

The semantics of activity identifiers are determined solely by the application, so the session-service does not police their use. This can lead to confusion if more than one outstanding activity is assigned the same identifier during a session-connection. Therefore, activity identifiers should be unique within a session-connection.

9.5.2.4 Use of Expedited Data

Excessive use of the expedited data transfer service can cause a subsequent resynchronization to be blocked. Therefore, this service should be used only very sparingly or not at all.

9.6 RELATIONSHIP BETWEEN THE APPLICATION AND SESSION LAYERS

The Session Layer provides a variety of functions that typically are not used simultaneously on a session-connection. Related functions are grouped into functional units that must be selected at session-connection establishment. The choice of which functional units to select depends on the requirements of the application.

The Session Layer provides many services that are useful for managing the dialogue between two AEs. It is very important to realize that these services are only tools: The Session Layer itself does not make any decisions about what to do in particular situations, e.g., whether a resynchronization should be of the "restart" or the "set" type. It simply executes the function requested by the session-service user.

An important responsibility of the application-protocol designer is determining how best to make use of the available session-services.

9.7 Session and Presentation Layers

The partitioning of functions into the Session and Presentation Layers represents a separation of concerns from the viewpoint of OSI protocol design; it does not reflect a simple hierarchical relationship between such functions. Consequently both Session Layer and Presentation Layer services are visible to a user of the presentation-service.

The complementary nature of the functions provided in these layers, coupled with the layered approach to protocol design, requires that Presentation Layer standards make Session Layer functions available to a presentation-service user in an essentially unmodified form. It is this complementary nature of the layers that gives rise to the concept of directly mapped services. In particular, the Presentation Layer provides a set of services that are directly mapped onto corresponding session-service.

CHAPTER 10

GENERIC APPLICATION SERVICE ELEMENTS

In ISO 7498, a distinction is made between common-application-service-elements (CASEs) and specific-application-service-elements (SASEs) on the basis that CASEs provide capabilities that are generally useful to a variety of applications. SASEs provide capabilities required to satisfy the particular needs of specific applications. This distinction is no longer in common usage, due to the difficulty of determining precise criteria for categorizing an ASE as a CASE or a SASE. However, it is still useful to recognize that some ASEs are generic in nature, in that they provide services that are useful in a wide variety of situations.

Included in this category are the Association Control (AC), Commitment, Concurrency, and Recovery (CCR), Remote Operations (RO), and Common Management Information ASEs. Each of these are described below, followed by a description of other more application-specific ASEs that have been or are being developed by ISO or CCITT.

10.1 ASSOCIATION CONTROL ASE

The Association Control ASE (ACSE) supports the establishment and release of application-associations (AAs), the identification of the application-context that is applicable to the association, and the transfer of user information between peer application-entities (AEs). It also provides the means for identifying the Presentation and Session Layer requirements for supporting the AA. All connection-oriented applications are expected to use the ACSE.

The ACSE supports two modes of operation: normal and X.410. The normal mode allows all the capabilities of the ACSE to be utilized and results in the transfer of ACSE semantics using the presentation-service. The X.410

mode allows ACSE service-users to interwork using the protocol specified in CCITT Recommendation X.410–1984 to support MHS. The use of this mode does not result in the transfer of ACSE semantics; it is intended only for use by message handling systems claiming conformance to the MHS (1984) Recommendations.

Addenda to the basic AC standard deal with connectionless-mode data transfer, application context management, and peer entity authentication.

10.2 COMMITMENT, CONCURRENCY, AND RECOVERY (CCR) ASE

This ASE supports a distributed application where two or more AEs participate and where one or more AAs are involved. This ASE provides a means for coordinating the activities on the separate AAs, where more than one AA is involved. It provides services for commencing and concluding protocol exchanges and related activity on each AA so that the entire sequence appears to other applications as atomic (i.e., indivisible), even in the face of failures of individual applications.

This ASE uses a two-phase commitment protocol involving a master and a number of subordinates that perform activities considered part of an atomic action. In phase 1, the master determines whether the subordinates are prepared to carry out, i.e., to commit to, the action. It is only following offers of commitment or refusal from all subordinates that the master decides whether to proceed. In phase 2, all subordinates are ordered to commit or to rollback. Commitment implies completion of the individual activities, while rollback implies cancellation.

An atomic action may involve a tree of activities, such that the initiation of one activity as part of the atomic action spawns another activity that in turn becomes a part of the atomic action. Thus, a CCR user (a) acts as a superior in relation to one or more subordinates, (b) acts as a subordinate in relation to a single superior, or (c) acts simultaneously as a subordinate to one superior and as a superior to one or more subordinates. The master of an atomic action is the initiator of the action and acts only in the role of superior.

The following are the main features of an atomic action:

- Commitment implies that the results produced by the atomic action have become permanent; no recovery capability exists at this level of operation for undoing the results produced once commitment has occurred.
- A superior may order rollback to the initial state at any time prior to ordering commitment.
- A superior may not order a subordinate to commit unless it has received an offer of commitment from it.
- If a subordinate has offered commitment, it may not refuse an order to commit.

- A subordinate may refuse commitment at any time up to making an offer to commit.
- The superior orders rollback for any subordinate that has refused commitment.

Among the OSI application protocols that make use of CCR are Job, Transfer, and Manipulation (JTM), Transaction Processing (TP), and Remote Database Access (RDA).

10.2.1 An Example

An example of the use of the CCR ASE is a job transfer that requires the transfer of three files to different participants. All of the transfers must be successful if the job is to proceed. The job transfer application in this instance is the master, and each invocation of the file transfer application is a subordinate.

Before each file transfer is initiated, the CCR C-BEGIN service is used to indicate to each file transfer subordinate that each transfer is part of a single atomic action. The file transfer subordinates then take responsibility for ensuring that the information relating to each particular transfer is kept secure, i.e., safe from communication and application failures. They are also responsible for ensuring that resources that are affected by the atomic action, e.g., the contents of a file to be updated, are protected from concurrent access for the duration of the atomic action.

As each file is transferred, the recipient does not actually update the target file; it saves the received information in such a manner that the information can survive an application failure. When the transfer is complete, the master indicates via the C-PREPARE service that it wants an indication from each subordinate of the success of the transfer. Each subordinate responds either with a C-READY if the answer is affirmative or with a C-REFUSE otherwise. Depending on the answers received from all the subordinates, the master can choose to commit or roll back the transfer. If the master chooses to commit, each subordinate must then complete the writing of the transferred information to the target file. If the master chooses to roll back, the transferred information is discarded.

It is also possible for either the master or one of the subordinates to request a restart of an activity if something wrong is detected before commitment proceedings are initiated.

10.2.2 Restrictions

CCR is only meaningful within the context of a single distributed application involving atomic actions. CCR cannot be used by an application that uses synchronization marks and resynchronization in a random manner unrelated to restart semantics. CCR cannot be used outside a session activity when use of the session activity functional unit has been negotiated.

Where a restart capability is visible in the service primitives of an application that uses CCR, the following restrictions apply to the combined sequence of service primitives:

- Application-service primitives cannot be used within an atomic action to restart to a point in time earlier than the start of the atomic action.
- Application-service primitives cannot be used following commitment or rollback to return to a point in time earlier than the point of commitment or rollback.

Where an application-service request primitive initiates an action whose completion (or failure) is signaled by an application-service confirm or indication primitive, a C-BEGIN cannot be issued between the two primitives. This restriction prevents ambiguity over the precise point at which the atomic action starts.

10.3 REMOTE OPERATIONS ASE

Some application-protocols are inherently interactive. One entity requests that an operation be performed while the other entity attempts to perform the operation and reports the outcome of the attempt. The specification and implementation of interactive protocols is facilitated by the concept of Remote Operations (RO). RO provides a uniform mechanism for representing operations and their outcomes. It uses the macro concept defined by ASN.1 to define Operation and Error data types as a vehicle for concisely specifying interactive protocols.

RO supports operations that always report results, operations that never report results, operations that report only success, and operations that report only failures.

One application-entity invokes operations provided by another by entering into an exchange of operation-protocol-data-units (OPDUs). There are four different OPDUs:

- The Invoke OPDU requests that an operation be performed. It is sent whenever one AE desires assistance from another. This OPDU carries the description of the operation to be performed.
- The ReturnResult OPDU reports the successful completion of an operation.
- The ReturnError OPDU reports the unsuccessful completion of an operation.
- The Reject OPDU reports the receipt and rejection of an invalid OPDU.

As RO provides the framework for interactive protocols, the developer of an interactive protocol need only specify the nature of the operation(s), the results, and the errors that are specific to that application. Aspects that are operation independent are already provided for by RO.

This ASE is an important one, for it is used as the basis for many application protocols, including the Directory Access Protocol (DAP), the Remote Database Access (RDA) protocol, and Distributed Office Applications such as Document Filing and Retrieval (DFR) and Printing (PR), which are being developed by ISO/IEC JTC1/SC 18.

The convenience of the ASN.1 macro notation as a means of specifying application-protocols has given rise to a set of descriptive conventions, called the Abstract Service Description Conventions (ASDC), which have been developed by CCITT within the context of their work on Message Handling Systems and Directories.

These conventions propose a radically different, object-oriented approach to the specification of distributed systems. At present, there is considerable controversy over the suitability of these conventions, as well as the suitability of the conventions described in Chapter 12, which have been used for the majority of OSI protocols. This controversy has become a matter of official study, and it is expected that an enhanced set of conventions for OSI application protocol specification will eventually emerge.

10.4 COMMON MANAGEMENT INFORMATION SERVICE ASE

The Common Management Information Service ASE (CMISE) provides generic services to be used by application-processes in peer open systems to exchange information and commands for the purpose of systems management. These services are intended to satisfy all the communication requirements of the various OSI management functions, described in Chapter 4. The use of these services by individual management functions would be distinguished by the nature of the managed objects that are the subject of communication and by the nature of the information that is conveyed using these services.

There are two types of information transfer service for management: (a) a management notification service and (b) a management operation service. For both types of service, the CMISE does not define the details of the notification or operation nor the consequent behavior of the communicating entities, as this is dependent on the nature of the managed objects involved. The general model of interchange follows the client–server model of remote operations. Each management interaction involves an "invoker" who initiates an interaction and a "performer" who is the target of the interaction.

In addition to the basic structuring capabilities provided by the notification and operation services, the CMISE provides additional structuring capabilities that enable (a) multiple responses to confirmed operations to be "linked" to the operation by the use of a linked identification parameter and (b) operations to be performed subject to a "synchronizing" condition. The latter allows operations to be synchronized across multiple managed objects, either on an atomic (i.e., all-or-none) or best-effort basis. The protocol that supports the CMIS services is based on the Remote Operations Service Element. Table 10.1 lists the services provided by this ASE.

10.5 FILE TRANSFER, ACCESS, AND MANAGEMENT ASE

The aim in the standardization of a file service is to allow the open interconnection of file users who wish to transfer, access, or manage files with elements that behave as if they store files. Anything that appears to be a system for the purposes of interconnection and conforms to the specified file protocols in the role of filestore provider is considered to provide a filestore.

10.5.1 Functional Units and Service Classes

The many capabilities of the File, Transfer, Access, and Management (FTAM) ASE are organized into functional units, as shown in Table 10.2. Three service classes group functional units according to the type of file processing associated with each class:

- File transfer class is intended for the transfer of entire files.
- File access class is intended for the manipulation of parts of files, e.g. individual records.
- File management class is intended for operations on files as a whole.

10.5.2 Use of FTAM

The FTAM ASE can be used as a vehicle for reliable transfer of large amounts of information between systems. It is usable for smaller amounts as well, but the considerable amount of dialogue involved in preparing for a transfer (connection establishment, file selection, file open, read or write request) makes FTAM less attractive in this case.

Table 10.1 Common Management Information Services

Service	Function
M-INITIALIZE	Establish a management association
M-TERMINATE	Terminate a management association
M-ABORT	Terminate abnormally a management association
M-EVENT-REPORT	Report occurrence of a management event
M-GET	Get attributes of a managed object
M-SET	Set attributes of a managed object
M-ACTION	Perform an action in a managed object
M-CREATE	Create a managed object
M-DELETE	Delete a managed object

Table 10.2 Services Associated with Each FTAM Functional Unit

Functional unit	Service(s)
Kernel	Association establishment Association termination (orderly) Association termination (abrupt) File selection File deselection File open File close
Read	Read bulk data Data-unit transfer End of data transfer End of transfer Cancel data transfer
Write	Write bulk data Data-unit transfer End of data transfer End of transfer Cancel data transfer
File access	Locate file access data-unit Erase file access data-unit
Limited file management	File creation File deletion Read attributes
Enhanced file management	Change attributes
Grouping	Beginning of grouping End of grouping
Recovery	Regime recovery Checkpointing Cancel data transfer
Restart data transfer	Restarting data transfer Checkpointing Cancel data transfer

The virtual filestore model used by FTAM provides for the representation of complex file structures. Thus the FTAM concepts and protocol are applicable to many applications requiring database access.

10.6 JOB TRANSFER AND MANIPULATION ASE

The purpose of the Job Transfer and Manipulation (JTM) ASE is to provide a set of communication-related services that can be used to perform work in a network of interconnected open systems. This work can include the running of traditional jobs. The JTM protocol not only covers the movement of job-related data (input and output) between open systems, but also provides for the movement of data concerned with monitoring job-related activity and for controlling and manipulating the progress of this activity. The JTM ASE uses the concept of a work statement as the data structure describing a distributed job. Two classes of service are identified: basic and full. Table 10.3 lists the services available in each class. The full class supports all services.

10.6.1 Use of JTM

The JTM ASE supports a set of related interactions between a controlling entity (called the initiation agency) and many other entities (variously called source, sink, and execution agencies). To do this, it needs to coordinate multiple associations. Hence, this application-protocol is more complex than FTAM. As a consequence of the distributed nature of this application, JTM can and does make use of the CCR capabilities described earlier. Thus JTM provides the framework for a wide range of applications requiring centralized control of many activities.

10.7 VIRTUAL TERMINAL ASE

The Virtual Terminal (VT) (basic class) ASE supports the interactive transfer and manipulation of graphic data by virtual terminal users. This graphic data is structured in a manner that models the class of character-box-oriented terminals. The structuring of graphic elements is limited to images consisting of character-box graphic elements arranged in a one-, two-, or three-dimensional array.

Table 10.3 Services Associated with Each JTM Service Class

Service Class	Service(s)	Function
Basic	J-INITIATE-WORK	Create work spec for document movement
	J-INITIATE-WORK-MAN	Create work spec for document manipulation
	J-DISPOSE	Pass a document to a sink or execution agency
	J-GIVE	Request a document from a source or execution agency
	J-END-SIGNAL	Signal end of an activity
	J-STATUS	Obtain information about status of an activity
	J-KILL	Terminate an activity, without documents
	J-STOP	Terminate an activity, possibly with do
	J-MESSAGE	Generate a USER-MESSAGE report
Full	J-INITIATE-TCR-MAN	Create work spec for manipulation of transfer control records
	J-INITIATE-REPORT-MAN	Create a work spec for report manipulation
	J-ENQUIRE	Obtain a list of document names
	J-HOLD	Request temporary suspension of an activity
	J-RELEASE	Cancel an earlier J-HOLD
	J-SPAWN	Specify that demand spawning is to occur

The transfer and manipulation of graphic data takes place within a virtual terminal environment defined by a set of parameters. Profiles are used to represent sets of predefined parameters as an aid in negotiating the characteristics of a virtual terminal environment. They can be used to represent the characteristics of commonly encountered virtual terminals.

The VT service permits the transfer and manipulation of data in a way that is independent of the internal representation of information used by each virtual terminal user; provision is made to control the integrity of the communication between users through the assignment of access rights to different sets of objects (e.g., a virtual screen and a virtual keyboard).

Both synchronous and asynchronous modes of operation are supported.

10.7.1 Service Subsets

Three subsets of the virtual terminal service have been identified. They differ only in the level of negotiation available in each subset. Each subset is a superset of the next lower subset. Table 10.4 lists the service subsets and the service facilities available for each.

10.7.2 Use of the Virtual Terminal ASE

This ASE is essentially a standalone one that is not amenable to incorporation within other applications. The VT negotiation mechanism is sufficiently powerful that the standard is not restricted to the virtualization of commonly encountered terminal characteristics. If an application required specialized characteristics yet remained faithful to the architectural framework of this standard (i.e., character-box graphic information in one-, two-, or three-dimensional arrays), then it could be accommodated by this standard.

10.8 MESSAGE TRANSFER ASE

The Message Transfer (MT) ASE supports reliable store-and-forward transfer of messages. It delivers messages to one or more recipients within a defined time period and, where required, performs syntax transformation on the contents of messages.

Table 10.4 Facilities Associated with Each VT Service Subset

Service Subset	Facilities
Kernel	Association establishment Association termination Data transfer Delivery control Token management
Profile switch negotiation	Switch profile negotiation
Multiple interaction negotiation	Multiple interaction negotiation

This ASE is the central ASE among the set of ASEs that form the ISO Message-Oriented Text Interchange System (MOTIS) and the CCITT Message Handling System (MHS), which are now equivalent. The other ASEs that can be present in a message handling system include:

- Message Submission, which may be used in submitting messages from a User Agent to a remote Message Transfer Agent
- Message Delivery, which may be used to deliver messages to a remote User Agent or to a Message Store (see below)
- Message Dispatch, which may be used to convey messages to a Message Store
- Message Retrieval, which may be used to retrieve messages from a Message Store
- Message Administration, which may be used to convey administrative information between User Agents, Message Stores, and Message Transfer Agents

10.8.1 Capabilities of the MT Service

The following list is the set of functions provided by the MT service:

1. The submission of a message for transfer to one or more recipients: The originator of the message can control various aspects of message processing, such as message priority, the need for notification of non-delivery, and deferred delivery.
2. The determination of whether a message could be delivered to one or more recipients if it were submitted (probe)
3. The delivery of a message to a specified recipient, along with indications of message characteristics
4. Nondelivery notification to the originator in the event that a message is not delivered to an intended recipient
5. Delivery notification in the event that the originator requested explicit confirmation of delivery
6. The ability to request cancellation of a message previously submitted for deferred delivery
7. The ability to temporarily limit the services that a user or the Message Transfer Service may invoke and the messages that may be submitted or delivered
8. The ability to make long-term changes to various parameters of a Message Transfer user held by the Message Transfer Service responsible for delivery of messages to the user
9. The ability to change the credentials used during association establishment for authentication purposes

Table 10.5 Services Associated with MT

Service	Function
Submit	Submit a message for delivery
Probe	Check that a potential message is deliverable
Cancel	Cancel a deferred message
Control	Set or modify user characteristics
Deliver	Deliver a message to its recipient
Notify	Notify origination of status of message
Register	Register user with MTA
ChangeCredentials	Change authentication credentials

Table 10.5 lists the services that are available.

10.9 INTERPERSONAL MESSAGING ASE

The Interpersonal Messaging (IPM) ASE is a companion to the MT ASE. It supports the interchange of electronic mail messages from one user system to another. Unlike the MT ASE, the IPM ASE operates on an end-to-end basis; the information conveyed by this ASE is meaningful only to the intended recipient(s) of a message and is not processed by intermediate systems.

The IPM ASE is intended primarily to convey information about the characteristics of interchanged messages that may influence the processing performed by the recipient—the type of information, the subject matter, its importance, its useful lifetime, etc. This is in contrast to the MT service, where the information conveyed is relevant primarily to the delivery of the message.

The IPM ASE allows various types of information to be conveyed in the message body, including character text, graphics, and facsimile-encoded images. The protocol procedures associated with this ASE allow message reception to be acknowledged and received messages to be forwarded to other destinations.

10.10 MESSAGE RETRIEVAL ASE

The Message Retrieval (MR) ASE is associated with the use of a Message Store (MS) in a manner complementary to the MT and IPM ASEs. The MR ASE supports the retrieval of messages from a remote MS (i.e., mailbox) to which the MT service has delivered messages. When the MT and IPM ASEs are used without an MS, messages are delivered directly to the recipient system, which means that the recipient system must be available for message reception at all times. In workstation-based environments, it is not always convenient or practical for the recipient system to be available for message reception. It is sometimes preferable that messages be delivered by the MT service into a remote mailbox (which is always available) and that the user retrieve messages at its convenience. It is in such situations that the MS is applicable.

The MR ASE supports the listing, summarizing, retrieval, and deletion of messages contained in the MS. Within the framework of its Distributed Office Applications Model, ISO/IEC JTC1/SC18 has identified a similar service, called Mailbox, that is intended to support additional capabilities beyond those associated with the MR ASE. Table 10.6 lists the services that are available.

10.11 DOCUMENT FILING AND RETRIEVAL ASE

The Document Filing and Retrieval (DFR) ASE provides the capability for users in a distributed system to access large-capacity data storage. This ASE is concerned with manipulation of documents as a whole and is independent of document content. It has similarities to FTAM (remote access to files) but differs in that it addresses manipulation of groups of documents and relationships among documents (called references) in addition to manipulation of single documents. Another difference is that it is based on the use of RO, unlike FTAM.

10.12 DOCUMENT TRANSFER, ACCESS, AND MANIPULATION ASE

The Document Transfer, Access, and Manipulation (DTAM) ASE is intended to support both bulk transfer of group 4 facsimile and mixed-mode Teletex documents as well as the interactive manipulation of remote documents that are structured according to the Office Document Architecture (ODA). This service is being developed within CCITT SG VIII, with the interactive capabilities oriented toward Videotex-based applications.

To support remote manipulation of documents, CCITT is defining a parallel structure to the existing ODA logical and layout structures, called "operational structure," which defines operations to be performed on constituents of the logical and layout structures. These operations are intended to support

Table 10.6 Services Associated with Message Retrieval

Service	Function
Delete	Delete a document
Fetch	Retrieve a message
List	List contents of message store
Perform	Perform specified action on message store
Register-MS	Register user with message store
Summarize	Summarize contents

activities like remote document editing, remote data entry using prompts, etc. and automatic generation of tables of contents, indexes, dictionaries, etc.

Work on DTAM services and protocols is at an early stage; it is expected that most of the development work will be done in the 1989–1992 timeframe.

10.13 PRINTING ASE

The Printing (PR) ASE provides the capability for multiple users in a distributed system to share expensive, high-facility imaging equipment. Documents sent to the printer might be represented according to the Office Document Interchange Format (ODIF), which is oriented toward office documents; the Standard Generalized Markup Language (SGML), which is being used in the publishing industry and has been adopted by the American Association of Publishers; or a page-description language like PostScript, Interpress, or the Standard Page-Description Language being developed within ISO/IEC JTC1/SC18/WG8. Work on the latter is at an early stage and no firm results are available, but it is expected to be based on one or more of the existing languages.

10.14 REMOTE DATABASE ACCESS ASE

The Remote Database Access (RDA) ASE supports access to databases from remote intelligent workstations and from other database systems. The model used for this service is that of a client process that interacts with a server process via the RDA service. The client process typically performs an information task, e.g., query processing, which requires access to information maintained within a remote database. The server process is co-located with the database of interest and is responsible for translating the protocol information conveyed by the RDA service into data manipulation procedure calls and then transmitting the results back to the client. The client process incorporates a query processor that formulates queries in a data manipulation language that the server process interprets.

An important feature of RDA is that it provides a set of generic services applicable to a wide variety of database systems and environments. These services support the interchange of information without constraining the nature of the database manipulation commands conveyed. This feature is included in recognition of the fact that the structure and content of databases can vary widely and are determined by database users (hence, the difficulty of developing standardized, widely applicable procedures for manipulating a database).

The strategy used is to design database languages (DBL) according to application and database characteristics and allow RDA to convey commands defined in terms of these languages. RDA cannot be used effectively by itself; it is meaningful only in association with a defined DBL.

DBLs are defined separately from RDA in a step called specialization. For example, ISO is defining a specialization of RDA for the relational data manipulation language Standard Query Language (SQL). Other data manipulation languages could be specified to suit the characteristics of particular databases or applications.

RDA makes use of the RO ASE; RDA protocol data-units are defined in terms of RO operations, using the corresponding macro notation.

RDA supports both simple and transactional database access; RDA transactions involve a number of operations on one or more databases that are atomic; i.e., they succeed or fail as a whole.

The set of services specific to RDA is listed in Table 10.7. In addition, CCR and Association Abort services are directly available to the RDA user if needed.

10.15 TRANSACTION PROCESSING ASE

The Transaction Processing (TP) ASE provides facilities to support distributed transaction processing and establishes a framework for coordinating across multiple resources in separate systems. It is intended to support transactions characterized by four properties, called the ACID properties.

- Atomicity implies that either all the operations of a unit of work are performed or none of them is performed.
- Consistency implies that the defined set of operations of a unit of work, if performed at all, is performed accurately, correctly, and with validity, according to the specification of the set of operations. Successful transactions should transform the bound data (i.e., the data that have some lifetime beyond the duration of the transaction) from one consistent state into a new consistent state.
- Isolation implies that the partial results of a unit of work are not accessible, except by operations that are part of this unit of work. With respect to concurrent units of work, the implication of this definition is serialization.

Table 10.7 Services Associated with Remote Database Access

Service	Function
r-Associate	Establish an RDA Association
r-Release	Terminate an RDA association
r-Open	Identify a data resource
r-Close	Terminate availability of data resource(s)
r-ExecuteDML	Execute single DBL statement
r-DefineDML	Define and store a DBL command
r-InvokeDML	Execute an already-stored DBL command
r-DropDML	Nullify one or more DBL commands

Table 10.8 Services Associated with Each TP Functional Unit

Functional Unit	Service(s)
Kernel	TP-BEGIN-DIALOGUE
	TP-P-REJECT
	TP-END-DIALOGUE
	TP-DATA
	TP-P-ABORT
	TP-U-ABORT
	TP-P-ERROR
	TP-U-ERROR
Shared control	
Polarized control	TP-GRANT-CONTROL
	TP-REQUEST-CONTROL
Handshake	TP-HANDSHAKE
	TP-HANDSHAKE-AND-END
	TP-HANDSHAKE-AND-GRANT-CONTROL
Commit	TP-COMMIT
	TP-COMMIT-CONTINUE
	TP-COMMIT-RESULT
	TP-DONE
	TP-COMMIT-COMPLETE
	TP-PREPARE
	TP-READY
	TP-ROLLBACK
	TP-ROLLBACK-COMPLETE
	TP-HEURISTIC
	TP-HEURISTIC-DONE
	TP-HEURISTIC-COMPLETE
Unchained transactions	TP-DEFER-NEXT-TRANSACTION
	TP-UNCHAIN-TRANSACTION
	TP-BEGIN-TRANSACTION

- Durability implies that all effects of a completed unit of work are not altered by any sort of failure.

The TP service allows three levels of coordination: NONE, SYNCHRONIZE, and COMMITMENT. When the level is NONE, the users of the TP-service are responsible for ensuring that the four properties are satisfied; further, there is no synchronization among TP-users. When the level is SYNCHRONIZE, TP-users may use synchronization services, but they remain responsible for transaction integrity. When the level is COMMITMENT, commitment mechanisms may be invoked to ensure transaction integrity.

The TP service resembles JTM in that it supports interactions among more than two systems and it also uses the CCR services for commitment purposes. Table 10.8 lists the TP services, grouped into functional units.

PART III

DEVELOPING AND USING OSI

CHAPTER 11

A METHODOLOGY FOR APPLICATION-PROTOCOL DEVELOPMENT

11.1 INTRODUCTION

This chapter describes the steps in the development of OSI-compatible specifications for ASEs. For each step, the nature of the information to be supplied, the level of detail, and the presentation format are defined. This methodology is intended to assist the protocol developer in conceptualizing a distributed application in OSI terms, identifying and formalizing the elements of service that a communicating system provides to the end user, specifying the protocol actions and states required to support the service, and identifying which services of lower layers are required. It is consistent with the ISO guidelines as stated in ISO TR 8509.

The application of each step of the methodology to the development of a sample ASE is described. The example used is interactive credit card authorization, which is one of a series of actions in a Card Message Communications Environment that are defined in ISO 8583. Interactive Authorization (IA) is concerned with the verification of information pertaining to a card-based financial transaction, e.g., a purchase of merchandise by credit card.

Note, however, that this example is simplified, used for illustrative purposes only, and *not* identical to the relevant parts of ISO 8583. The example makes use of messages as defined in ISO 8583 and does *not* attempt to redefine the application model or approach to distribution. It maintains the ISO 8583 model in which the application has control over all message flow. Thus, the protocol that results from this example may not optimize OSI resource usage or performance.

IA is one component of a larger application, namely bank card message processing. For the purposes of this example, it is considered to be a stand-alone ASE.

Where appropriate, references are made to ISO and CCITT Application Layer standards, e.g., FTAM and MHS, to illustrate specific features of the methodology.

Note: Tutorial material is set to a narrower measure than regular text and is signaled by a triangle at the beginning and end and by a rule in the outside margin.

11.2 OBJECTIVE OF METHODOLOGY

The objective of the methodology described in this chapter is to develop Application Layer service and protocol specifications that are compatible with the OSI Reference Model and consistent in organization and presentation style with OSI standards developed by ISO/IEC JTC1/SC21.

It is not an objective of this methodology to describe how to design distributed applications. Such applications include an information-processing component and a communications component; only the communications component is of concern here. It is recognized that the communications component cannot in general be designed in isolation and that an understanding of the overall application is required. However, there are many possible approaches to the design of an overall application, and no consensus exists on the "best" one to use. The methodology identifies only what information must be known a priori before service and protocol standards development can begin. How this information is obtained is outside the scope of this methodology.

▶ 11.3 OVERVIEW OF THE INTERACTIVE AUTHORIZATION EXAMPLE

This section introduces the Interactive Authorization (IA) application and the business requirements that must be determined prior to the use of the methodology. IA is an activity related to financial transactions involving bank cards. It is one of the functions supported by ISO 8583. A high-level model for bank card–related processing recognizes that four parties may be involved: the Cardholder, Card Acceptor, Acquirer, and Card Issuer. These parties and their relationships are illustrated in Figure 11.1.

The Cardholder is always the initiator of a financial transaction and is typically a person. The Card Acceptor may correspond to a clerk in a store, to a Point-of-Sale (POS) machine, or to an Automatic Teller Machine (ATM). The Acquirer is normally the merchant's financial institution, which may also act, in certain cases, as the agent of the Card Acceptor for interactions involving a Card Issuer. The Card Issuer is the financial institution that issued the bank card to the Cardholder and has authority to accept or refuse transactions initiated by the Cardholder.

In this example the case of intermediate agents who act on behalf of the

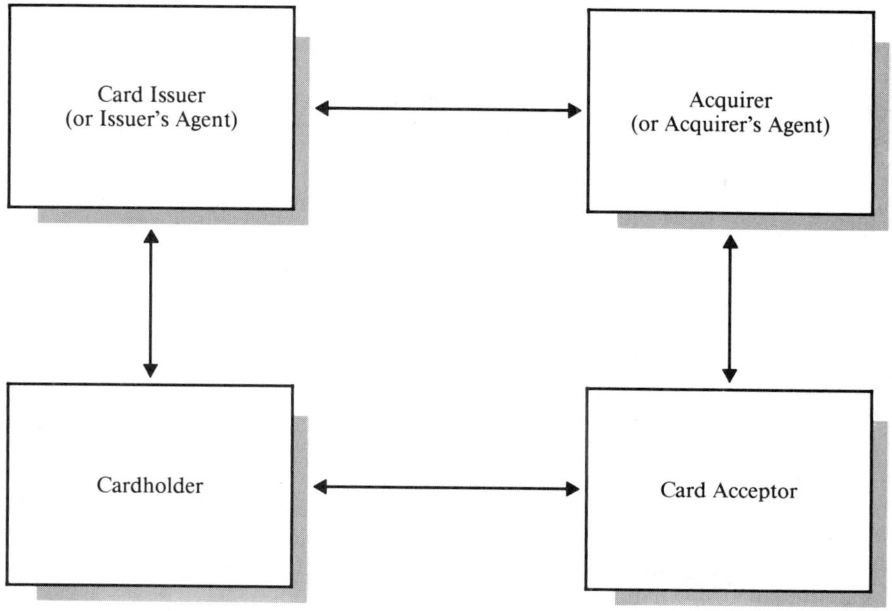

Figure 11.1: Parties involved in an IA application (business relationships).

Acquirer or Card Issuer is not included. From a communications protocol point of view, there is no difference between the real party and the party's agent.

In this environment, the purpose of an interactive authorization (hereafter simply called an authorization) is to obtain an approval or guarantee for a financial transaction to proceed. An authorization request flows from the Card Acceptor to the Acquirer and then to the Card Issuer. The response flows in the opposite direction along the same logical path as the request. The act of "authorizing" can be viewed as an operation performed at a location that is remote from the source of the request.

An authorization is not intended to convey sufficient data to permit the posting of a transaction to the Cardholder's account for the purpose of issuing a bill or statement. An important aspect of this application is its real-time nature, with its strict upper limit on response time between issuance of a request for authorization and receipt of a response. An example of an authorization is a request for approval of a credit card purchase.

The above is a very brief overview of the business environment in which authorization transactions exist. Many variations upon this theme exist in real systems, and a variety of security, integrity, and recovery features would be required. This description "sets the stage" for the specification of communication requirements by providing a general outline of the problem and the basic assumptions made.

11.4 STEP 1: DEVELOPMENT DISTRIBUTED APPLICATION MODEL

The first step of the methodology is to identify which application-processes in the distributed application require interaction, in the OSI sense, with other processes. Thus, a mapping must be made from the high-level business model to a distributed application model, taking into consideration the interactions among the distributed processes.

Where an application involves two or more application-processes, it is necessary to analyze the possible physical and organizational mappings to determine:

- Which processes need to interact via a communications service. For example, if two processes are always co-located in the same physical system, there is no requirement for a communications protocol between them.
- How many different ASEs are required. For example, if the interactions between subsets of processes differ considerably in nature, more than one ASE may be required to satisfy the overall communication requirements of the application.
- Whether each identified ASE needs to be standardized. For example, if two processes that require an ASE for communication are both located within the same organization or the same administrative domain, a standardized protocol may not be necessary.

Business considerations will come into play in this analysis, e.g., security needs or QOS requirements. If a requirement for more than one ASE is identified, then the methodology is repeated for each such ASE. Each requirement must also be examined to determine if "generic" ASEs exist that will satisfy the need and can be adopted, e.g., file transfer using FTAM.

11.5 STEP 1 FOR THE MHS EXAMPLE

One example of this form of analysis is provided in the CCITT X.400 (1984) series of Recommendations for Message Handling Systems (MHS). Recommendation X.400 defines the MHS distributed applications model as having three types of processes: Users, User Agents (UA), and Message Transfer Agents (MTA). This model recognizes the possibility of different physical and organizational mappings (see Figure 11.2). The model identifies four types of interactions:

- Among User Agents (Note that Figure 11.2 does not explicitly illustrate the UA–UA interactions.)
- Among Message Transfer Agents

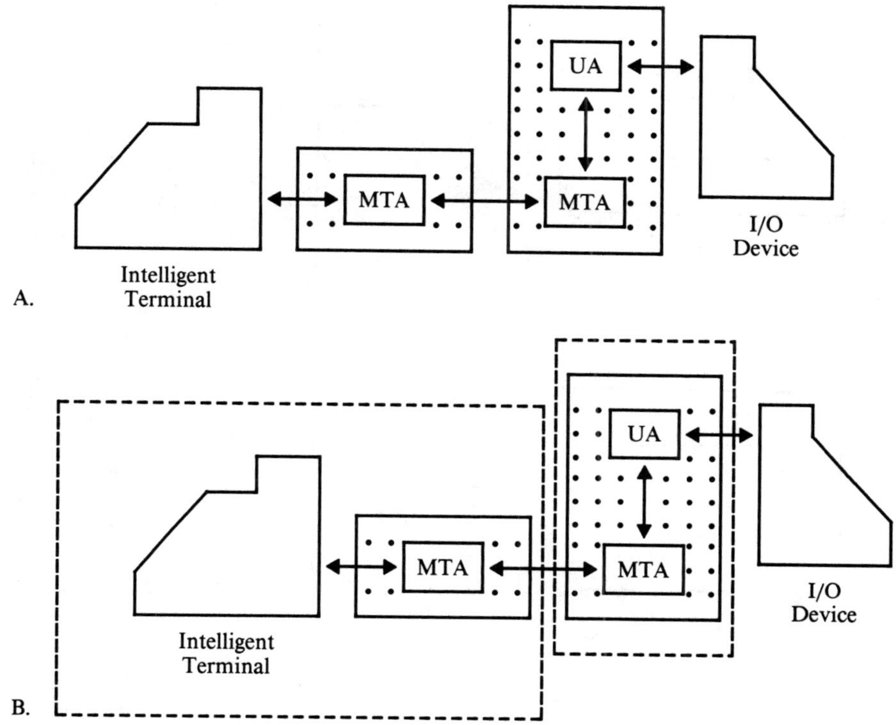

Figure 11.2: Example of physical mapping (A) and organizational mapping (B) for Message Handling Systems. Dashed rule indicates organizational boundaries.

- Between a User Agent and a Message Transfer Agent
- Between a User and a User Agent.

In recognition of the different possible physical and organizational mappings, the first three of these interactions are candidates for standardization. As each type of interaction has distinct characteristics, it is appropriate to develop separate protocols for each. As a result, three different MHS protocols (P1, P2, and P3) have been developed.

11.6 STEP 1 FOR THE INTERACTIVE AUTHORIZATION EXAMPLE

In the business model of the IA application, there are four parties, each performing a different role. The distributed application model derived from

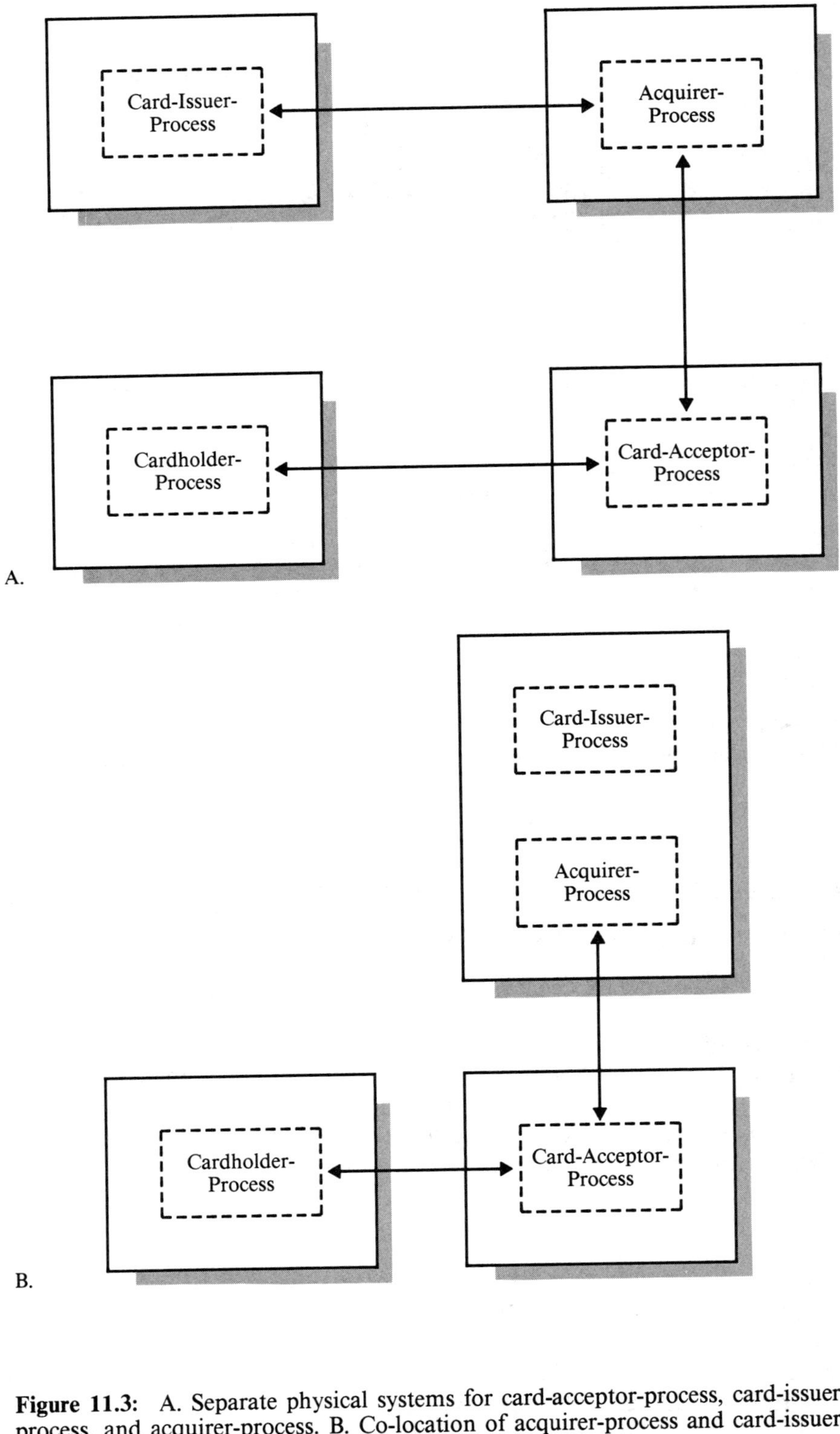

Figure 11.3: A. Separate physical systems for card-acceptor-process, card-issuer-process, and acquirer-process. B. Co-location of acquirer-process and card-issuer-process. Solid lines indicate a physical system. Dashed lines indicate a process.

the business model recognizes four different processes: the cardholder-process, the card-acceptor process, the acquirer-process and the card-issuer-process. Each of these processes represents functions typically performed by one of the business parties.

Many physical and organizational mappings for these processes are possible, particularly when intermediate agents and failure avoidance functions are taken into account. This example considers only two physical mappings: one where the card-acceptor-process, the acquirer-process, and the card-issuer-process are located in different physical systems, and another where the acquirer process and the card issuer-process are co-located (see Figure 11.3).

For the first of these physical mappings, there is a possible requirement for two standardized system-to-system IA protocols: card-acceptor-process to acquirer-process and acquirer-process to card-issuer-process. Organizational mappings would then be considered in determining which protocols actually need to be standardized.

Various organizational mappings are possible for the first configuration of physical systems (see Figure 11.3A). In one mapping, each process would belong to a different organization (i.e., is in a different management domain), so both protocols are candidates for standardization. In another mapping, the card-acceptor-process and the acquirer-process would belong to the same organization, so there may not be a need for a standard protocol between these two systems (i.e., they need not be open in the OSI sense). In a third instance, all processes except the card-holder-process belong to the same institution; with this mapping, no protocols need be standardized.

For the second physical mapping (see Figure 11.3B), there is a communication requirement only for the interaction between the card-acceptor-process and the acquirer-process. Depending on the organizational mapping, there may or may not be any requirement for protocol standardization.

As this example is based on ISO 8583, which applies only to interactions between Acquirer and Card Issuer, only the Acquirer-to-Issuer protocol will be considered further.

It has been stated that, in some cases, no requirement exists for standard protocols. This does not suggest that use of standard protocols may not be beneficial, but simply that no interorganizational exchanges are involved.

11.7 STEP 2: SHARED CONCEPTUAL SCHEMA DEVELOPMENT

From this step onward, the methodology addresses the development of a single application protocol.

A distributed application involves the cooperation of two or more application processes. For this cooperation to be meaningful, they must share a common understanding of the environment in which the communication is to take place. Conceptually, they are said to have a shared *universe of discourse.* This shared universe of discourse is the intersection of the universes of discourse of each individual process, as illustrated in

Figure 11.4. The universe of discourse for an individual application-process models all aspects pertinent to its information-processing objectives. This includes both local and communications-related aspects.

The description of a universe of discourse is called a conceptual schema. This description is in terms of *objects* in the universe of discourse and the *operations* that can be carried out on these objects. The use of the term objects in this context corresponds to intuitively meaningful aspects of the universe of discourse. Two types of objects may be distinguished. Processing objects are those that may initiate operations on other objects. Information objects are simply collections of data elements and associated operations that are initiated by other objects; they do not themselves initiate operations on other objects.

In the case of a distributed application, the shared conceptual schema describes only the information that must be known to both processes in order to work together successfully. The shared conceptual schema defines both the static and dynamic properties of individual objects and the relationships among them. The objects are represented as collections of subordinate objects and data elements.

Since the focus in this step of the methodology is on the semantics (i.e., the meaning) of the information and not on its syntactical representation, natural language descriptions are generally suitable. Syntactical representations of this information are dealt with during the protocol specification stage of the methodology. A process of successive refinement is typically used for defining objects in the shared conceptual schema. First, the major objects are described at a high level of abstraction; then their internal structure is defined in progressively greater detail.

Communication between application processes participating in a distributed application is for the purpose of operating on (e.g., creating, modifying) the objects in the shared universe of discourse. Therefore, the shared conceptual schema must describe these operations. At this level of detail, it is sufficient to describe operations simply in terms of the type of processing that can be performed on objects. The emphasis is on *what* operations are permissible, not on *who* can perform them or *how* they are executed. The detailed descriptions of the information that is to be inter-

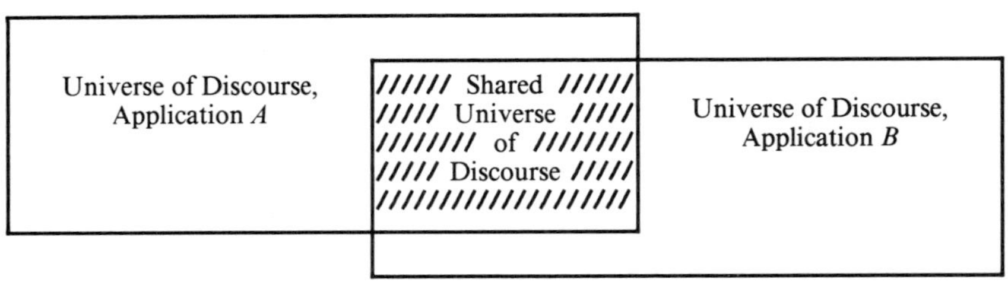

Figure 11.4: Shared universe of discourse.

changed and the communication procedures that facilitate the interchange are provided in the service definition, protocol specification, and application-context definition. This detailed information also forms part of the conceptual schema and serves as a further refinement of the view developed in this step.

11.8 SHARED CONCEPTUAL SCHEMA FOR EXISTING OSI STANDARDS

11.8.1 File Transfer, Access, and Management

In the case of the FTAM standards, the principal information object is the virtual filestore. The virtual filestore is an abstract representation of a file system that provides a common model for use in describing files and their attributes. It hides the differences in the way real (i.e., physical) systems actually store and provide access to data. Each system that implements FTAM is responsible for developing a mapping between the abstract representation of a file system and the actual characteristics of the local system.

The principal components of the virtual filestore are files. Files have attributes, some of which describe general properties, such as filename, and some of which describe the structure of the file, e.g., flat, hierarchical, etc. The complete filestore definition provided in ISO 8571/2 includes a definition of all file attributes.

The set of operations permissible on the virtual filestore include operations on complete files (create select, change attribute, read attribute, open, close, delete, deselect) and operations for accessing information within a file (locate, read, insert, replace, extend, erase).

11.8.2 JTM

In the case of the JTM standards, the principal information object is the work specification. This specification defines the work to be performed as part of a job. It contains fields that, for example, provide for identifying the work to be performed, authorizing that work, identifying who is to perform the work, identifying what reporting information is to be supplied, and specifying further work to be performed when initial work is completed. A work specification also may contain one or more documents that convey the actual information that is to be processed by a recipient JTM user. For example, the actual Job Control Language to be processed by a particular computer system would be contained in a document. Any document type can be transferred between JTM users, as long as there exists an abstract syntax for it. JTM operations pertain to controlling the transfer of work specifications, manipulating reports, and manipulating work specifications. For example, the work manipulation operations include selection, modification, killing, stopping, and displaying work specifications and associated subjobs.

11.9 STEP 2 FOR THE INTERACTIVE AUTHORIZATION EXAMPLE

11.9.1 Shared Conceptual Schema

As determined in step 1, the protocol under consideration operates between two application-processes: the acquirer-process and the card-issuer-process. The principal information object for this application is the Card Authorization Record (CAR). This object represents all pertinent information related to the authorization activity, permitting a decision to accept or reject the authorization request. In real systems, further information concerning failure and recovery processing would be needed.

The CAR object is similar in nature to an MHS message or JTM work specification in that it is a data structure exchanged between systems.

Note that from an implementation perspective, there may be other important objects that exist locally but are not visible to the other party. Such objects are not relevant to the protocol development process and are not part of the shared conceptual schema (although they are a part of the overall universe of discourse).

An example of such an object is the customer file maintained by the Card Issuer, which contains the information that determines whether an authorization request is accepted or rejected. This information is not visible to or directly accessible by the Acquirer and therefore does not play a role in the definition of standards for this application. How an authorization decision is taken is of no concern to the Acquirer—from its perspective, the decision could be based on information maintained by a human operator. The Acquirer is interested only in getting a response to its request. In contrast, if an authorization decision were to be made by the Acquirer based on information retrieved from the customer file, then this file becomes a visible object for this application.

11.9.2 Data Elements

The CAR is required to contain the following items of information:

- Transaction identifier, which uniquely identifies a specific transaction
- Transaction type identifier, which identifies the kind of business transaction that the initiator is performing (e.g., Automated Banking Machine, Point-of-Sale Terminal, etc.)
- Account information, which identifies the customer account
- Identification of the Transaction party identifier, which identifies the Acquirer and Card Issuer (and optionally the Card Acceptor)
- Currency information, which identifies the currency of the transaction
- Transaction amount, which is the value of the transaction being performed

• Transmission information, which provides a time stamp for interchanged messages

From this set of requirements can be derived the data elements identified in ISO 8583. Some of these items could be selected from standard or commonly used structured data elements that are not banking specific (e.g., transaction identifier, participant names, currency codes, and so on). Others must be defined specifically for bank use (such as account information).

11.9.3 Operations

The following operations are defined for the IA application and are relevant to the Card Authorization Record:

• *Authorization,* which determines whether a financial transaction is authorized to proceed
• *Authorization Completion,* which indicates that authorization actions have been completed
• *Authorization Completion Acknowledgment,* which acknowledges the authorization completion operation

It is possible, in an OSI Environment, to develop a protocol that removes the need for the Authorization Completion operation *from the communications perspective.* Specific application requirements may dictate a separation of these actions for business reasons.

11.10 STEP 3: SERVICE DEFINITION PREPARATION

The previous step defined the high-level shared conceptual schema for the distributed application. It is now appropriate to begin describing the interactions among the application processes using the OSI formal approach. This involves the preparation in this step of a service definition and then in the next step of a protocol specification. The purpose of the service definition is to describe, in an abstract yet precise way, the user view of the communication capabilities being provided to the user by the ASE.

11.10.1 Elements of a Service Definition

The following information should be present in a service definition standard:

• *Service model:* A model of the application described in terms of a collection of service users that communicate via a service provider. The service model defines the relationships among the service-users and determines the mode of interworking among the service-users.

- *Identification of services:* A list of services with a brief description of their purpose, semantics, and classification according to service type.
- *Groupings of services:* Collections of services that are meaningful in terms of service subsets, service classes, or functional units.
- *Service primitives:* A definition of service primitives, including all parameters and their characteristics.
- *Sequences of service primitives:* All constraints on the sequencing of service primitives must be identified.

11.10.2 Service Model

This model describes all communications activity in terms of interactions between the service-users and the service provider. Protocol mechanisms within the service provider convey the information relating to these interactions between the systems.

A convention used in service models is that the AE that initiates associations with one or more entities is always called the initiator, while all other AEs are called responders.

11.10.2.1 Relationships Among Users

Relationships among service-users may be defined in terms of either the control of the services or the nature of the processing performed by a particular user. The types of relationships based on the control of services include:

- *Peer-to-peer:* Each service-user can autonomously initiate application-associations with another user.
- *Master–slave:* One user can initiate an application-association, while the other user can only respond. Typically, once an application-association has been established, only the initiator can invoke services. In certain cases, a responder may also be allowed to invoke a service, but normally these are restricted to the reporting of exception conditions, such as a local system failure.

The types of relationship based on the nature of processing include:

- *Client–server:* One service-user manages a resource that the other service-user wishes to access. (*Note:* A client–server relationship does not necessarily imply a movement of data (e.g., remote operations.)
- *Source–sink:* There is movement of data from the source service-user to the sink service-user (e.g., FTAM).
- *Initiation–execution:* One service-user is capable of executing some operation that another user wishes to have performed. An example of this type of relationship is JTM.

These various types of relationship are not mutually exclusive. Indeed, all of them may be possible for a single ASE.

11.10.2.2 Modes of Interworking

The nature of the interactions between the service-users and the service provider will be influenced by the mode of interworking of the AEs. There are three distinct modes of interworking: connection-mode, connectionless-mode, and store-and-forward. The decision as to which mode is appropriate is related to the QOS requirements of the application.

The following series of questions will assist in the analysis of the mode of interworking needed by the application.

Connection-mode Interworking. Does the application require reliable transfer of large amounts of data? Does it require negotiation of interworking characteristics? Does it require an ongoing dialogue between the communicating partners? Is the nature of interworking synchronous? If so, then the connection-mode approach to interworking is most likely the appropriate choice. Connection-mode interworking may be achieved via single or multiple associations with multiple associations being used when there is parallelism in the communications activity.

Connectionless-mode Interworking. Does the application have a requirement for low data transfer delay and for the transfer of small amounts of data? Is reliability of data transfer a secondary requirement? Is there a need to send the same information to multiple destinations? Is negotiation of communications characteristics unnecessary? Is the nature of interworking asynchronous? If so, then the connectionless-mode approach to interworking may be suitable.

Store-and-Forward Interworking. Does the application have a requirement for transfer of small to medium amounts of data to one or more destinations that may or may not be always available? Is transfer delay of secondary importance? Is the nature of interworking asynchronous? If so, then a store-and-forward mode of interworking may be appropriate.

11.10.3 Identification of Services

Services represent the visible capabilities of the service provider and together comprise the ASE service.

11.10.3.1 Criteria for Selection of Services

Although there is no precise rule for selecting services, the following process is recommended:

1. Allocate a service for each operation identified in the high-level shared conceptual schema.

2. If the communication is to be connection-mode, then services are required for controlling the application-association. Three such services are usually needed: one to initiate the application-association, one to terminate it gracefully, and one to abort it unconditionally. Normally, these should be provided using ACSE (see Section 10.1). These services may also provide for the exchange of information concerning variable aspects of the application-association, such as selection of application-context or provision of accounting information upon termination of the application-association.
3. Allocate a service for service provider functions that are not directly related to operations identified in the conceptual schema but do satisfy a communications requirement of the application. Such communications requirements are derived from an analysis of the application and an intuitive appreciation of the underlying functionality needed to support the desired object operations. For example, if the application requires coordination of activities taking place over more than one application-association, then the CCR ASE may provide that coordination on behalf of the service-users.

11.10.3.2 Description of Services

Three items of information are required in order to fully specify services: a list of service names, their corresponding service type, and a definition of the semantics of each service. A tabular format is generally most effective for presenting the first two, while descriptive text is appropriate for the last item.

Service names should adhere to the following conventions:

- Capital letters should be used.
- The first one or two letters should identify the application.
- The application identifier should be separated from the function identifier by a hyphen.
- A descriptive name should be given to the service

A service primitive is formed by appending the primitive name (not capitalized) to the service name.

As an example, the following FTAM service opens a file:

F-OPEN

where F refers to the FTAM application and OPEN is the function name.

A component service primitive of that service is

F-OPEN request

where "request" is the primitive name.

Services may be classified into types that indicate whether the service is confirmed, unconfirmed, or provider-initiated. The service definition should identify what provider-initiated services are required (e.g., information on the status and activities of the service provider).

11.10.4 Groupings of Services

Services can be grouped as functional units, service classes, and service subsets.

Functional units represent small, meaningful groupings of services. The criterion for membership in a specific functional unit is that a particular member would not be useful if the other members were not also available.

Service classes represent combinations of functional units. There are no precise criteria for selecting a class. Selection may be done on the basis of gradation of functionality (for example, for a basic class that is a subset of a full class), or it may be done on the basis of differentiation of functionality (different classes define different aspects of functionality). A class may include certain functional units as options and require others. The use of optional functional units would be negotiated during association establishment.

Service subsets are logical groupings of functional units that include a kernel functional unit and any other set of functional units.

11.10.5 Service Primitives

Service primitives must be defined both in terms of their role in performing the service and in terms of the impact of the parameters on the meaning of the results. The definition, usage, and range of values must be provided for each parameter of each service primitive of each service. Also, for each service, the service-user that may issue the request service primitive must be identified.

The definition of each parameter states its meaning. Only one definition need be provided for a parameter that appears more than once in the specification.

The usage of each parameter states whether the parameter is mandatory, optional, or conditional. A mandatory parameter must always be present when the service primitive is invoked. An optional parameter may be present if appropriate. The interpretation of the absence of a parameter is parameter dependent and must be explained as part of the specification. A conditional parameter is one whose usage is dependent on the presence or value of other parameters. This dependency must also be explained as part of the specification.

In certain cases, a parameter of a service primitive is constrained to be identical to that of a previous primitive of the same service. For example, a filename associated with a "file open" indication must be identical to the filename provided with the "file open" request. All such constraints must be stated explicitly.

The tabular format shown in Table 11.1 is helpful to illustrate this convention. In this example, a parameter of an indication or response service primi-

Table 11.1 Example of a Service Primitive Parameter Table

	Service Primitives (Delete file service)			
Parameter	F-DELETE request	F-DELETE indication	F-DELETE response	F-DELETE confirm
Diagnostic			Mandatory	Mandatory
Delete password	Optional	Optional (=)		
Charging			Optional	Optional

tive that is constrained to take on the same value as its predecessor primitive is indicated with an equals sign in parentheses. A blank space under a service primitive indicates that the corresponding parameter is not applicable. The range of values for each parameter must be specified, along with any default value, if applicable. A formal definition of parameter syntax in terms of simple types, such as integers, strings, boolean, etc., is desirable. The use of the ASN.1 syntax notation for this purpose is recommended and is in general use throughout the ISO/IEC JTC1 standards.

Since some services can be invoked by either service-user and others by only one, information must be supplied for each service that specifies which is allowed.

11.11 STEP 3 FOR THE INTERACTIVE AUTHORIZATION EXAMPLE

11.11.1 Service Model

The service model for the interactive authorization ASE is shown in Figure 11.5. There are only two service-users: the Acquirer and the Card Issuer.

11.11.1.1 Roles of the Users

Within the scope of the IA application, the Acquirer is always the initiator and the Card Issuer always the responder. There is a master–slave, initiation–execution relationship between these two users: The Acquirer asks the Card Issuer to perform an authorization operation, and the Card Issuer is expected to respond to that request.

11.11.1.2 Mode of Interworking

The IA application has a requirement for fast response time. The number of interactions between an Acquirer and Card Issuer for any specific

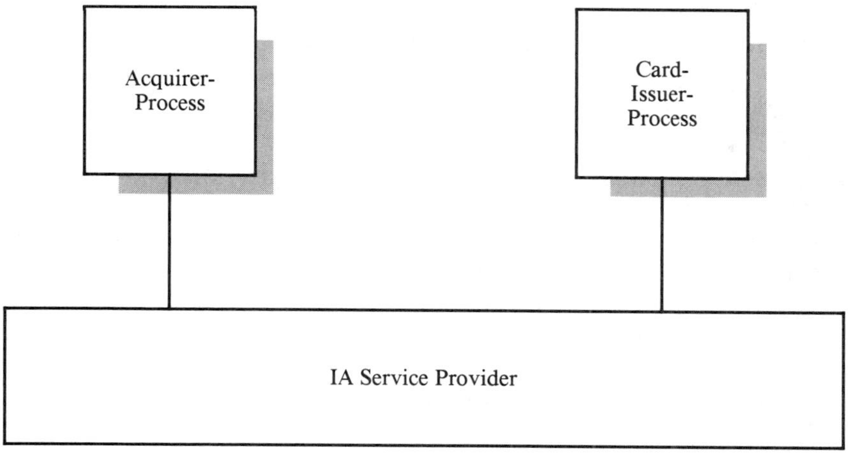

Figure 11.5: OSI view of IA application.

financial transaction is typically two, with the size of messages relatively small. These characteristics suggest the use of either connectionless-mode or connection-mode interworking.

A connectionless-mode service has the advantage of potentially smaller communication delay because of lower overhead. It has the disadvantage that its reliability is totally dependent on the characteristics of the network used. Presently there are no higher-level error recovery capabilities specified in existing connectionless-mode protocols, and there is no opportunity for negotiation of communication characteristics as these are fixed by a priori agreement.

> Note: In this application the use of Completion and Completion Acknowledgment operations would allow application mechanisms to compensate for unreliable connectionless-mode services.

A connection-mode service may result in increased communication delay, but this is in large measure due to the additional error recovery capabilities that are important for the IA application. The connection-mode service also provides for dynamic negotiation of application-association characteristics, which can be advantageous if requirements are changeable. Potentially, the most serious drawback is the connection establishment delay, which can be significant if a network connection must be established for each authorization request. Delay can be reduced somewhat by maintaining a network connection established indefinitely and creating new AAs and presentation, session, and transport connections for each authorization transaction. Another alternative is to establish an association only once and keep it indefinitely. This eliminates delay in connection establishment on a per-transaction basis, but at the cost of permanently allocating communications resources, such as buffers.

In the IA example, no choice of supporting service is made, since both connection-mode and connectionless-mode approaches may be appropriate. It is possible to defer the choice of the supporting service because there are no specific requirements for negotiation of characteristics. It might even be possible to use both connection-mode and connectionless-mode services for a single transaction; connectionless-mode services could be used for normal message flow to take advantage of the low overhead, while connection-mode services could be invoked for additional reliability if it is found necessary to invoke the "repeat" service elements.

If a requirement had existed for negotiation of AA characteristics, then connection-mode interworking should be selected, in which case ACSE would be needed. For the purposes of this example, no requirements for CCR or RTS have been identified.

Note: In practical interchanges between large banks in a single country, the same AA is likely to be used for a stream of authorizations from many Card Acceptors. The third alternative defined above is the most probable solution. The other alternatives may prove effective in low transaction frequency situations (e.g., between banks in different countries).

11.11.2 List of Services

Table 11.2 lists the services and their service type. The initials BC have been chosen to represent the bank card application, of which the IA-application is a part. The services were arrived at in the following way: The BC-INITIALIZE, BC-TERMINATE, and BC-ABORT services support the establishment and release of associations (they map directly onto ACSE); and

Table 11.2 Services for Interactive Authorization

Service Name	Service Type
BC-INITIALIZE	CONFIRMED
BC-TERMINATE	CONFIRMED
BC-ABORT	UNCONFIRMED
BC-AUTHORIZE	CONFIRMED
BC-AUTHORIZE-REPEAT	CONFIRMED
BC-COMPLETE	UNCONFIRMED
BC-COMPLETE-REPEAT	CONFIRMED
BC-COMPLETE-ACK	UNCONFIRMED

The choice of services of Table 11.2 places the responsibility for initiating repeat operations upon the service-user. A basic IA ASE would not include the repeat functions. A full specification would require more complete understanding of the meaning, i.e., the semantics, of this action to the application.

An alternative mapping could have been selected where repeats were provider-initiated, perhaps under the control of a parameter in the initial authorization request.

the BC-AUTHORIZE, BC-COMPLETE, and BC-COMPLETE-ACK services correspond to the operations that were identified in the shared conceptual schema. The BC-AUTHORIZE-REPEAT and BC-COMPLETE-REPEAT services have been added in recognition of the necessity for the initiator to force action on the part of a responder when an answer has not been received within a reasonable time.

11.12 SERVICE GROUPINGS

Functional units may be defined for this ASE. One logical selection is shown in Table 11.3. The use of a particular functional unit is negotiated at the time when the AA is established. Once a functional unit has been selected, its use becomes mandatory; for example, if the completion functional unit is selected, then a BC-COMPLETE request must be issued whenever a BC-AUTHORIZE confirm is received. There is no requirement to identify service classes or subsets.

11.13 DEFINITION OF SERVICE PRIMITIVES

At this point, consideration should be given to the use of an existing ASE for all or part of the required task, if possible. In particular, for this example, the RO ASE (see Section 10.3) would be considered for use with the IA operation.

> Note: In this example, we proceed to develop a completely new protocol for tutorial purposes.

The service primitives for this example may be defined by extending the parameters provided in ISO 8583 into a more formal definition using ASN.1 syntax notation (see Chapter 12).

Table 11.3 Functional Unit Example

Functional Unit	Service	Constraints
Kernel	BC-INITIALIZE BC-TERMINATE BC-ABORT BC-AUTHORIZE	Must always be selected
Completion	BC-COMPLETE	
Ack	BC-COMPLETE-ACK	Can be selected only if completion functional unit is selected
Authorize Repeat	BC-AUTHORIZE-REPEAT	
Complete Repeat	BC-COMPLETE-REPEAT	Can be selected only if completion functional unit is selected

11.14 SEQUENCES OF PRIMITIVES

Valid sequences of primitives are generally specified using a combination of text, state transition diagrams, and time sequence diagrams. Time sequence diagrams do not normally specify all possible sequences of primitives but are suited for specifying certain constraints that cannot be easily stated using text or state transition diagrams. In some cases they may be used primarily to illustrate the text and serve as a guide to the reader; such diagrams should be placed in an appendix that is not part of the standard.

Figures 11.6 and 11.7 show the state transitions possible for authorizations at each of the user–provider interfaces. Note that in these figures there are four possible states from which the interface can return to idle after an implementation-dependent timeout. Three of these, namely, AUTHORIZE RESPONSE RECEIVED, AUTHORIZE COMPLETION, and AUTHORIZE COMPLETION ACK, are states in which no more authorization processing may be performed (depending upon the selection of functional units). For example, the AUTHORIZE RESPONSE RECEIVED state represents completion of processing when the COMPLETION AND COMPLETION ACK functional units are absent. Figures 11.6 and 11.7 apply to a single transaction; many transactions may occur during an association and may overlap.

The time sequence diagram in Figure 11.8 shows the sequence of events associated with an authorization with completion acknowledgment, where the BC-AUTHORIZE response primitive is issued after receipt of an BC-AUTHORIZE-REPEAT request primitive. In this case the BC-AUTHORIZE response and confirm primitives serve to complete both the BC-AUTHORIZE and BC-AUTHORIZE-REPEAT services.

> Note: It is important to define all possible event sequences. Time sequence diagrams can be used as tools to determine these sequences. Only three examples of time sequence diagrams are provided here.

The time sequence diagram in Figure 11.9 shows a sequence with authorization and authorization completion without acknowledgment, in which a repeat request is issued after an BC-AUTHORIZE response. No repeat confirm is issued to the Acquirer, since the prior BC-AUTHORIZE confirm completes both outstanding services.

The last time sequence figure (Figure 11.10) shows an authorization where a repeat is requested after reception of the authorization confirm. In this case, the full repeat functional unit is involved.

11.15 STEP 4: APPLICATION-PROTOCOL SPECIFICATION PREPARATION

This step specifies an application-protocol to support the ASE defined in the previous step. An application-protocol is a set of rules and formats that determines the communication behavior of the AEs that support an application. A separate application-protocol specification is normally provided for

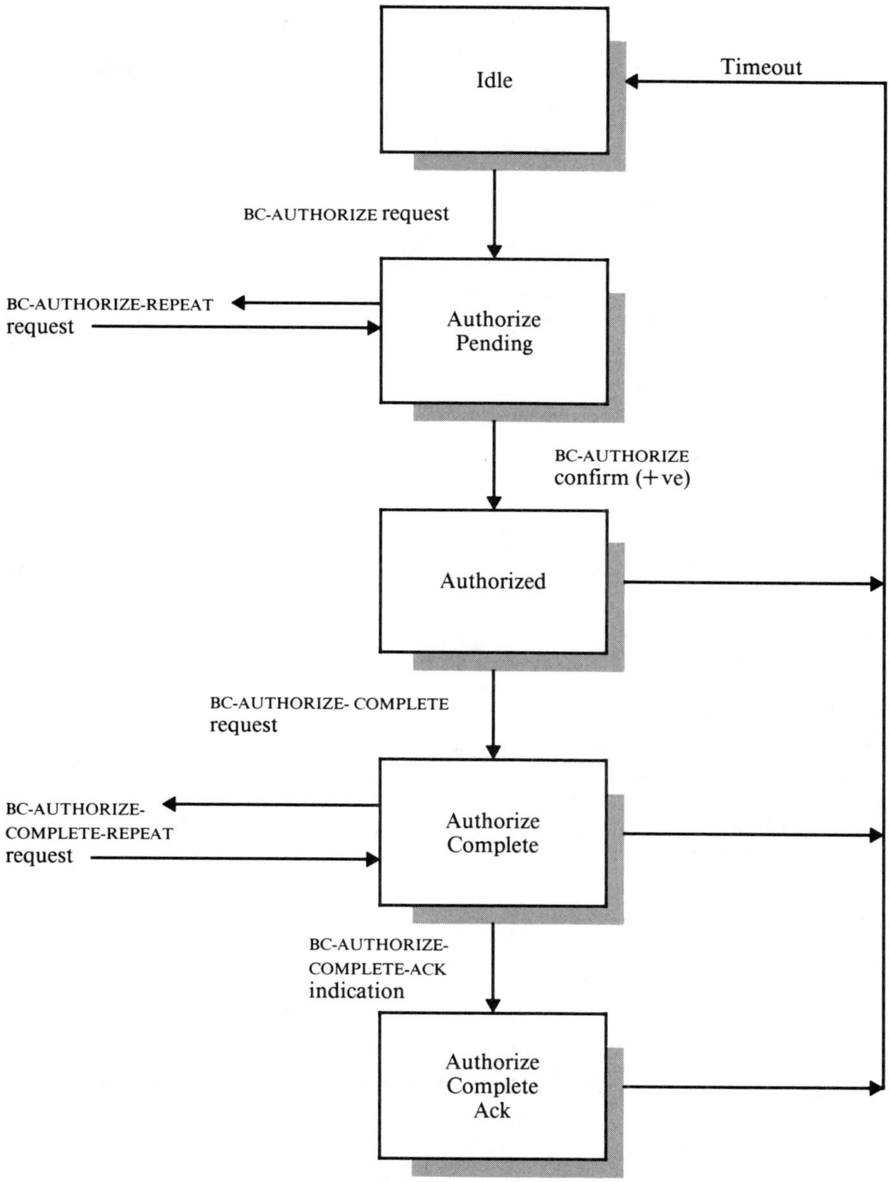

Figure 11.6: Authorization state transitions at the interface between the Acquirer and the service provider.

each ASE of the communicating AEs. The specification method described here is based on a model that is applicable to all OSI protocols. This section first provides some background material on the essence of a protocol specification and then describes each of the various elements that comprise it.

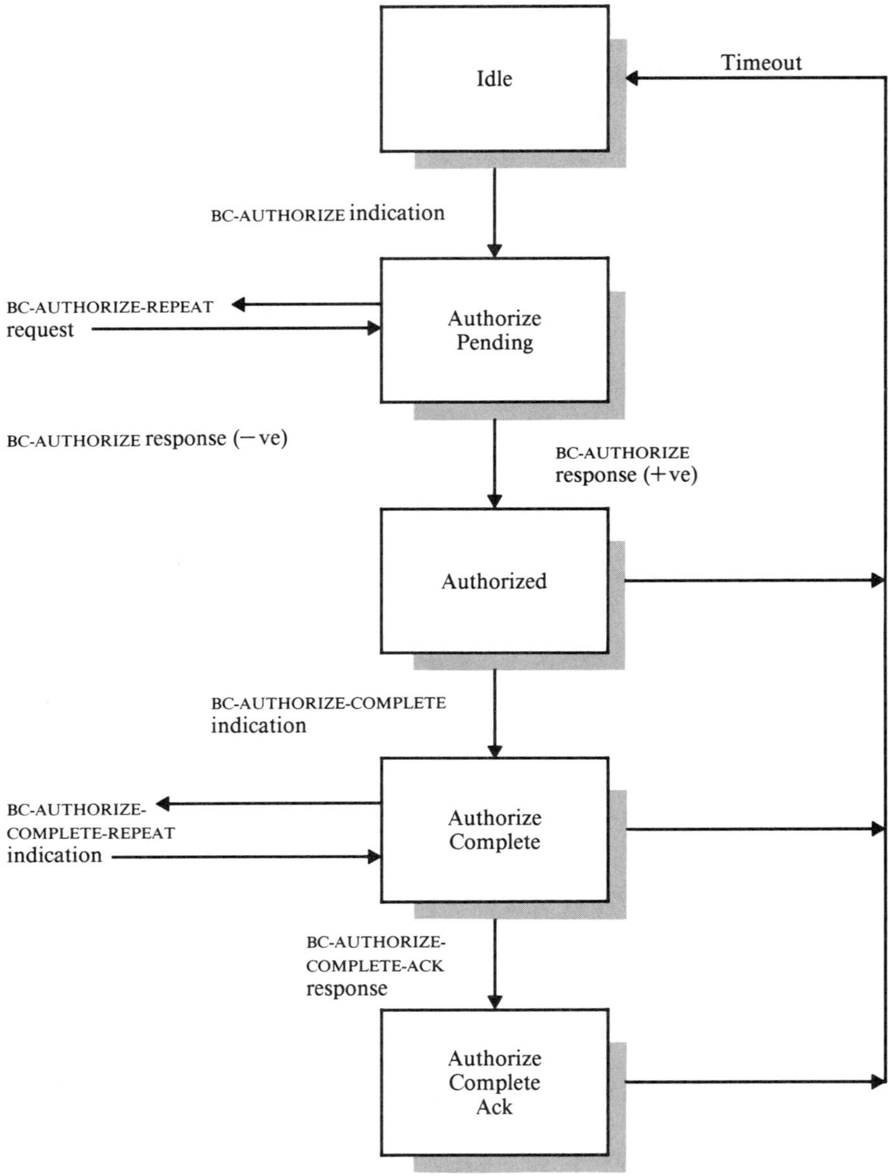

Figure 11.7: Authorization state transitions at interface between Card Issuer and service provider.

11.15.1 Model of Protocol Operation

The operation of an application-protocol is modeled as the interaction of two (or more) protocol machines (PMs) each of which forms part of a separate AE. The two PMs communicate by means of the services available at their lower boundary, in such a way as to provide the services required at their upper boundary. These concepts are illustrated in Figure 11.11.

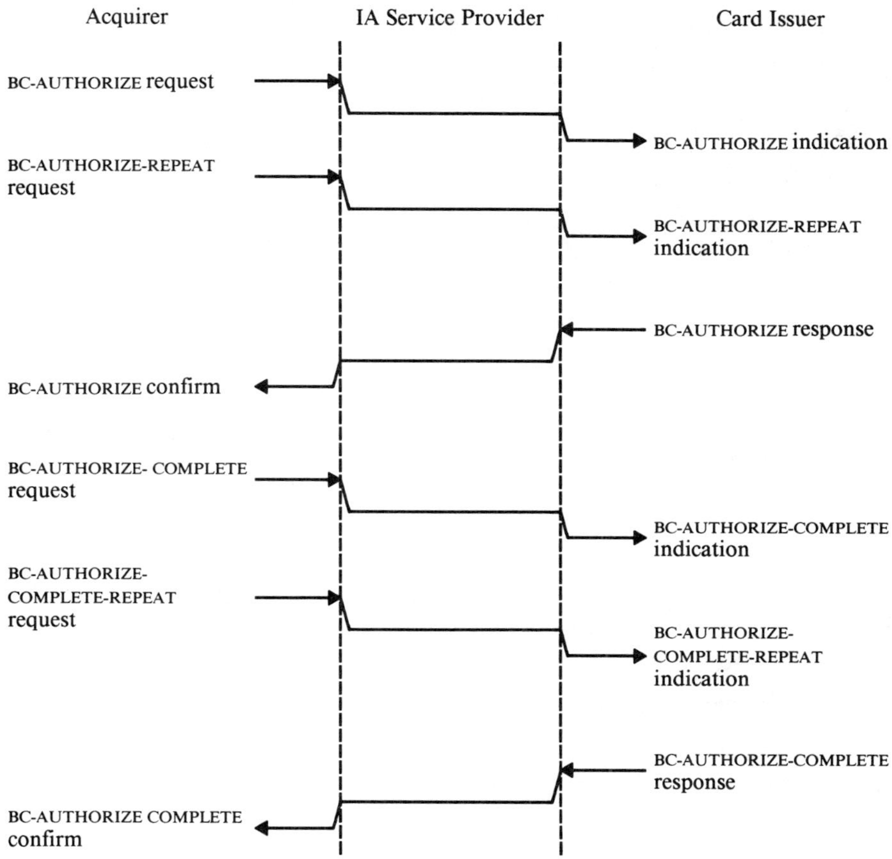

Figure 11.8: Time sequence for authorization with completion acknowledgment.

The behavior of each PM is defined in terms of the following:

1. The stimuli it receives, namely:
   a. Receipt of request or response service primitives from the upper service-user
   b. Receipt of indication or confirm service primitives from the lower service provider
   c. Local events, such as error indications
2. The action it takes, namely:
   a. Issuance of indication or confirm service primitives to the upper service-user
   b. Issuance of request or response service primitives to the lower service provider

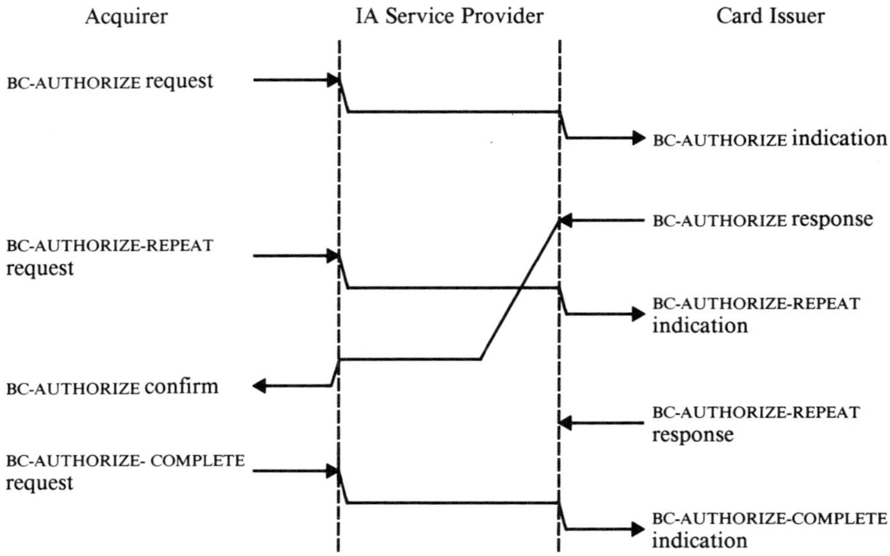

Figure 11.9: Time sequence for authorization without completion acknowledgment.

3. The information it retains, namely:
   a. Information associated with the lower connection-endpoint (this information is lost if the connection provided by the lower service ceases to exist)
   b. Information associated with the upper connection-endpoint (this includes information about the functionality requested by the service-user, e.g., the ability to recover from errors)

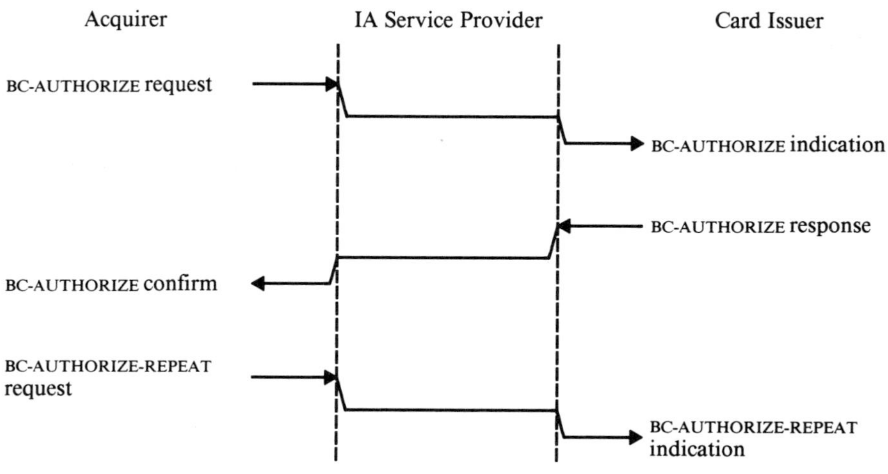

Figure 11.10: Time sequence for authorization with repeat request.

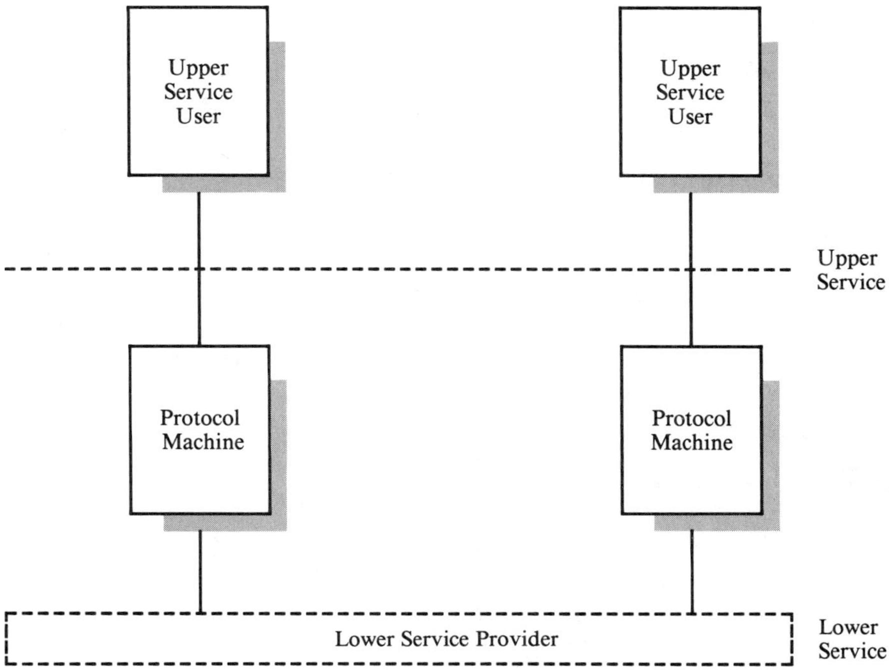

Figure 11.11: The protocol model.

11.15.2 Elements of a Protocol Specification

The following information must be provided as part of a protocol specification:

- List of services provided by the ASE
- Services assumed from the lower service provider
- Identification of functions
- Mapping between service primitives and APDUs
- Description of state information
- Description of APDUs
- Elements of procedure
- Mapping to supporting services
- Detailed description of APDUs
- Formal description of protocol (optional but advisable)

- Conformance statement
- Protocol state tables
- Definition and naming of application-context(s) and syntaxes

A formal protocol standard will include sections for each of the above topics. The following provides more detail concerning the contents of each section.

11.15.2.1 Services Provided to the User

This part of a protocol specification briefly outlines the services provided by the protocol, preferably summarizing them in tabular format. Reference may be made to the corresponding Service Definition in which the ASE service is specified in detail.

11.15.2.2 Services Assumed from the Lower Service Provider

A brief description of the services assumed from the lower service provider should be given, and a summary should be provided in tabular format. A reference may be made to the appropriate Service Definition in which these services are specified in detail.

As a minimum, the lower service provider in a connection-mode environment must be capable of providing the services defined by the ACSE, the Presentation Layer, and the Session Layer kernel functional unit. Each functional unit of a protocol may have differing requirements for additional services, in terms of either other ASEs or other functional units of the Presentation and Session Layers. These requirements must be stated for each functional unit.

In specifying an application-protocol to realize an ASE, a variety of common ASEs may be available in addition to the basic services of the OSI Presentation Layer (and lower layers). In general, the use of generic ASEs to satisfy as many requirements as possible is desirable. Complex combinations of ASEs may be assembled and coordinated by the OSI Application Layer. Chapter 10 provides a more detailed overview of the services available from other ASEs which will assist in the selection process.

11.15.2.3 Identification of Functions

A function is an activity performed by the protocol entity to support the service(s) it provides. The activity may or may not be performed as a direct result of user interaction. As an example, the management of sequence numbers to support a reliable data transfer service is a function of a transport-protocol. The operations of a function are not, however, directly accessible by the user.

Each protocol or protocol class is distinguished by the functions it performs. Although most functions are unique to a particular protocol, the following must be performed by all protocols:

- Mapping of service primitives and parameters into PDUs
- Ensuring the progress of the protocol, i.e., ensuring that an action initiated by the protocol does not take forever to complete (this is typically dealt with by the use of timers)

11.15.2.5 Description of State Information

Every protocol entity maintains a "major" state that reflects the state of the entity's protocol machine. It is this state that governs the actions of the protocol when events occur. In addition, a protocol entity may maintain other state information, such as the association status of the lower service provider, names of P-contexts, and checkpoint numbers, that affects the behavior of the entity in certain situations. This section describes all state information maintained by the protocol entity in terms of its purpose and its representation (an integer, a character string, etc.).

11.15.2.6 Description of APDUs

This part of the protocol specification includes tables that outline the contents of the APDUs. It outlines all the functions of the protocol. Each function supported by the protocol is described by a statement of its purpose, capabilities, limitations, related services, and an outline of its procedure.

The functions may be grouped according to functional units, phasing of the protocol, protocol classes, or whatever is the most natural organization. A session-protocol, for instance, will have connection establishment, data transfer, and connection release phases and it would have functions like token management, resynchronization and expedited data transfer.

11.15.2.4 Mapping Between Service Primitives and APDUs

APDUs are the units of information exchanged between peer application entities. APDUs typically are complex data types consisting of mandatory and optional data elements.

This part of the protocol specification uses tables to describe the mapping between the service primitives and the APDUs of the protocol. A brief description of the name and purpose of each APDU type is stated before presenting the tables. For each APDU there should be a table that enumerates the fields that are meaningful to the operation of the protocol. The tables include a brief description of each field and state whether the field is mandatory, user optional, provider optional, or conditional.

11.15.2.7 Elements of Procedure

This part states the high-level relationships between the upper services, the APDUs, and the lower services. It describes all events affecting the protocol state machine. This includes the effects of service parameters on the procedures of the protocol. It does not, however, describe in detail the mapping to the lower services. This information is provided in the subsequent section.

When an APDU is generated by a protocol entity, the values of the types in the APDU are set by the sender to:

- Reflect the values of the parameters of the service primitive that caused the transmission of this APDU
- Reflect the state of the entity sending the APDU
- Correspond to literal items in the APDU definitions provided in the abstract syntax specification

APDUs are transmitted as the user-data of a request service primitive that is issued to the lower service provider. The receiver of an APDU recognizes it on the basis of its "data type definition." A received APDU must also contain all the mandatory types in the order given, and it must not contain any types not present in the definition in order to be accepted. An APDU must be contained entirely within a single service primitive. There may also be other constraints on the detection of a valid APDU that are particular to the protocol and must be specified. An entity signals a protocol error if it receives a sequence of data types that does not form a defined APDU when an APDU is expected.

This part of the protocol specification is divided into subsections, one for each procedure—connection establishment, connection release, etc.—handled by the protocol. A specification subsection describes relevant service primitives and APDUs for the procedure. For the case of APDUs, the following activities are addressed:

- *Sending the APDU:* The conditions for sending the APDU and the resulting effect are stated. The service primitives associated with the APDU should be identified.
- *Receiving the APDU:* The effects in terms of protocol actions, issuance of service primitives, and/or changes in the state machine are described.

The handling of each of the fields of an APDU must be specified. The subsection describes both the initiating and the responding entities.

11.15.2.8 Mapping to Supporting Services

This part of the protocol specification consists of tables and text stating the detailed mapping of the parameter values of the upper layer services and the APDUs of the protocol onto the parameters of the lower layer services. There may be more than one mapping. If so, each mapping is described separately.

11.15.2.9 Detailed Description of APDUs

This part of the protocol specification defines the composition and encoding of the APDUs, with a subsection for each APDU. Each subsection describes its APDU in terms of the following:

- *Contents:* This lists the data types contained in the APDU.
- *Structure and encoding:* The structure of the APDU is shown using a diagram to identify its fields and their ordering within the APDU. Each field of the APDU is described in terms of its range of values and the meaning associated with each value.

The structure and content of the APDUs is described using an abstract syntax notation. The ASN.1 syntax defined in ISO 8824 is preferred (see Chapter 12). This abstract syntax notation defines complex data types in terms of a small collection of basic data types that are application independent. It is necessary as part of the syntax specification to indicate which basic data types and which structured types are used.

The encoding of APDUs is specified by identifying or describing the encoding rules that result in a transfer syntax. If the abstract syntax is specified using ASN.1, a transfer syntax is implicitly defined by the ASN.1 encoding rules. If the abstract syntax is not specified using ASN.1, then it is necessary to define a transfer syntax. Such a transfer syntax defines the encoding of the abstract syntax into a bit stream. More than one transfer syntax may be defined for an application protocol to suit different requirements, such as encryption or data compression.

11.15.2.10 Formal Description of the Protocol

Up to this point the description of protocol behavior has been accomplished in the form of a natural language description. A formal specification should be supplied, especially if no state transition tables are to be included. Otherwise, this section is optional. Three different formal description techniques (FDTs), Estelle, LOTOS and SDL are described in detail in Chapter 12.

11.15.2.11 Conformance Statement

The conformance statement is a critical part of the protocol specification as it determines the degree to which variability of protocol implementation is permitted. It defines the conditions under which an implementor can claim that his or her implementation conforms to the standard. There are two ways that conformance requirements can be described:

1. The conformance requirements in a protocol specification can be defined in terms of:
   a. *Mandatory requirements*, which must be observed in all cases
   b. *Conditional requirements*, which must be observed only when the conditions set out in the standard apply
   c. *Options*, which can be selected to suit the implementation, so long as any requirements on which the option depends or that depend on the option are observed

2. The statements of conformance requirements in a standard can be positive or negative:
   a. *Positive*—they state what must be done.
   b. *Negative* (prohibitions)—they state what must not be done.

The statement of conformance requirements is divided into three subsections: (a) static conformance requirements, (b) dynamic conformance requirements, and (c) protocol implementation conformance statement (PICS) requirements.

Static conformance requirements specify what capabilities the implementation must include. These requirements may be stated at a broad level, for example, the grouping of functional units and options into protocol classes, and/or at a detailed level, for example, the range of values that must be supported for specific parameters or timers. Static conformance requirements and options can be of two varieties:

- Those that concern the capabilities to be included in the implementation of the particular protocol
- Those that concern multilayer dependencies which place constraints on the capabilities of the lower layers of the system in which the protocol implementation resides

Static conformance requirements that are common to many application-protocols include:

- Support at least the kernel functional unit
- Act in the role of initiator or responder or both
- Support the encoding that results from applying the basic ASN.1 encoding rules to the abstract syntax specification, for the purpose of exchanging protocol-control-information.

Other protocol-specific requirements are typically included.

Dynamic conformance requirements specify choices of procedure that determine how a protocol implementation must behave during instances of communication. Requirements that are common to many application-protocols include:

- Follows all the procedures relevant to each functional unit that the system claims to implement
- Supports the mapping onto the lower service provider as defined in the specification

In addition to the subsections describing the static and dynamic conformance requirements of the protocol, there is also a subsection containing the Protocol Implementation Conformance Statement (PICS) requirements.

The PICS states the capabilities and options that have been implemented and any features that have been omitted. It is needed to test the implementation for conformance against the relevant requirements, and against those requirements only. This part of the protocol specification includes the PICS proforma, which consists of a series of tables to be filled out by the implementor in order to produce a PICS.

The PICS is not part of the protocol specification; it is a document, prepared by an implementor, that acts as the basis for conformance testing. The conformance statement for the protocol specification states only what information is to be provided in the PICS. The PICS proforma for a specific protocol should contain:

- Definitions of special symbols, abbreviations, special terms, and appropriate references
- Instructions for completing the PICS
- A form to be completed to give the necessary documentary information, either explicitly or by reference to the system overview
- One or more tables (or other kinds of form, if necessary) to be completed to state the capabilities of the implementation in detail, including:

  Name of feature, APDU type, timer, parameter, and any other capabilities
  A column stating whether each is mandatory, optional, negotiable, or conditional
  A column stating the relevant references to the standard
  A column giving the permitted range of values, if appropriate
  A column to give the supported range of values, if appropriate

The PICS proforma should also follow these guidelines:

- The structure and terminology should follow that of the protocol standard.
- It should cover all functions, elements of procedure, parameters, options, APDUs, timers, and other capabilities identified in the protocol standard, including mandatory as well as optional and conditional ones.
- The name and version of the protocol and data should be stated on each page.
- For consistency, the abbreviations to be used are:

  m: mandatory
  o: optional
  c: conditional
  n: negotiable
  x: exclusion of capability
  —: not applicable
  s: ability to send
  r: ability to receive

B: binary number
D: decimal number
H: hexadecimal number
O: octal number
N: numeric string
A: alphanumeric string
y/n: yes/no

- The PICS proforma should give a clear indication of the preferred data types (number bases, string types, octets, bits, seconds, minutes, etc.) for responses using the above abbreviations.

The PICS requirements subsection should include any other requirements not addressed in the proforma.

11.15.2.12 Protocol State Tables

If no formal description of the protocol is provided, a comprehensive set of state tables is required to describe the behavior of the protocol machine (PM) as completely as possible. The tables describe PM operation in terms of incoming events (e.g., receipt of a service primitive or an APDU) and actions. An action may consist of one or more outgoing events (e.g., issuance of a service primitive or the sending of an APDU) and local actions (e.g., update of a checkpoint counter). Actions may be conditional on specified predicates; i.e., the action will take place only if the predicate is true. An example of a predicate is the result parameter of a confirm service primitive that indicates a successful operation. Otherwise, actions are unconditional, in which case they will always take place when the trigger event occurs.

A typical state table entry will specify the current state, an incoming event, a predicate, an action, and a resulting state. It may not be possible to specify all actions explicitly using state tables. If such is the case, all actions not explicitly specified must be described using accompanying text and figures. An example of such an action is the behavior of the PM when an invalid incoming event is detected. As such a condition is possible for each state, it would be very cumbersome to cover these in the state tables. It is simpler and clearer just to state what action is taken generally when the condition is detected.

11.15.2.13 Definition and Naming of Application-Context(s) and Syntaxes

Application-context is the name given to the set of rules that governs the exchange of information in an application-association. An application-association has only one application-context (although the rules defined by it may change during the lifetime of the corresponding association). A simple application requires a single application-context that satisfies all the requirements of the application. In other cases, the application is sufficiently complex for more than one application-context to be needed; for example, in the JTM standard, a different context is identified for each of the basic and full classes of protocol.

An application-context will always include a specification of a set of ASEs (by reference to the relevant specifications). Other items that may be specified by the application-context include:

- Specifications for the logical structure of relevant information, i.e., abstract syntaxes other than that for APDUs
- Inter-ASE dependencies and coordination rules
- Additional rules related to the selection, use, and sequencing of APDUs
- Designation of and rules for the use of application functions, such as the directory
- Rules for changing the rules

Each application-context is assigned a unique name that is registered with an ISO registration authority (see Chapter 12) for application-context-names. An example of a name is ISO 8832-JTM-BASIC.

Each type of abstract syntax defined as part of this step must also be assigned a name so that it can be used for the identification of a presentation-context. Any transfer syntaxes defined for the abstract syntax must also be allocated unambiguous names. Both abstract and transfer syntax names must be registered with an ISO registration authority.

11.16 STEP 4 FOR THE INTERACTIVE AUTHORIZATION EXAMPLE

11.16.1 Overview of the Protocol

11.16.1.1 Protocol Model

The protocol model described in Section 11.15 is applicable to this application. Each of the elements that the protocol specification should contain is addressed below.

11.16.1.2 Services Provided

The following services are supported by the IA protocol:

- BC-INITIALIZE
- BC-TERMINATE
- BC-ABORT
- BC-AUTHORIZE

- BC-AUTHORIZE-REPEAT
- BC-COMPLETE
- BC-COMPLETE-REPEAT
- BC-COMPLETE-ACK

11.16.1.3 Services Assumed from Lower Service Provider

As discussed in step 3, the IA ASE could use connection-mode or connectionless-mode supporting services. Both possibilities are considered here.

In terms of connection-mode supporting services, there is no requirement for any Application Layer services other than ACSE services. As there is no requirement in this application for the interchange of substantial amounts of data, the Session Layer functional units related to synchronization and activities are not needed. The Major Sync or Activity functional unit may be useful to clearly delineate separate transactions occurring serially during an application-association. However, for the purpose of this example, it is assumed that this is not necessary.

In order to minimize the delays associated with executing an authorization, the minimum number of protocol exchanges is desirable; thus, a full-duplex form of dialogue is preferred. This form of dialogue has the additional advantage that it readily permits multiple authorizations to be in process concurrently; there is no need to manage the turn explicitly.

Table 11.4 lists by functional unit the connection-mode supporting services that are sufficient for this application.

In a connectionless-mode environment, the supporting services are the UNIT-DATA service of the ACSE and of the Presentation, Session, and Transport layers.

Table 11.4 Connection-mode Supporting Services Required for Interactive Authorization

Functional Unit	Services
Kernel	A-ASSOCIATE
	A-RELEASE
	A-ABORT
	P-DATA
	P-DEFINE-CONTEXT
	P-DELETE-CONTEXT
Repeat	P-DATA
Completion	P-DATA
Completion Ack	P-DATA

Table 11.5 Service Primitive Mapping

Service Primitive	APDU
BC-AUTHORIZE request	Authorization Request
BC-AUTHORIZE response	Authorization Request Response
BC-AUTHORIZE-REPEAT request	Authorization Request Repeat
BC-COMPLETE request	Authorization Complete Confirmation
BC-COMPLETE-REPEAT	Authorization Complete Confirmation Repeat
BC-COMPLETE-ACK	Authorization Complete Response

11.16.1.4 Functions Provided

The IA application protocol includes the mandatory functions for performing APDU mapping and ensuring progress of the protocol. There are two different subprotocols associated with the IA application. The association management subprotocol is responsible for establishing associations in a connection-mode environment. There is only one invocation of this subprotocol for each AE-invocation. The IA subprotocol is responsible for managing individual authorization transactions. There may be many such subprotocols operating in parallel over the same AA.

11.16.1.5 Mapping Between Service Primitives and APDUs

The IA service primitives map onto APDUs as shown in Table 11.5.

11.16.1.6 Application-Protocol-Data-Units

These APDUs can be constructed based on the rules given in Section 11.15.2.6.

11.16.1.7 Description of State Information

Conceptually, a different IA PM is invoked for each financial transaction for which authorization is desired. Therefore, state information must be maintained for each such PM, as well as for the single association management PM, when connection-mode supporting services are used. Each PM is distinguished by using data elements (defined in ISO 8583) called the System Trace Audit Number, perhaps in conjunction with the Primary Account Number. The states associated with the IA PM are shown in Table 11.6.

11.16.2 Elements of Procedure

The behavior of the association management subprotocol is described separately from the IA subprotocol. The main function of this subproto-

Table 11.6 IA Protocol States

IDLE	No authorization is in progress
I-AUTH-PD	Authorization pending, initiator; waiting for IA-AUTHORIZE response PDU
R-AUTH-PD	Authorization pending, responder; waiting for IA-AUTHORIZE response service primitive
AUTH-RESP-RCVD	Authorization response received
AUTH-COMPL	Authorization completion
AUTH-COMPL-ACK	Authorization completion acknowledged

Different names have been associated with the PM states than were associated with the service states, even though there is a direct correspondence between the two. This serves two purposes: First, it distinguishes between the fact that the set of events that drive the protocol state machine include PDUs and service primitives (and possibly internal events, such as timeouts), while the service state machine is driven by service primitives; second, there frequently are more protocol states than service states, due to factors like error conditions, retransmissions, etc.

col is to establish the appropriate application context for the IA protocol and to select the functional units that are to be used. The IA subprotocol is described in terms of the input events and the actions that should be taken according to the current state of the PM. The PM behavior is different for the initiator and responder.

CHAPTER 12

RELATED TOOLS AND FACILITIES

This chapter introduces a number of support facilities for the OSI Environment. Although most topics apply to all layers, the implications for application-protocol development are emphasized.

12.1 ABSTRACT SYNTAX NOTATION ONE (ASN.1)

The Application Layer requires a way of describing its data in an abstract way that does not constrain how the data are encoded for processing and transfer. The description mechanism must be powerful enough to describe a wide variety of data structures of varying complexity. It is desirable that the description mechanism be readily amenable to encoding so that the transformations performed by the Presentation Layer can be kept simple. These objectives are satisfied by ASN.1.

ASN.1 defines an abstract syntax notation that enables the definition of complicated data types and also the specification of their values. This is done without determining the way an instance of this type is to be represented during transmission.

ASN.1 specifies a number of built-in types and associated values. It also provides type constructors for developing complex data structure types (called structured types), with corresponding complex data values derived from these basic built-in types. Common built-in types include boolean, integer, bit string, and octet string. The common constructors are sequence, set, and choice; they define the three typical ways in which data types can be combined to form more complex data types.

An important objective of ASN.1 is to support the representation of Application Layer and Presentation Layer protocol-data-units and to facilitate encoding. For this reason, it provides a means for associating identification tags with data types. This is in contrast to the data structure definition facilities of Estelle and LOTOS, which were not intended expressly for PDU representation.

Various types of character string are supported, including ISO IA5 strings, numeric character strings, printable character strings (a basic 74-character set), teletex character strings, videotex character strings, and graphic character strings. The latter permits the use of any character set in the ISO Register of Character Sets, as established by ISO 2375.

Standardized representations of date and time (generalized time and universal time) are provided.

An important built-in type is the Object Identifier. This type is used typically to represent the value of an information object when the range of values is not known a priori or when it is not desirable to standardize the range of values. In such cases, the possible values of the object identifier are assigned by a registration authority, which for international standards will be ISO, CCITT, or ISO and CCITT acting jointly. An example of the possible use of Object Identifier is in the Message Handling environment, where the heading of each message must identify the type of information contained in the body part. As a general purpose message system must be able to support a wide variety of body types, e.g., character text, graphics, and facsimile, it is appropriate that the abstract syntax definition of a message heading specify the body type using the Object Identifier construct. As various legitimate body types are identified, they can be registered with the appropriate CCITT registration authority.

ASN.1 provides two other features for the specification of complex syntaxes:

- The *External type*, which allows one abstract definition to refer to other abstract syntaxes that have already been defined; this in effect permits nesting of abstract syntaxes.
- A *macro definition capability*, which permits the definition of a new notation with which a user can then construct and reference ASN.1 types or specify values of types. An example of the use of this feature is the Remote Operations protocol, which is specified using a set of ASN.1 macros.

In an addendum to ISO 8824 and 8825, a number of potential extensions to ASN.1 have been specified:

- Enabling the definition of a default as IMPLICIT or EXPLICIT for tagging
- Providing a notation to specify upper and lower bounds on integers, minimum and maximum lengths of strings, and minimum and maximum iteration counts in sets and sequences
- Adding new types for scaled integers and for floating point
- Defining an enumerated type to replace the current clumsy use of integer in certain circumstances

- Providing support for pointer types
- Adding features for unambiguous identification of ASN.1 modules, for listing the symbols imported into a specification from an external module, and for listing the symbols that can be exported to other modules.

These extensions will make ASN.1 a more complete tool for the specification of abstract syntaxes.

12.2 REGISTRATION AUTHORITIES AND PROCEDURES

For two open systems to interwork, it is not sufficient that they both implement the same set of protocols. There are a number of other aspects of which the two systems must be cognizant. One obvious example is knowing the title or address of the destination AE that an initiating system wishes to reach. Another example is the Originator/Recipient Name (O/R Name) used in Message Handling Systems to uniquely identify the senders and recipients of messages. While the structure of these names may be standardized, the actual names must be allocated by some accepted authority (called, in this case, a naming authority) as and when needed (i.e., there is no need to use the standards voting process for each assignment).

Registration is the act of allocating an unambiguous name for a structured amount of information. A registration authority is an organization that has been assigned the responsibility for ensuring that each name is unambiguous and for recording the registered information. It may also be responsible for ensuring completeness and accuracy of the information to be registered. When ISO acts as a registration authority, it specifies the formal procedures that an applicant must follow. As a simple example, ISO registers standards; that is, it assigns numbers that are the unique name for the structured amount of information called a standard. Thus, the need for named information is quite general and not unique to OSI. When information to be registered is not relevant to all of OSI, for example, when a set of names is relevant only to the banking industry within a country, then the registration authority may be assigned to a body other than ISO.

Another type of OSI-related information for which registration is required is the application-context-name. Knowledge of the application context is crucial to proper interworking of two AEs; therefore, application-context-names must be known to and unambiguous for the interested parties. This is achieved by registering names with an authority responsible for ensuring unambiguity of application-context-names and making public the set of registered application contexts.

Registration is also necessary for abstract and transfer syntaxes. Application- and presentation-entities rely on a protocol-based negotiation mechanism to reach agreement with their peer entities on the subject of their communication and its representation during the period of the dialogue. This negotiation is based on the ability to unambiguously identify a syntax known to both peer entities; it is achieved through reference to a reserved or registered name for that syntax. Registration is needed because there may be more syntaxes than are standardized by ISO.

For a particular ASE, there may be other requirements for registration authorities. For example, in the Job Transfer and Manipulation (JTM) ASE, document types that can be interchanged using JTM must be registered.

12.2.1 Registration Procedures

The successful application and use of OSI standards requires that certain objects and/or unambiguous names be registered with some authority. To achieve successful communication between open systems, standards are required to specify the form or structure of these names, the extent of domains in which they are unambiguous, and the authority or procedures required to register the names of newly defined syntaxes. This requirement applies to the following types of names:

- Transfer syntaxes
- Abstract syntaxes
- AE-titles
- SAP-addresses
- Application-contexts
- Document types
- AP-type-title
- AE-type-title
- System-title

The process of registering a name for an object requires, first, that a specific Registration Authority be established and then that a proposal be submitted to that Registration Authority to register the proposed name. Specific Registration Authorities responsible for individual naming domains will be registered with and coordinated by the general OSI Registration Authority. As an illustration of the type of information that is associated with a register entry, a register of abstract syntaxes would contain the following information for each registered syntax:

- An unambiguous name for the abstract syntax (assigned by the Registration Authority) and a list of any registered aliases
- A reference to the definition of the abstract syntax
- References to those registered transfer syntaxes capable of supporting the information representation requirements of the abstract syntax
- The identity of the organization that requested the registration of the object

- The date of registration
- Status information, e.g., version and obsolescence data
- Variable features of the registered object, i.e., options of one or more forms

A register entry for transfer syntaxes would contain similar information, with the references to transfer syntaxes in the third item above replaced by references to the registered abstract syntaxes that the transfer syntax supports.

12.3 THE DIRECTORY SERVICE

12.3.1 Basic Directory Functions

The OSI directory service provides a common method for the storage, manipulation, and retrieval of information concerning communications. It fulfills two essential needs of OSI:

- It makes "user friendly" names available to clients (i.e. users and applications).
- It makes the OSI self-configuring in the sense that addition, removal, and changes in the physical location of objects need not affect the operation of OSI systems.

The directory service provides its clients with the following capabilities:

- *Name-to-attribute binding,* which binds (i.e., logically relates) a name to the information related to the object to which the name refers. Name-to-address binding is a special case of name-to-attribute binding. This capability is analogous to a "white pages" telephone book.
- *Name-to-list-of-names binding,* which binds one name to a list of names, for use, for example, in electronic mail, routing tables, or hosts having multiple access points. This can be considered a "distribution list" capability.
- *Attribute-to-set-of-names binding,* which lists the names of objects that have a given attribute. One example of this is a "yellow pages" telephone book, which can be used, for example, to find the names of all people in a certain town who are plumbers. Finding the names of all printers in a company that have Elite typefaces and wide carriages is another example.

The set of all information processing systems that provide directory services, together with the information they hold, can be viewed as an integrated whole, called the Directory. The Directory distinguishes between various categories of data based upon their semantic classes and does not rely on syntax alone to make the various types of information distinctive. For example, "567" can be, in one situation, part of the network-address for a resource and, in another environment, a password to access a resource. The Directory allows for alternative names for the same object, including (a) names that "describe" the object by including a collection of its attributes and (b) aliases, which allows very different names to denote the same object. Names can permit spelling variations in the values of any of the attributes forming the name. These characteristics go to providing the "user-friendly" capabilities of the Directory.

12.3.2 Functional Model of the Directory

The functional view of the Directory System Model is shown in Figure 12.1. It shows the concepts of Directory User, Directory User Agent (DUA), and Directory Service Agent (DSA). Directory information is distributed among the DSAs. A user wishing access to directory information first interacts with its DUA, which acts as its agent; the DUA understands the access procedures to the DSA and formulates the request in a form that the DSA can process. A DSA may use information stored in its local database or interact with other DSAs to carry out requests. Alternatively, the DSA can direct a requestor to another DSA that can help carry out the request.

A DSA may be located in the same system as the requesting DUA or in a separate system. When co-located, the interface between the two is a local implementation matter. When separated, a standardized protocol is used to access the DSA. Thus, there are two different protocols involved in the Directory Service: The Directory Access Protocol (DAP), which permits a DUA to access a remote DSA, and the Directory System Protocol (DSP) which governs the interactions among DSAs.

The Directory protocols are application-protocols.

12.4 FORMAL DESCRIPTION TECHNIQUES (FDTs)

Experience has shown that natural language descriptions of complex systems invariably lead to misinterpretations and a variety of problems that frustrate the intended purpose of the specification. These problems are particularly compounded when the specified system is distributed and its various parts are required to interwork despite being implemented within entirely separate organizations using different technologies. The international telephone network is a typical example of such a system. It functions with a multiplicity of equipment, supplied by various manufacturers, implemented on a global scale and operating with commendable success. Computerization of telecommunications systems has driven the development of new and better tools and methodologies for the description and analysis of requirements for systems. A Specification and Description Language (SDL) was developed by the CCITT in 1976, specifying a graphical method to describe an extended finite state automaton. This language has since been extended and revised and has been published in 1989 as CCITT Recommendation Z.100. It now includes linear as well as graphical syntax forms.

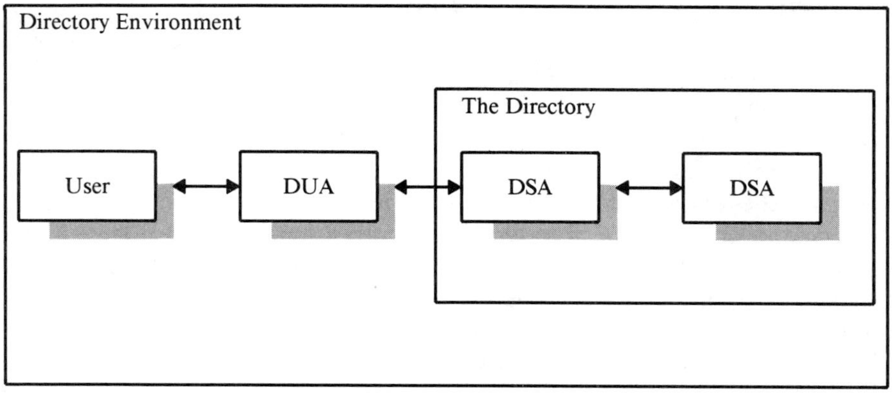

Figure 12.1: Functional model of the directory. (⟷ denotes an interaction)

With the advent of OSI in the late 1970s, the search was begun to find a formal description technique that could be used for the specification of OSI protocols and services. In spite of a strong advocacy by CCITT for the use of SDL or an enhanced SDL, ISO members pursued the development of a Pascal-like formal description technique, Estelle, and LOTOS, based on the Calculus of Communicating Systems (CCS). All three techniques are now published as international standards.

12.4.1 Estelle

Estelle is derived from Extended State Transition Language. It is a formally defined language for describing distributed or concurrent processing systems, and in particular those that employ OSI. An Estelle specification defines a hierarchically structured system of state machines that communicate by exchanging messages through bidirectional channels connecting their interaction points. Since Estelle employs (extended) Pascal programming language concepts that are relatively well known, the Estelle developers thought that the widespread use and knowledge of Pascal would help achieve rapid acceptance of the technique, with a minimum learning period within the target user population. Experience to date has not quite proven this to be the case: Estelle has in fact become relatively complex, and there is limited interest in its use in some quarters.

The basic goal of Estelle is to provide a tool that can be applied to OSI protocol and service specifications and thereby remove ambiguities inherent in standards described in a combination of natural language prose, state tables, and other informal ways. As experience with OSI and FDTs developed, other desirable qualities have been identified. These include the possibilities of using the formal nature of Estelle specifications for the semiautomatic derivation of implementations.

The relative ease of developing implementation code from an Estelle specification has been taken by some as evidence that Estelle specifications are always implementation-oriented and thus direct the user toward a particular implementation approach. Those with a preference for a more abstract specification technique where influence toward a particular implementation is absent perceive this as a disadvantage. Others find it an advantage and welcome the ease of following the structure of a formal specification to develop an implementation. However, an implementation is not constrained to follow an Estelle specification and is required only to exhibit the external behavior corresponding to a possible behavior of the Estelle specification as observed at its external interaction points. In practice, the level of abstraction in an Estelle specification can vary from abstract to quite implementation oriented.

Estelle is fully defined in ISO 9074.

12.4.2 LOTOS

LOTOS (Language of Temporal Ordering Specification) is based on the concept that protocol systems can be described by defining the relation between events in the externally observable behavior of a system. The formal mathematical model of LOTOS is based on a modification of CCS, which was developed at the University of Edinburgh. CCS provides a powerful analytical technique for concurrent systems.

In LOTOS, distributed systems are modeled as a set of communicating processes. A system as a whole is a single process that may consist of many interacting subprocesses. These subprocesses may in turn be refined into sub-subprocesses, etc., so that a specification of a system in LOTOS is essentially a hierarchy of process definitions. The behavior of each process may be thought of as having a treelike structure. The root of the tree represents the initial state of the process. The edges of the tree represent events, which are units of synchronized interaction between two processes. The tree structure thus represents process behavior as a sequence of possible choices ordered in time according to the depth of the nodes in the tree.

The CCS model on which LOTOS is based focuses on the dynamic aspects of process behavior and does not define the mechanism to use for the representation of data. LOTOS uses ACT ONE as the mechanism for defining data types and values; ACT ONE is based on the theory of abstract data types.

LOTOS is fully defined in ISO 8807.

12.4.3 Specification and Description Language

Of the three FDTs presented in this section, SDL has been an international standard for the longest time, and has a solid base of users, especially in the telephony environment. Graphical SDL was first published as a CCITT Recommendation in 1976 and has undergone substantial modification and enhancement since then. It was published by CCITT in 1989 as Recommendation Z.100, which includes substantive Annexes incorporating the two alternative syntactic forms, Graphical Representation (SDL/GR) and Phrase Representation (SDL/PR), and other formal definition parts.

As with Estelle and LOTOS, the objective of SDL is to provide a precise formal method for use in specification of systems. SDL is of the same generation of FDT as Estelle in that it is of the finite state automaton type.

SDL incorporates a rich variety of concepts for precisely defining a system at various desired levels of hierarchical decomposition. This may vary from overview level to detailed substructure level. The basic functionalities include the concepts of channels, blocks, and processes. Channels are the media through which signals are exchanged between blocks. Blocks are connected to each other and to the environment by channels. The blocks themselves represent the structuring modules in SDL and contain the processes.

In SDL the system boundary denotes the separation of the specified system, and the environment signal instances permit the exchange of information across the boundary. Each block in an SDL system contains a definition of the process types that may be contained therein.

The stimulus–response type of specification, where a system specification is seen as the sequence of responses to any given stimuli, is particularly easy to follow for first-time users of FDTs, especially in the SDL/GR form. There is an intuitive comprehension of what the representation means, coming from a general familiarity with state-transition diagrams and flow-chart concepts.

SDL/GR and PR forms, which are concrete representations of the same SDL semantics, are also helpful for those wanting to learn a programming-like form of FDT.

12.4.4 Future Developments

The three FDTs are fully accepted by ISO and CCITT as applicable to OSI. It is now up to the standardization groups to take advantage of these FDTs in their specifications. Experience seems to show that the discipline of learning and using FDTs is not readily embraced by most. However, now that these FDTs have reached a stable state as international standards, their use may increase.

Work continues on adding enhancements to the FDTs, especially to add a graphical form to LOTOS (G-LOTOS). This is being developed to satisfy users who find a graphical form more user friendly than the linear form.

An important FDT-application document entitled “Guidelines for the Application of Estelle, LOTOS and SDL” has been published as a guideline by ISO and as a manual by CCITT.

An interesting new area of work in FDTs is Architectural Semantics. This work, still at an early stage, is intended, among other things, to provide a common basis for uniform and consistent comparison of formal descriptions of the same standard in different FDTs. The core work is independent of any FDT and any particular architecture.

12.5 INTERNATIONAL STANDARDIZED PROFILES (ISPs)

In the development of OSI standards, many different technical, economic, and political requirements had to be met in order to achieve the necessary basis for international agreement. This has resulted in standards that have classes, options, and multiple functional units. In many cases they are open to different interpretation of the specifications. FDTs are helpful in addressing the issue of interpreting the precise meaning of a specification, but they provide no help at all in regard to a universal choice of classes and options and combinations of protocols to make up a useful implementation.

This fact was not recognized or dealt with in OSI development until serious seven-layer implementation work began in the 1985 time frame. Until that time, practical systems were largely concerned with lower layer implementations. Options and compatibility within the related layers were handled in the traditional fashion, driven by the telecommunication service providers, who offered specific services with published specification details and test facilities to assist in the development of compatible products. International interconnection issues have traditionally been handled by multiple bilateral testing and adjustment in this environment. However, the completion of the OSI upper layer protocols, rich in ASE options, beyond the exclusive pervue of any particular national or international monopoly service provider, demanded new approaches and new global infrastructures. One of these, conformance testing services, is dealt with in Chapter 13. Another, the subject of this section, is the establishment of International Standardized Profiles (ISPs) and Functional Profiles (FPs). These define combinations of base standards to provide specific functionalities. Specific options and classes are identified, leaving as little as possible free for selection by implementors.

12.5.1 Basic Concepts

Figure 12.2 illustrates how a seven-layer Functional Profile is built up from selections of classes, subsets, options, and parameters standardized for the various layers of OSI. This is identified by the vertically joined modules forming a seven-layer slice of OSI standards, and providing a functionality, such as file transfer over an X.25 packet network using Transport Class 2 and an RS-232-C connector at the Physical Layer. Presentation Layer and Session Layer options would similarly be precisely identified in the ISP/FP.

Ultimately an ISP is the defining specification from which internationally recognized conformance test suites and testing services are developed. Therefore, they are vital links in the route to interoperable open systems. Rather than repeating the base standard specification, ISPs refer to their relevant parts needed for building the target functionality.

This referencing requirement introduces a need for registration mechanisms to register objects being referenced in base standards. The specification of such objects is maintained by Registration Authorities, which are being established internationally in the 1989/90 time frame.

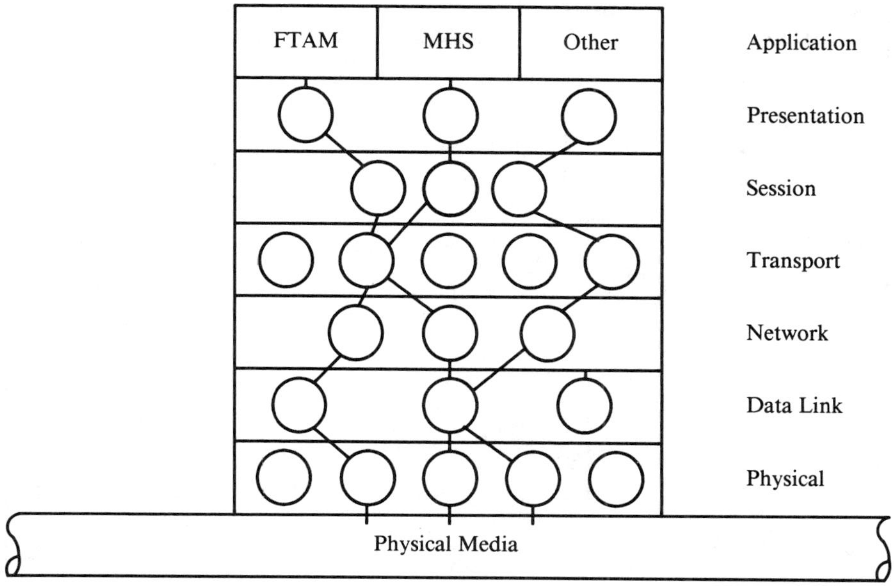

Figure 12.2: Functional Profiles.

It is important to note that an International Standardized Profile may refer to one or more OSI base standards. Its definition includes:

- A statement of purpose and scope of the required functionality
- An illustration of the utility of the Profile
- Reference to a single set of base standards
- Specification of the application of each referenced base standard
- Conformance statement

In the case of the last item, the concepts of static and dynamic conformance, outlined in Chapter 13, also apply to ISPs.

12.5.2 Taxonomy of ISPs

In OSI, the structure and classification within which Functional Profiles must fit are defined. This taxonomy gives a basic level specification of the profile and draws upon specific areas of expertise related to the base standards. The classification scheme for ISPs identifies at least six distinct classes of OSI Profiles:

F—Interchange Format and Representation Profiles
A—Application Profiles using connection-mode transport-service
B—Application Profiles using connectionless-mode transport-service

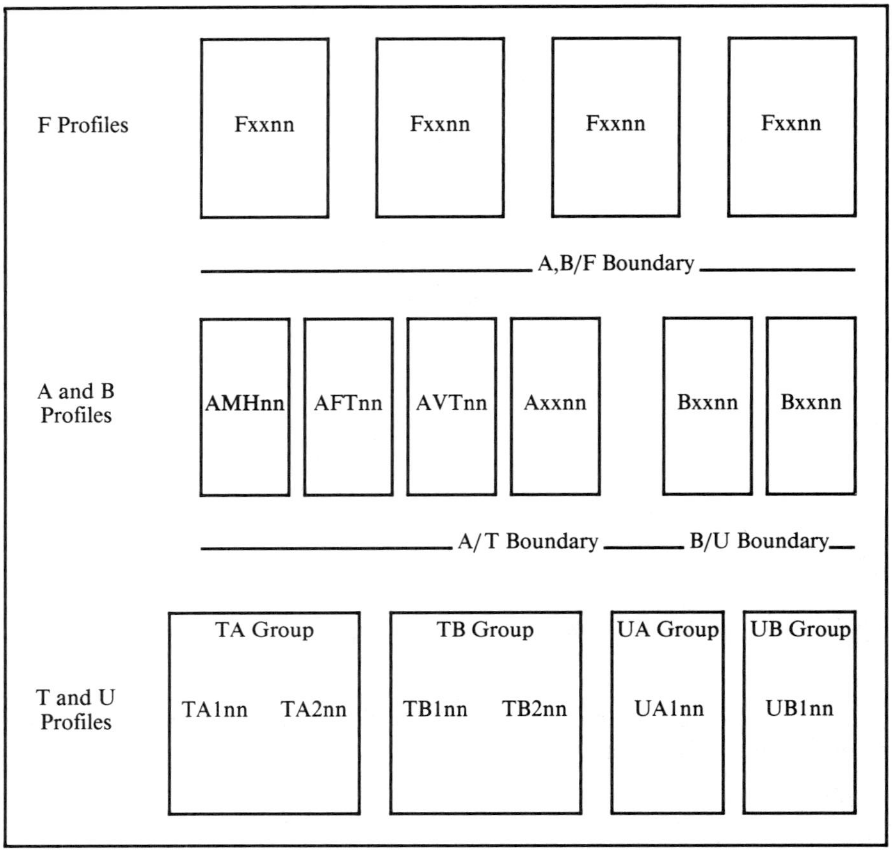

Figure 12.3: Examples of relationships between profiles in the OSI taxonomy. This figure illustrates logical structuring possibilities, not the relationships among specific identified profiles.

T—Connection-mode Transport Profiles, related to subnetwork type
U—Connectionless-mode Transport Profiles, related to subnetwork type
R—Relay function between T- or U-Profiles

Note that T- and U-Profiles are further subdivided into groups having related or compatible functionalities. The evolution of OSI and the development of standards in the context of Open Distributed Processing (ODP; see Chapter 14) will no doubt require extension of this taxonomy.

Figure 12.3 illustrates relationships between Profiles in the main subdivisions of the taxonomy. It also suggests the combinations that can be made by selections from different classes. An A- or B-Profile must be used in combination with a T- or U-Profile. The separately identified boundaries between classes in Figure 12.3 illustrate the possibility of combining any pair of A- and T-Profiles, one from each of the two classes, where a common boundary exists, e.g., A/T boundary. Similarly, combinations of A- or B-Profiles with

F-Profiles will be selected for specific required functionalities. However, the A/F and B/F boundaries are distinguished from the A/T and B/T boundaries in that they are not characterized by a single service definition.

12.5.3 Status of ISP Work

In the international standardization arena a Technical Report (TR 10000) will be issued by ISO/IEC JTC1 covering the Taxonomy Framework for ISPs and the taxonomy of profiles. The full documentation envisaged will provide a comprehensive classification of OSI Functional Profiles, organized identification of functionalities, status of ISP completion and target schedule, and supporting organizations at the "major organization level" (Corporation for Open Systems [COS], Promoting Conference for OSI [POSI]/Japan, etc.). A definition for European functional standards (Memorandum M-IT-02) also exists, as does a National Institute of Standards and Technology (NIST) Workshop Taxonomy.

CHAPTER 13

CONFORMANCE TESTING CONCEPTS

13.1 INTRODUCTION

This chapter provides an introduction to conformance testing as it applies to OSI. OSI applications cannot easily be achieved without a highly disciplined approach to checking the conformance of implementations. This in turn cannot be achieved without appropriate reliable and measurable conformance statements made concerning a particular OSI standard. These statements must set forth clearly and concisely the optional capabilities and required behavior of an implementation. The conformance testing methodology itself must provide a means for precisely defining test configuration, test stimuli, and possible responses.

The ISO has addressed these issues during the development of OSI standards. Its work towards standardizing conformance testing has resulted in a five-part standard, to be designated ISO 9646, Parts 1–5. This standard goes beyond basic conformance testing requirements and includes important considerations in standardization of test suites, practical development of executable test suites, and operation of test laboratory services.

13.2 CONFORMANCE

The development of OSI protocol standards was already well advanced before the important concepts of conformance and conformance testing were identified. Conformance clauses form an essential part of OSI standardization. They attempt to state concisely and unambiguously the functionality requirements, without which an implementation cannot be claimed to conform to the standard. Since the international effort to develop a conformance testing methodology and framework has been to some extent separate and out of phase with protocol standards development, a substantial retrofitting of conformance clauses will be needed. This is especially true for those OSI standards completed prior to 1986. Developers and suppliers of real physical systems must be able to state exactly to what their products are conforming. Conversely, buyers of real systems must have a precise way of stating their requirements. For OSI these two needs must be harmonized if the benefits of market aggregation and system interoperability are to be realized.

The approach taken by ISO to this complex conformance issue has been to decompose the problem into manageable pieces. Three types of conformance requirements have been identified:

- Mandatory requirements that must be met under all circumstances
- Conditional requirements that must be observed when the appropriate conditions are applicable
- Optional requirements that must be observed only if selected; the implementor is free to make the selection

Furthermore, conformance to a standard can be stated positively, i.e., stating what shall be done, or negatively, i.e., stating what shall not be done. While this may appear simple at first glance, the sheer complexity of OSI standards results in nested requirements within these classifications. For example, in the transport-protocol (ISO 8073) it is mandatory to implement either class 0 or class 2. In addition, if class 4 is implemented, then class 2 must also be implemented, and so on.

Conformance requirements have been further classified into static and dynamic requirements. *Static* conformance requirements are constraints placed on the OSI standards relating to such things as grouping of functional units and options into protocol classes, parameter ranges and timer values, and multilayer dependencies. *Dynamic* conformance requirements relate to detailed allowable behaviors of an implementation in instances of communication (hence the term *dynamic*). The exchange of (PDUs) during call establishment, for example, would be governed by dynamic conformance requirements.

The Protocol Implementation Conformance Statement (PICS) has become the vehicle for recording a statement of the capabilities and options that have been implemented for a given protocol. The PICS specifies the capabilities and options implemented and is used to determine what tests apply to a given implementation. It should contain the following information:

- Which static conformance requirements are met
- Details of multilayer dependencies, if any
- Any other information needed to support the testing process or help in assessing the test results

13.3 CONFORMANCE TESTING

The objective of conformance testing is to determine if a given implementation conforms to the specifications stated within the protocol standard. Conformance testing requires standardized test suites for each OSI protocol standard. Four types of conformance testing have been identified:

- *Basic interconnection tests*
- *Capability tests*, which test static conformance claims
- *Behavior tests*, which test dynamic conformance claims
- *Conformance resolution tests*, which are not standardized but may be used for in-depth probing

An important vehicle for recording additional information about an implementation under test (IUT) and its testing environment is the Protocol Implementation Extra Information for Testing (PIXIT). Thus, a client submitting an IUT to a testing laboratory would provide a PIXIT. The PIXIT may contain, for example, information needed by the test operator to run the appropriate test on the specific system, further precision on the PICS information, or administrative-type information. PIXIT and PICS information should not conflict. A comprehensive PIXIT proforma is developed by the testing laboratory based on the skeleton PIXIT proforma in the standard (ISO 9646, Part 5). The PIXIT proforma is in the form of a questionnaire that, when completed by the IUT supplier, becomes a PIXIT. The PICS proforma, on the other hand, is always provided as an integral annex or as a part of the protocol standard, and the proforma information is provided by the equipment (IUT) supplier.

13.4 ABSTRACT TEST SPECIFICATION

Figure 13.1 shows the conceptual testing architecture for OSI implementations. In this model, a tester can be either co-located with the system under test or remotely connected via telecommunication links. OSI protocols define the behavior of protocol entities in terms of PDUs, and the abstract service primitives (ASPs) above and below these entities. Therefore, the points of control and observation (PCOs) focus on the behavior of these elements. The possible PCOs enable the following distinctions to be made:

- Whether it is the ASPs or the PDUs that are observed and controlled
- The layer identity of the ASPs or PDUs concerned
- Whether they are controlled and observed within the system under test (SUT) or in a system remote from the SUT.

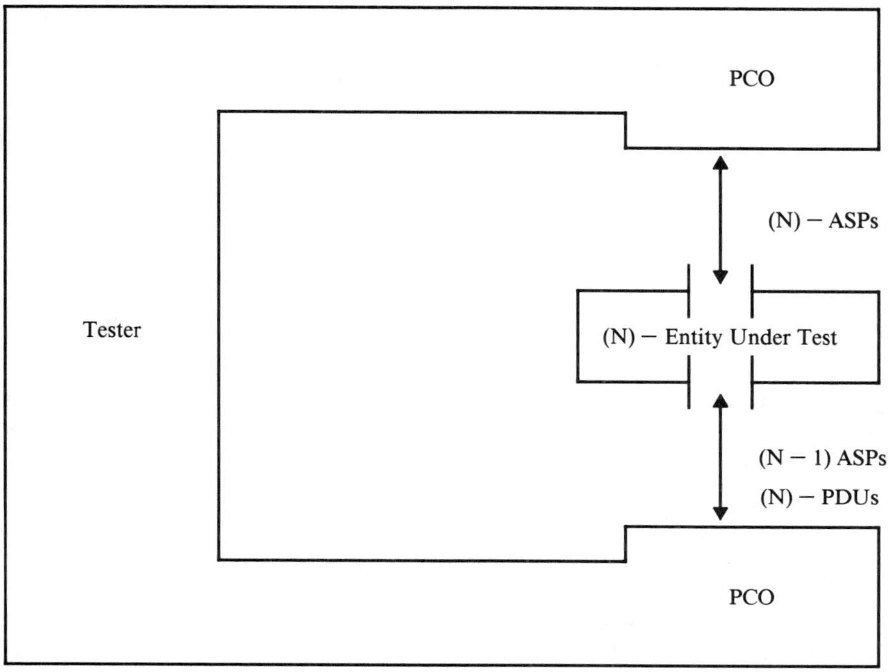

Figure 13.1: Conceptual testing architecture.

Conformance testing utilizes the concepts of *upper* and *lower testers*, since it is the combination of events at both upper and lower service boundaries in OSI that affects the protocol entity. Testers applied at these boundaries, properly coordinated, will provide the necessary mechanism to stimulate and observe the protocol entity behavior. Figure 13.2 illustrates the concept of upper and lower tester, showing also the use of test coordination procedures needed for ensuring cooperation between the testers.

Four categories of abstract test methods have been standardized: one local and three external. The choice of category of abstract test method depends on the stage of development of implementation.

The *local test methods* (Figure 13.2) are useful for systems under development, where the major testing functions are done in the same system as that in which the IUT is executing.

The three external test methods are specified for testing full or partial end-systems in which the major testing functions are done in a system that is different from the one in which the IUT is executing. The *distributed test method* (Figure 13.3) applies when it is necessary to allow complete freedom for the implementation of the test coordination procedures between the SUT and the lower tester but to specify in detail the control and observation requirements at both ends. The *coordinated test method* (Figure 13.4) applies where it is possible to implement a standardized test management protocol in

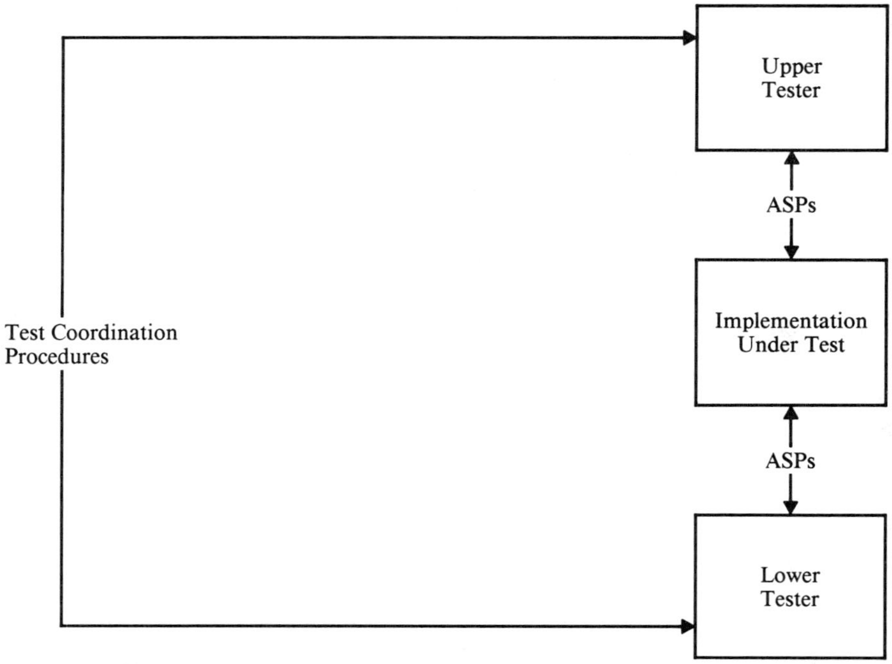

Figure 13.2: Local test methods.

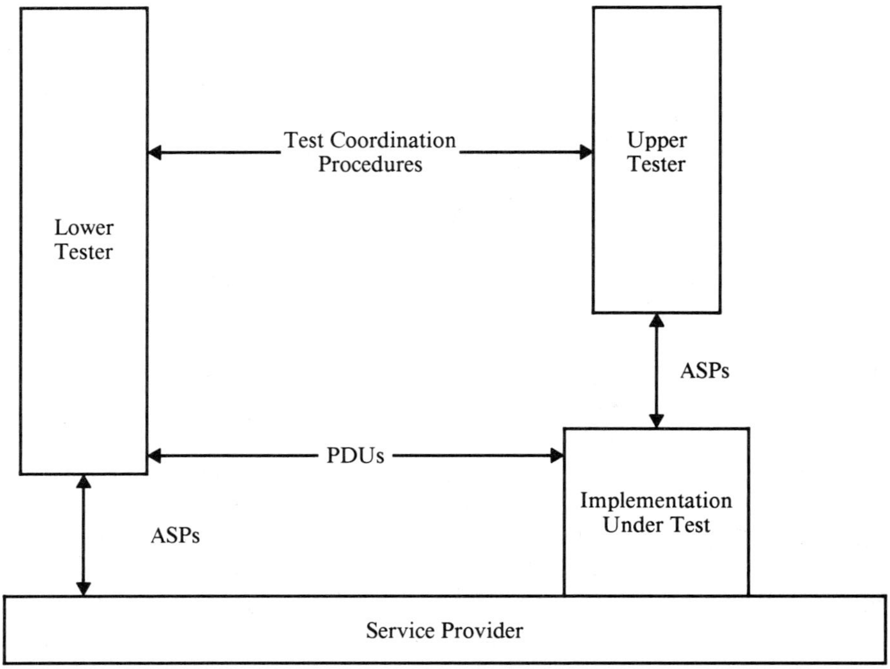

Figure 13.3: External distributed test methods.

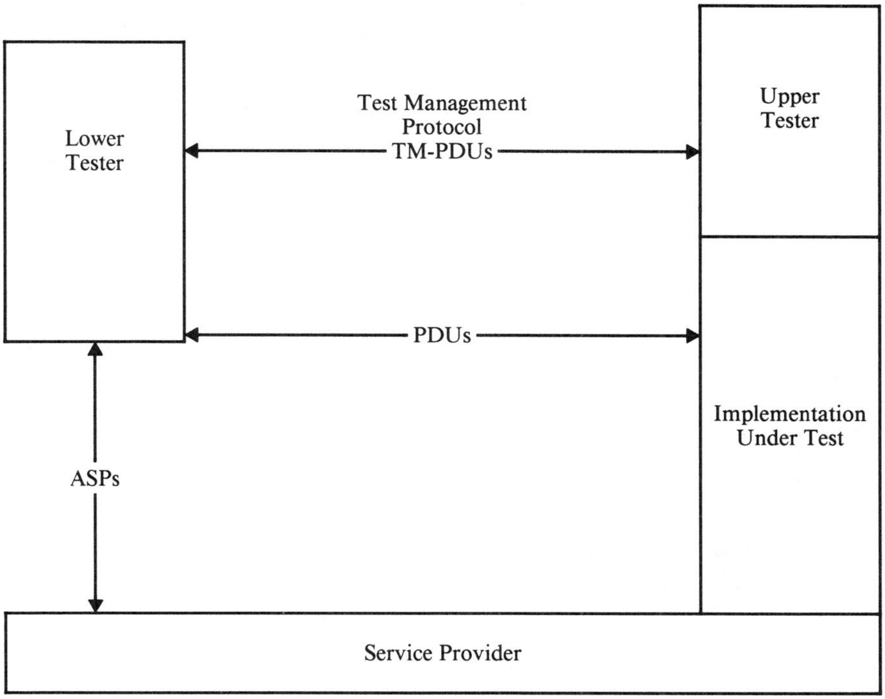

Figure 13.4: External coordinated test method.

an upper tester in the SUT, above the IUT, with control and observation only at the lower tester. The *remote test method* (Figure 13.5) applies when it is possible to use some SUT functions to control the IUT during testing, instead of using a standardized upper tester. Each test method has variants that can be applied to single or multilayer IUTs. Single-layer test methods are the most appropriate for testing the majority of protocol conformance requirements.

13.5 CLASSES OF IUTs

The classes of systems that need to be considered for conformance testing are seven-layer open systems, partial open systems, and relay open systems. For each of these systems, the four categories of test methods have variants that can be applied to single-layer and multilayer IUTs. In addition, for single-layer testing of a multilayer IUT in which the individual service boundaries within the IUT are not accessible, an embedded variant of the test methods has been defined. Examples of single-layer and multilayer testing using the local test methods are described in the following sections.

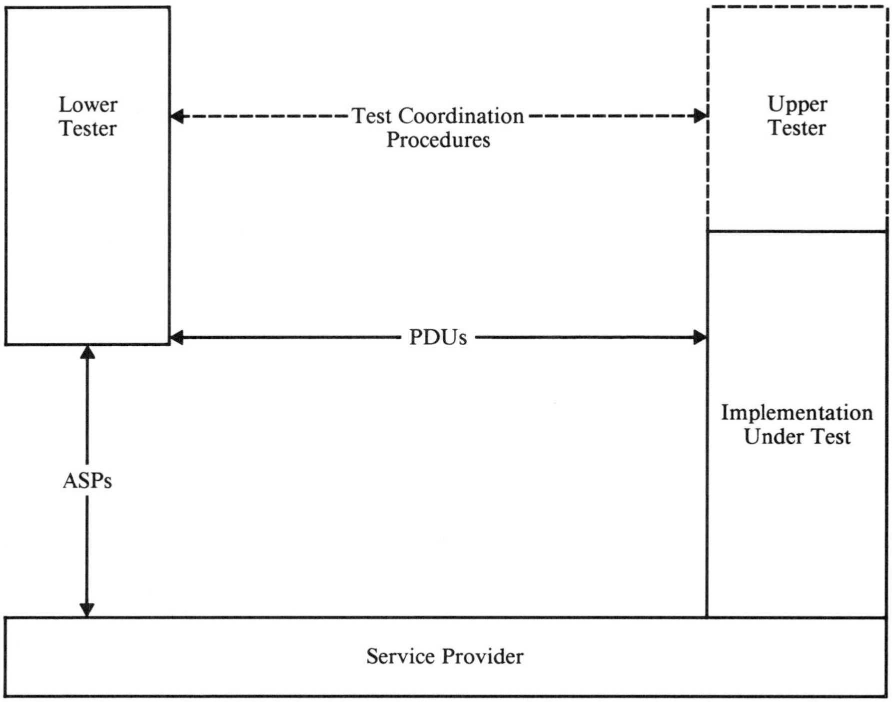

Figure 13.5: External remote test method.

13.6 SINGLE-LAYER TESTING

For single-layer testing using the local test method, the points of control and observation are defined as being at the service boundaries above and below the (N)—entity under test. The lower tester is considered to observe and control the (N−1)-ASPs and (N)-PDUs, while an upper tester observes and controls the (N)-ASPs. This is illustrated in Figure 13.6.

Procedures for single-layer testing using the other three categories of test methods can be similarly deduced.

13.7 MULTILAYER TESTING

For the case where testing is required for several layers at once, without accessing the interlayer interfaces, the multilayer methods are used. In the local multilayer test method the points of control and observation are at the service boundaries directly above and below the IUT. The test events are specified in terms of (N+n)-ASPs above the IUT and the (N−1)-ASPs and (N)- to (N+n)-PDUs below the IUT. Figure 13.7 illustrates this case.

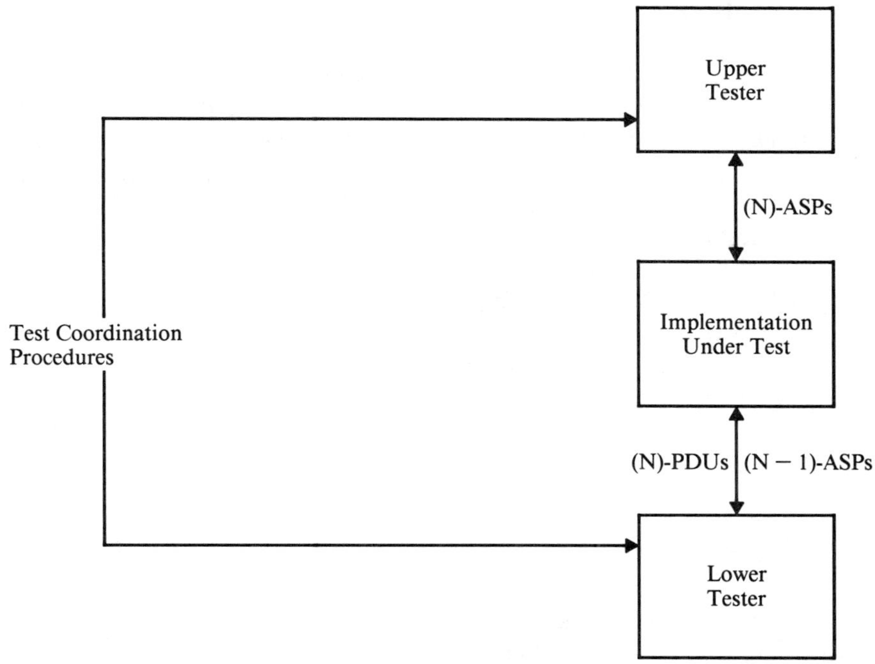

Figure 13.6: The local single-layer test method.

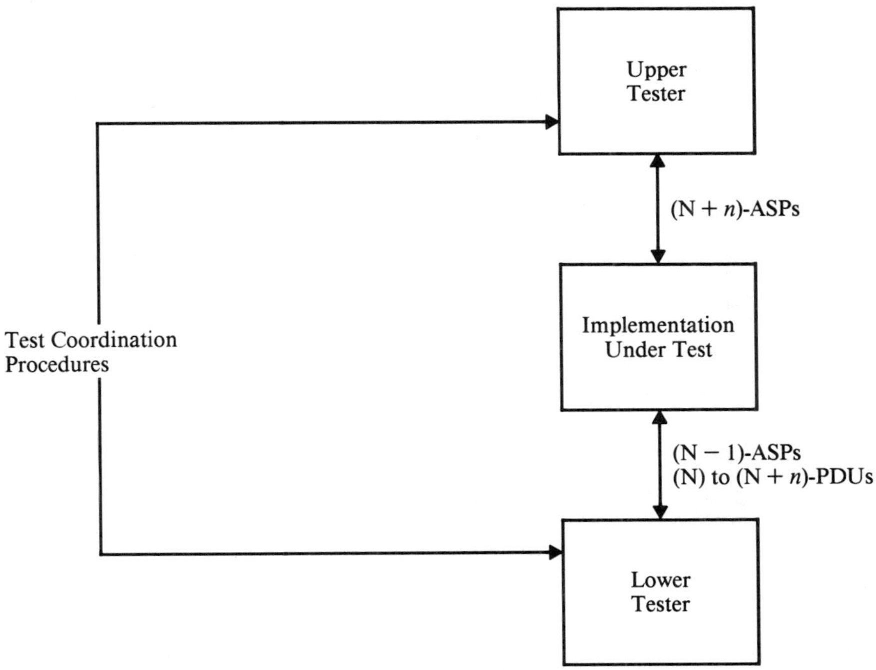

Figure 13.7: The local multilayer test method.

13.8 EMBEDDED TEST METHODS

The embedded single-layer test methods specify procedures for testing a single layer within a multilayer IUT. This is done by including the specification of the protocol activity in the layers above the layer being tested but without specifying control or observation at the service boundaries embedded within the multilayer IUT. This is illustrated in Figure 13.8 for the local single-layer embedded test method in which layer (N+*i*), embedded within the layers (N) to (N+*n*), is being tested.

Procedures for multilayer testing using the other three categories of testing methods follow the same principles.

13.9 TEST SUITES

Test suites are complete sets of test cases, possibly combined into nested test groups, that are necessary to perform conformance testing for an IUT or a protocol within an IUT. Test suites have a hierarchical structure in which test events (e.g., the transfer of a single PDU to or from the IUT) are basic building blocks (see Figure 13.9). Each test case has a narrowly defined purpose focusing on a single conformance requirement. A test case comprises at least one test step, which defines the series of events covered by the test purpose. Test steps may be nested to an arbitrary depth. A partial list of test cases which a test suite designer would specify is as follows:

- Capability tests (for static conformance)
- Behavior tests of valid behavior
- Behavior tests of syntactically invalid behavior
- Behavior test of inopportune behavior
- Tests focusing on PDUs sent to the IUT
- Tests focusing on PDUs received from the IUT
- Tests focusing on interactions between what is sent and received
- Tests related to each protocol mandatory feature
- Tests related to each optional feature implemented
- Tests related to each protocol phase
- Variations in the test event occurring in a particular state
- Timing and timer variations

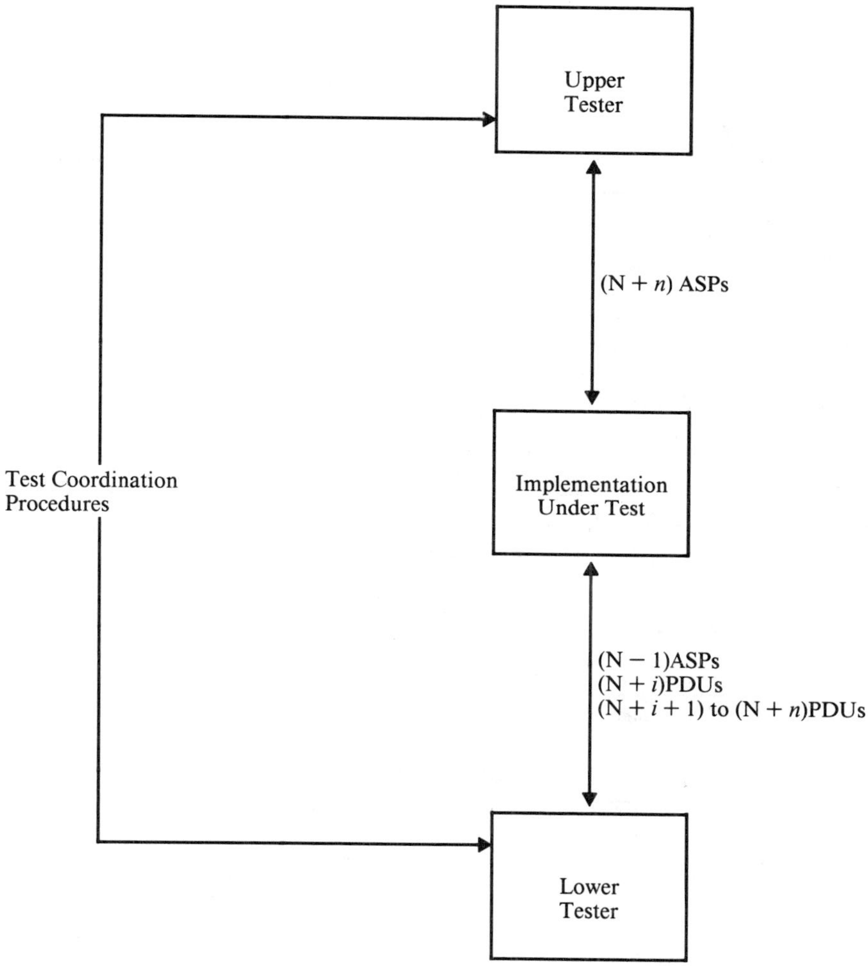

Figure 13.8: Local single-layer embedded test method.

- PDU encoding variations
- Variations in combinations of parameter values

13.10 SPECIFICATION OF ABSTRACT TEST CASES

A basic decision required before beginning to develop a test case specification is to select an appropriate notation. ISO has formulated a notation for the specification of test suites using the techniques of both trees and tables. This technique, designated the Tree and Tabular Combined Notation (TTCN), is not a formal technique but is easily understood and by design is well suited for test case specification. Proposals to study formal approaches in conformance testing and test specification using formal description techniques such as

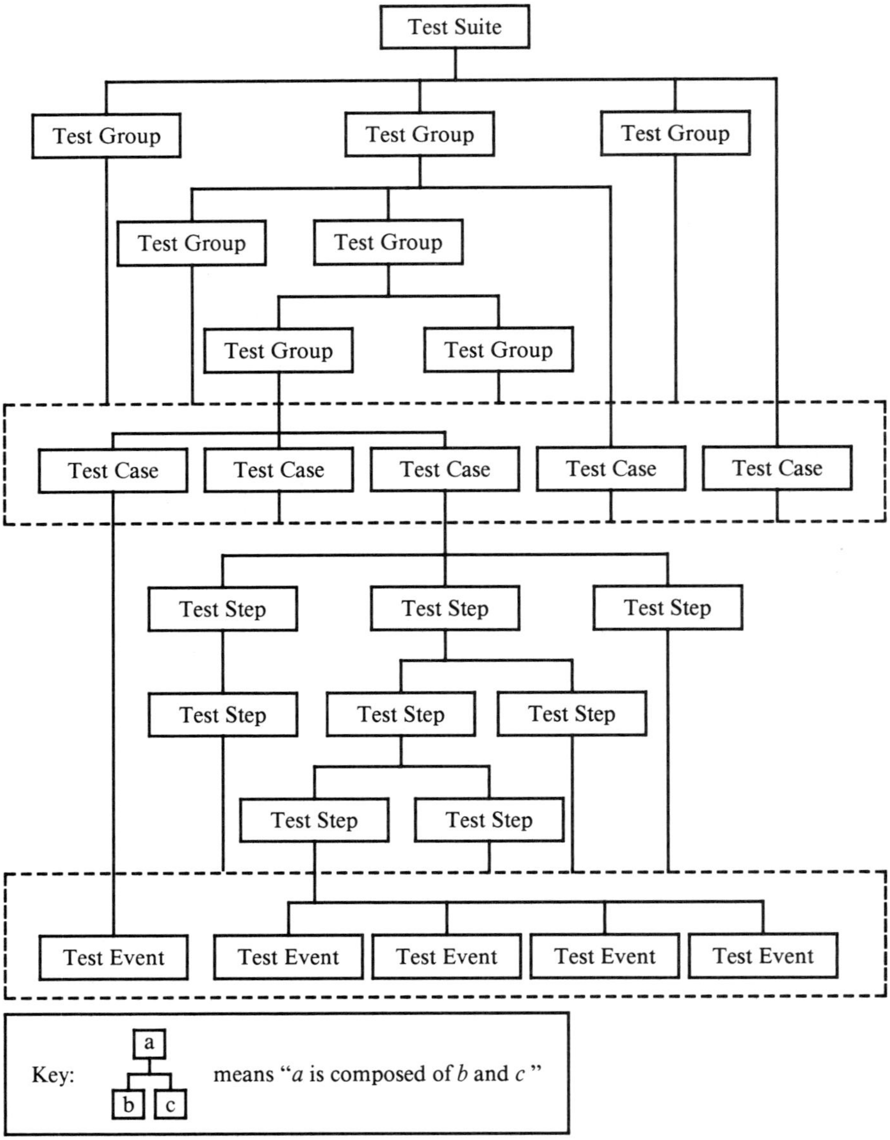

Figure 13.9: Test suite structure.

LOTOS (ISO 8807) or Estelle (ISO 9074) are now being considered by ISO. LOTOS and Estelle are characterized by being well defined and having formal semantics. TTCN, on the other hand, enjoys several important advantages. TTCN is a test-oriented notation that can express the hierarchical structure of the test suite and include the relevant aspects of the testing methodology. When expressed in TTCN, a test suite specification is complete, requiring no additional documentation. TTCN imposes a tree structure on test case specification by limiting loop constructs in behavior specification. TTCN permits all possible outcomes in response to an event to be specified by assigning explicit verdicts so that test results are easily recognized and the tests properly terminated.

Test suites written in TTCN include four major components: a suite overview, a declarations part, a dynamic part, and a constraints part.

The *suite overview* contains information needed for the general presentation and understanding of the test suite. It is written in a proforma of the type shown in Figure 13.10.

The *declarations part* contains the set of events to be used in the test suite and the appropriate set of ASPs and PDUs involved in the tests. The declarations are written in a proforma of the type shown in Figure 13.11 for ASPs.

The *dynamic part* contains a proforma of the type shown in Figure 13.12. Such a proforma contains the trees of dynamic protocol behavior. Behavior trees display paths of events across the page and alternative events at the same level of indentation. In the example in Figure 13.13, event 1 could be followed by event 2 or event 3. If it is followed by event 2, then event 4, or if

Suite Overview			
Suite Name: Reference to Standards: Reference to PICS: Reference to PIXIT: How Used: Test Method(s): Comments:			
Test Case Identifier	Test Case Reference	Page	Description
<test case identifier>	<test case reference>	<number>	<free text>
Test Step Identifier	Test Step Reference	Page	Description
<test step identifier>	<test step reference>	<number>	<free text>
Default Identifier	Default Reference	Page	Description
<default identifier>	<default reference>	<number>	<free text>

Figure 13.10: Suite overview proforma.

ASP Declaration		
ASP: <ASP>	PCO: <PCO> (list)	Comments: <free text>
Service Control Information		
Parameter Name	Type	Comments
<parameter name> and ID	<type and value>	<free text>

Figure 13.11: ASP declaration.

Dynamic Behavior				
Reference: <test cases or test step reference> Identifier: <identifier> Purpose: <free text> Defaults Reference: <defaults reference>				
Behavior Description	Label	Constraints Reference	Verdict	Comments
<Behavior description in tree form>	<label>	<constraints reference>	<verdict>	<free text>
Extended Comments: <free text>				

Figure 13.12: Dynamic behavior declaration proforma.

event 3, then event 5. Events in a real system could include a Connect Request, Data Indication, or Disconnect. The sequence of events and the individual paths in the behavior trees are specified in detail using an abbreviation notation and a small set of constructs that impose a tree structure on the specification.

The *constraints part* specifies, in tabular form, the value for each ASP parameter and PDU field. These field and parameter values are the constraints placed on ASPs and PDUs. Each constrained ASP or PDU is assigned a constraint name that must be given in the Constraints Reference column of the dynamic behavior proforma if that ASP or PDU appears in an event line.

In addition to the human-readable form of TTCN described here, a machine processable form, called TTCN.MP, has also been defined. TTCN.MP provides a formal syntax for TTCN expressed in BNF notation. The main purpose of TTCN.MP is to ease portability of abstract test suites and aid in the derivation of executable test suites.

13.9 TEST REALIZATION

Test realization is the process of producing a means of testing based on a specific standardized reference abstract test suite. A means of testing is a combination of equipment and procedures for carrying out test selection on the basis of PICS entries, test parameterization on the basis of PIXIT entries, test derivation from abstract specification to executable form, test execution, and test log generation. A test realization process is required to preserve the correspondence between the elements of the resulting executable test suite and the elements of the reference abstract test suite at all levels of the test suite hierarchy down to the individual test events. It is also required to preserve the mapping between the test cases and the entries in the PICS, and to ensure correct verdict assignments to all outcomes.

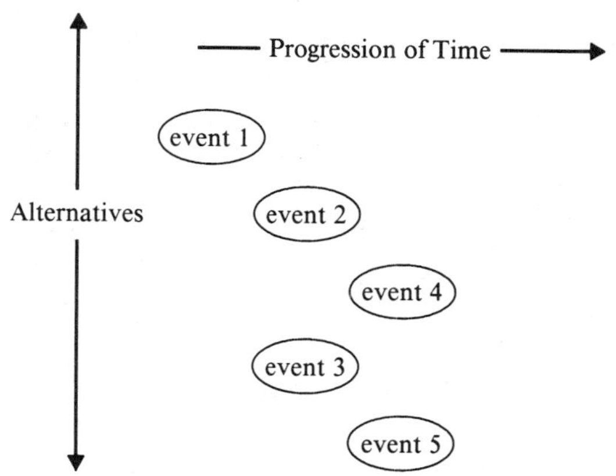

Figure 13.13: Event paths in dynamic protocol behavior.

Comparability of test results from different test laboratories is an essential part of practical conformance testing. Production of a means of testing is, therefore, required to include a means of generating an appropriate conformance test log. Such a log must include a capability of logging every test event with relative time stamping and associated verdict assignments. A complying means of testing would include a means of converting the logged data into human-readable form.

13.10 TEST PROCEDURES

Conformance testing involves a number of steps combining both static and dynamic test phases, resulting in a test report. An example of the various steps in actually testing a system, illustrated in Figure 13.14 are:

1. Static conformance review
2. Test selection and parameterization
3. Basic interconnection testing (optional)
4. Capability testing
5. Behavior testing
6. Analysis of test results
7. Final conformance review, synthesis, conclusions, and conformance test report production.

In an actual situation, provision is also needed for "negotiated exits." These are points where the concerned parties can decide that the results of the previous step are inadequate to justify continuing the test.

13.11 TEST RESULTS

Organizations offering conformance testing services may be expected to provide standardized test reports containing the test results. Two types of test reports are useful: a system conformance test report and a protocol conformance test report. The former would include identification of the list of standards against which testing has been carried out; it would clearly identify areas of conformance and, if applicable, of nonconformance. A protocol conformance test report would be provided for each protocol tested; it would identify the test cases executed and the verdicts assigned.

13.12 INTEROPERABILITY TESTING

It is important to recognize that successful conformance testing of an implementation does not imply a 100 percent guarantee that an implementation

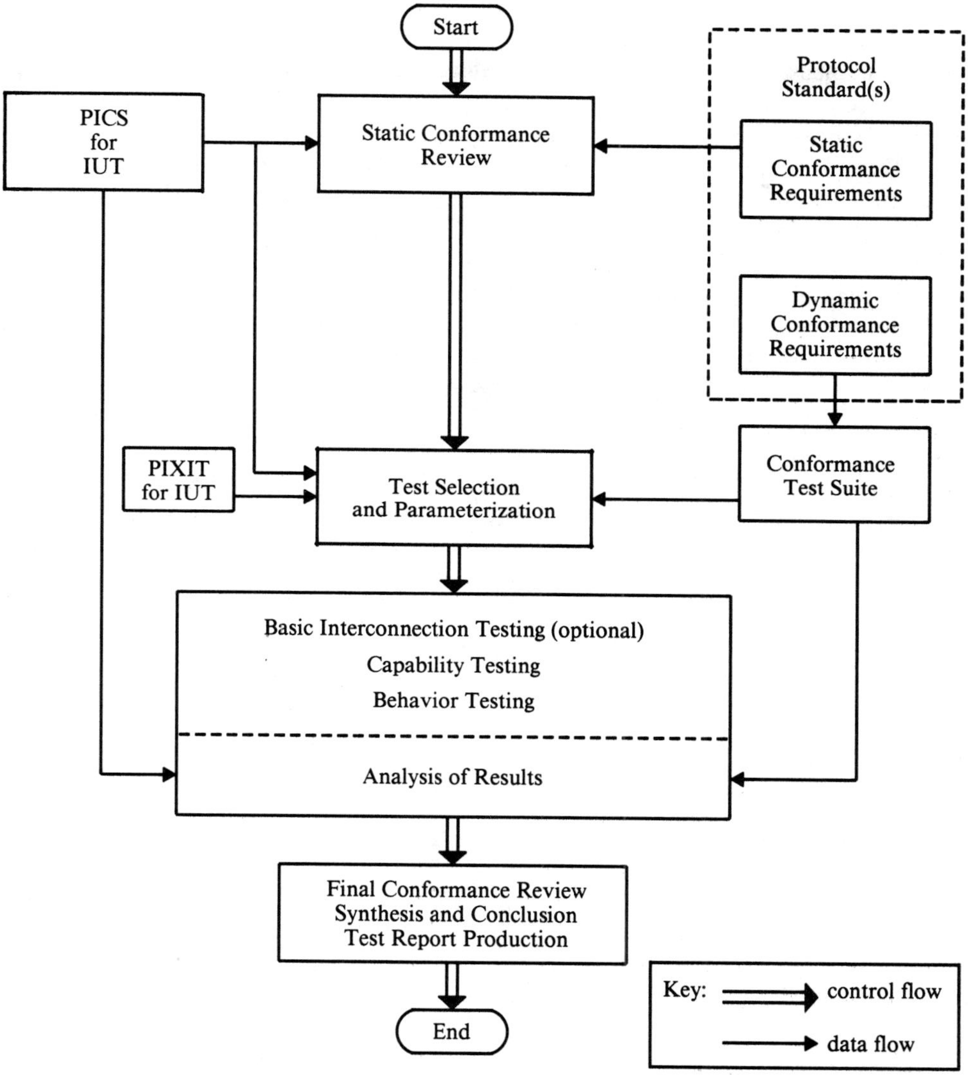

Figure 13.14: Conformance assessment process.

will interwork with a similarly tested implementation. Comprehensive interoperability testing would be required to provide complete confidence of real interworking capabilities. This stems from the sheer complexity of OSI protocol standards and the impracticality of exhaustive conformance testing.

Interoperability testing is concerned with verifying the correct operation of two implementations against each other. It tests areas not covered by conformance tests, such as incompatible selections of optional protocol parameters, or areas of testing not covered in standard conformance test suites.

Interoperability testing can be passive or active. In the passive case, the behavior of two interconnected systems can be observed as they perform normal tasks during a trial period. In the active case, a tester would be placed between two implementations for inspection and possible modification of PDUs in order to exercise the two implementations more rigorously.

Successful interoperability testing provides a high degree of confidence that actual system interoperability will be achieved in operational use. It is particularly feasible when a limited number of vendor products is involved. However, in situations where large numbers of different vendor products are involved, interoperability testing could prove to be a major task.

Standardization of interoperability testing procedures has not yet been addressed by the international standards bodies. It may prove necessary to develop such standards both to avoid reinventing procedures each time interoperability testing is performed and also to produce uniform results with widely understood meanings.

In general, both for conformance testing and interoperability testing, harmonization of test center operations, test suites, and strict version control procedures will be indispensable in working toward real open systems interworking in a multivendor environment.

PART IV

FUTURE DIRECTIONS FOR OPEN SYSTEMS

CHAPTER 14

OPEN DISTRIBUTED PROCESSING

This chapter provides an introduction to a new area of standardization called Open Distributed Processing (ODP). It also describes an object-oriented methodology that can be used for modeling the communications behavior of distributed systems. It should be recognized that this area of standardization is very new and results have not yet stabilized.

14.1 OPEN DISTRIBUTED PROCESSING

14.1.1 Definition

ODP comprises that class of information processing activities in which discrete components of the overall processing activities may be located in more than one system, at more than one geographical location, or where there is any other reason that necessitates formal communication among the components. ODP is considered to be a subset of the overall area of information processing. OSI is in turn considered to be a subset of ODP.

14.1.2 The Basic Reference Model for ODP

A new Working Group has been established within ISO/IEC JTC1/SC21 to develop a Basic Reference Model for ODP. This Reference Model is intended to provide a framework for the coordination of current and future standards activities relating to distributed processing.

14.1.2.1 Scope

The scope of ODP is not limited to communication standardization activity; it includes graphics and database standards and the development of functional specifications of interfaces to distributed processing services. Some participants hope that this work will lead to the definition of language bindings for standardized distributed processing services, similar to the work being done with the Graphical Kernel System (GKS). Possible target areas are distributed database processing and distributed graphics processing. This would lead to the eventual possibility of source code portability for distributed processing software.

The management of ODP is also within the scope of the work. This encompasses the infrastructure needed to control and monitor ODP activity.

14.1.2.2 Field of Application

ODP provides support for all commercial and industrial distributed application systems. The field of application specifically includes

- Office systems
- Data-processing systems
- Database systems
- Real-time systems
- Integrated data/text/voice/image systems
- Communication command and control information systems

Real-time distributed systems include both transaction processing systems and industrial process control systems.

14.1.3 Relationship Between ODP and OSI

The Reference Model for ODP is complementary to and makes use of the communication resources that are contained in the OSIE. This can be illustrated by considering a simple model of application processing.

Application processing can be viewed as the task or set of tasks carried out by a collection of ODP components that are interrelated and jointly managed. This set of components can be classified into three overall types of objects: data processing, data storage, and communications. Data processing is the task of modifying the state of data storage, and communications is the method by which data processing components may directly communicate with each other. This leads to the following relationship between the three types of objects:

```
Data Storage                                              Data Storage
     |                                                         |
Data Processing   <-->   Communications   <-->   Data Processing
```

The distinction between the ODP model and OSI is that the ODP model examines the interface between OSI and its users. The ODP model does not examine the OSI interface (the Application Layer) itself in as much detail as does OSI, but rather gives a user's view of how the Application Layer is constructed and how to use it. Similarly, the ODP model covers the types of users of OSI, classifies the types of applications that would use OSI, and specifies their communications requirements. The model then shows how various communications constructs (e.g., transaction processing, remote procedure calls) may be implemented and used over OSI. The ODP model addresses how connection-mode, connectionless-mode, and store-and-forward communications may be integrated into distributed open systems.

The OSI model provides the definition of the communications services available to the application-process. The ODP model deals with the coordination and cooperation among application-processes involving communication, possibly OSI, in order to perform a distributed application.

From the perspective of application design, an application developer would use the ODP model as a means for describing in a high-level abstract manner the relationships and interactions among the components involved in a specific application. From this description, the requirements for communications can be extracted and then mapped onto OSI services. Depending on the application, this mapping could be done onto existing services, onto new services, or onto a combination of both.

14.2 METHODOLOGY FOR MODELING DISTRIBUTED APPLICATIONS

At present the work on ODP is just beginning, so no consensus exists on the methodology for modeling distributed applications. This section describes one possible object-oriented approach that is derived partly from existing OSI techniques.

14.2.1 Overview

The modeling methodology described here is based on the object-oriented approach used in the work on Remote Operations (RO) and the Directory. This technique is not only applicable for the modeling of distributed applications; it has gained favor as a general-purpose technique for software engineering. The description of interactions between system components is supplemented by the concepts of state transition records and completion records. These concepts provide mechanisms for defining the control of the behavior of objects.

This methodology describes a distributed application in terms of "objects" that perform "operations." Interactions between objects are described in terms of operation invocations. A "binding" must be established between objects to enable operations to be invoked. It is important to realize that although the "operation" formalism is used as the basic modeling tool for describing interactions between objects, this does not necessarily imply the use of ROSE as the only means for conveying such operations between open systems.

"Operation classes" represent the four different types of operations. A "dialogue" is a group of related operations involving two objects; a "job" is a set of operations involving two or more objects; a "transaction" is a special type of job with particular characteristics. The conveying of information between objects pertaining to operations is achieved via an operation support environment, which can be viewed as providing "services" to individual objects.

14.2.2 The Object Model

14.2.2.1 Definition

An *object* consists of data and a set of operations to modify and interrogate the data. The data can only be accessed by the operations associated with the object and are generally referred to as the *state of the object.*

The set of operations performed by an object forms the *operational interface* to that object. Operations are specified at a level of abstraction that defines what happens, not how it happens. Thus, the operational interface is separate from the internal implementation and concrete data structure of the object.

There are no shared data among objects, but data can be passed between objects as parameters of operations.

The object-oriented form of application modeling provides location independence; i.e., the description of the interactions between two objects remains the same whether they are co-located in the same system or distributed over separate systems. This property makes the object model particularly suitable for modeling distributed applications.

The state data that form an object are described abstractly in terms of primitive and composite data types, using an appropriate notation. For example, high-level programming languages like Pascal and Ada allow for the definition of data in terms of data types. For database systems, data definition languages exist for defining the structure of data. For OSI applications, the notation that is commonly used is ASN.1.

14.2.2.2 The Nature of Operations

In the object model, the generic structure of an operation is an elementary request–reply interaction. The request element is referred to as the invocation of the operation. The reply element consists of two alternatives, referred to as the result and the error.

The invoke causes the specified operation to be executed, with parameters passed where necessary. It has the following structure using BNF notation:

Invoke : : = operation-type arguments

where

operation-type	distinguishes among the different operations of the object
arguments	the parameter values supplied by the invoker

The reply has the following structure:

Return Results : : = results

or

Return Error : : = error-type error-parameter

where

results	the parameter values returned by the invoked operation
error-type	identifies the type of exception
error-parameter	provides additional diagnostics

This clear separation of normal and exceptional outcomes is a natural way of simplifying application structure. It helps to ensure that error management is well specified and comprehensively implemented. The outcome of each operation is either the predefined normal outcome or one of the predefined exception outcomes.

An operation is *total* if it includes predefined outcomes for all possible cases, including error cases. This does not imply that the return error reply can never occur; it simply implies that all possibilities are accounted for; i.e. there is no error return of type "unknown." If every operation on an object is a total operation, then the object is *robust*.

14.2.2.3 Object Binding

For operation invocation to be possible, a relationship must be established between the object that wishes to invoke an operation and the object that will execute the operation. Such a relationship is called a *binding* and may be established directly or indirectly.

Direct binding occurs when the invoking object interacts directly with the target object to establish the binding. The target object may be viewed as supporting two mutually exclusive sets of operations: One set consists of only the "bind" operation, which, when completed, makes available the other set of operations and makes itself unavailable. This second set includes an "unbind" operation that makes this set unavailable but makes the "bind" operation available once again. Thus, there is in effect a switching of operation sets. The second set is only available once a direct binding is established. The first set is available when the second set is not; however, for the first set to be accessible, some form of relationship must exist. This relationship is achieved via an indirect binding.

In indirect binding, the relationship is established via a third party. In the software environment, such a binding is typically established by a linker that provides the mapping between separately compiled program units that refer to each other. In a distributed processing environment, a directory can provide the mapping. Conceptually, an object wishing to make itself available publishes its operational interface in a directory; e.g., it provides a name and addressing information. This is called exporting its interface. An object wishing to access another object searches the directory and imports the operational interface of the target object. This dual act of exporting and importing the operational interface constitutes an indirect binding. As indirect bindings represent a less tightly coupled relationship between the objects, they may not be appropriate in all situations.

With both types of binding, it is possible to control access to the target object. With direct binding, this control is provided by the target object itself. With indirect binding, control is provided by imposing constraints on directory access; additional access control may also be imposed by the target object on each operation.

14.2.2.4 Object Types

A set of objects with a common, characteristic, externally visible behavior is referred to as an *object type*. The operations of an object type are called *type operations*. An object type is referred to by its type name. All instances of an object type have the same type operations. An instance is referenced specifically by an instance name, and generically by its type name. The Directory Service standard supports both type names and instance names.

14.2.2.5 Concurrency

The object model naturally permits concurrency between objects. Interaction between objects occurs only by invoking operations, and execution only affects data belonging to the object in which the execution occurs. Therefore, executions in separate objects will not interfere with each other and can occur concurrently.

When two operation requests are made to the same object, one request may be queued pending completion of the other (sequential execution), or both operations may execute concurrently (concurrent execution), depending on the implementation. If concurrent execution of operations is supported, internal concurrency control may be required to protect the consistency of the data within the object.

14.2.2.6 Operation Classes

Operations can be distinguished according to the expected form of the return: Result or Error, Error (if any) but not Result, and neither Result nor Error. There are two possible operation modes from the viewpoint of the invoking object. In the *synchronous* mode, the object invoking an operation may continue to issue further invocations without waiting for any reply. Four operation classes can be defined according to the operation mode and expected return:

1. Synchronous mode with Result or Error
2. Asynchronous mode with Result or Error
3. Asynchronous mode with Error (if any)
4. Asynchronous mode without return

14.2.3 Levels of Description

Modeling a distributed application is normally achieved by a process of successive refinement. At the initial stages, the emphasis is on the identification of the principal objects that are meaningful to the application and on their interrelationships, based for example on a functional decomposition of the application. At this stage, it is not necessary to precisely identify all the individual operations that make up the interactions among the objects; it is sufficient to identify operation groups (e.g., dialogues, jobs, and transactions, as described in Section 14.2.4), where these convey the sense of the interaction between the objects.

At the next stage, these objects may in turn be refined into a more detailed set of objects and individual operations to reflect a finer level of granularity of application detail. This iterative process can proceed to any level of nesting needed to accurately reflect the natural structure of the application. Once all objects and operations are identified, the final step in this process is to define the internal details of the identified objects. This last step may not be necessary if the internal behavior of an object can be deduced from its operational interface. Figure 14.1 illustrates this process for a simple directory application. In Figure 14.1A, representing the first step in the modeling process, two objects are identified: the directory user and the directory provider. Operations are identified for searching and updating the directory. In Figure 14.1B, representing the second level of decomposition, the directory provider is decomposed into a number of directory agents, reflecting the distributed nature of the directory database. Additional operations are identified to support the interactions among the directory agents.

Figure 14.1 also illustrates the concepts of *operation chaining* and *operation decomposition.* Operation chaining occurs when an operation on one object triggers the invocation of an operation on another object. This chained operation may in turn cause another operation to be invoked. Operation decomposition occurs when an operation on one object triggers multiple operations on other objects. The result is a hierarchical *processing tree,* with the object performing the initial operation at the root of the tree; each subordinate operation must be completed before its superior operation can finish, and coordination among subordinate operations may be required (see Section 14.2.4). Figure 14.1B illustrates a processing tree.

14.2.4 Operation Groups

Three types of operation groups are distinguished: dialogue, job, and transaction.

A.

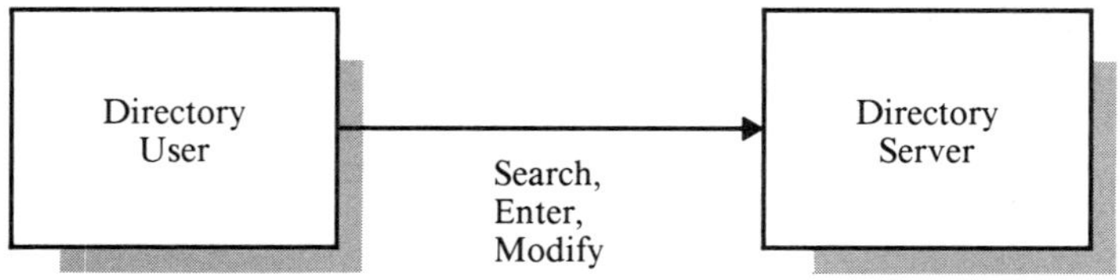

B.

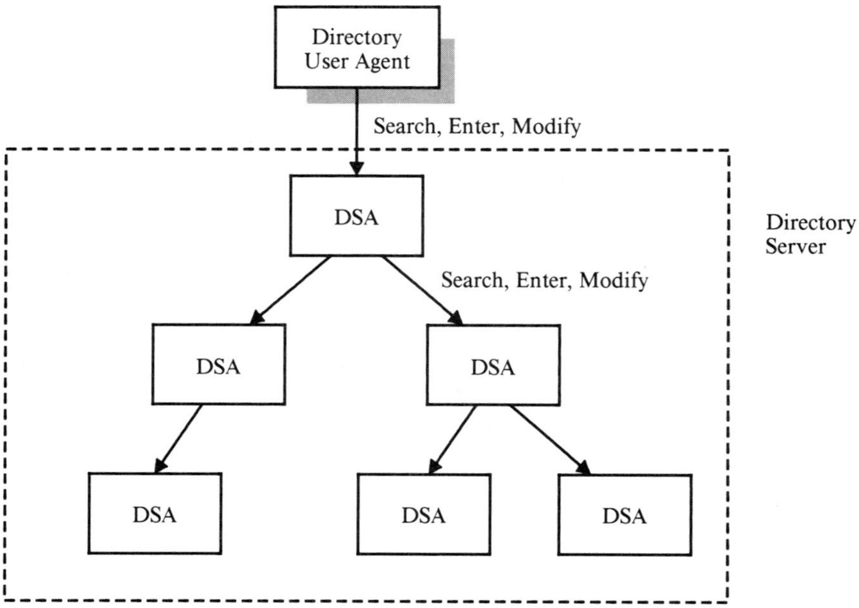

Figure 14.1: A. Simple model of directory application. B. Processing tree for directory application.

A *dialogue* is a conversational form of interaction consisting of a sequence of related operations involving two objects. In the general case, either object participating in a dialogue can invoke operations, but the situation where a set of related operations is invoked by the same object also qualifies as a dialogue. An example of a dialogue is the transfer of a file, where operations for selecting and opening the file, reading/writing file contents, and deselecting and closing the file are involved.

There are three types of dialogue: simple, synchronized and transaction oriented. In simple dialogue, the objects need only to exchange information between themselves, without synchronization or commitment, e.g., a database enquiry. In synchronized dialogue, explicit synchronization occurs between objects in the course of processing. Examples of synchronization are half-duplex operation with explicit handing over of the right to send data or the insertion into a data stream of synchronization marks that are to be acknowledged. A transaction-oriented dialogue has commitment semantics, as explained below in the discussion of transactions. It is a special type of synchronized dialogue.

A *job* is a set of operations involving two or more objects. The relationships among the objects participating in a job are represented by a processing tree, as described earlier. There is only one root object for a job. A job may be viewed as a collection of related dialogues. In the simplest case, a job consists of a single dialogue.

A *transaction* is a special form of job with particular semantics. It is an atomic unit of work that comprises a sequence of operations that guarantees the mutual consistency of the resources concerned in the work, called the bound data; the unit succeeds or fails as a whole. A typical transaction has the ACID properties of Atomicity, Consistency, Integrity, and Durability, as described in Chapter 10 in the section on transaction processing. All the dialogues within a transaction are of the transaction-oriented type. Together, they form a transaction tree, which may be a subtree of a larger job tree.

The transaction processing style of interaction is distinguished from other forms of jobs such as batch processing or time-sharing by its emphasis on atomicity, timely response (i.e., CPU processing time in milliseconds and response time in seconds) and high availability, (i.e., accessibility to a large population of users and low downtime). Not all transactions have all of these properties; for example, atomicity does not apply to a transaction involving nonrecoverable data, such as an audit trail. This fact makes a rigorous definition of a transaction difficult. The decision as to whether a particular job qualifies as a transaction when some of the above properties do not apply is a subjective one.

Figure 14.2 illustrates the relationship among these three types of groups. In this figure, a transaction is shown as consisting of three dialogues, and the transaction as a whole is nested within a larger job.

In general, a job may consist of many dialogues, transactions, and nested jobs. A transaction can have transactions nested within it as well. There is no limit to the level of nesting.

14.2.5 Relationships Among Objects

The following types of relationships among objects may be identified:*

Peer-to-peer: Each object can autonomously invoke operations on the other object.

Client–server: One object manages a resource to which the other object wants access. A shared file server is an example of a provider that interacts with various objects who wish to retrieve files.

Source–sink: There is movement of data from the source object to the sink object. The distinction between this relationship and the client–server one is that the client–server relationship does not necessarily imply

*These distinctions have no formal meaning, but can be helpful for understanding.

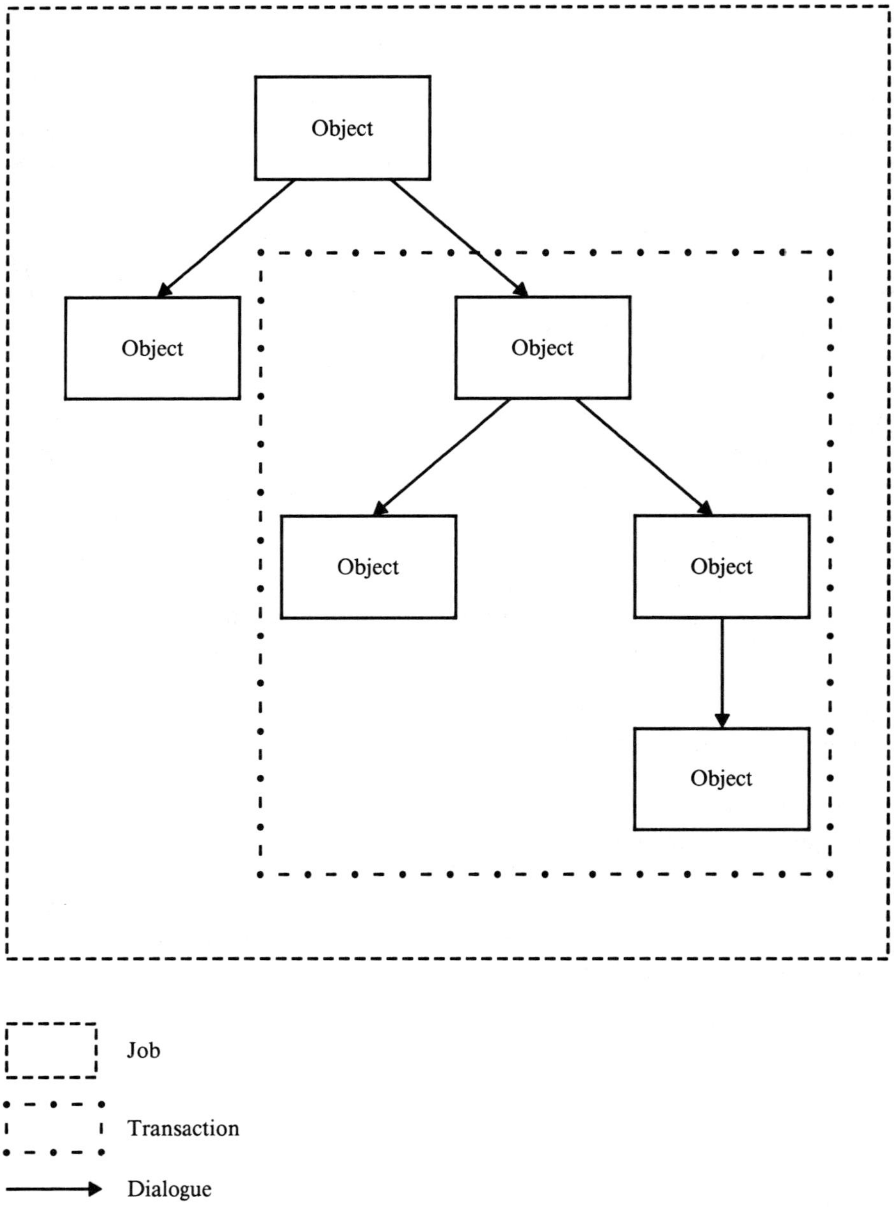

Figure 14.2: Relationship between dialogue, transaction, and job.

movement of data. For example, a request to delete a file is a legitimate client–server interaction but not a legitimate source–sink one. A request to transfer a file to the requestor qualifies as both.

Initiation–execution: One object is capable of executing a set of operations that another object wishes to have performed. An example of this type of relationship is a remote job entry application.

These various types of relationship are not mutually exclusive. Indeed, all of them may be possible within a single application.

14.2.6 Control of Operations

14.2.6.1 State Transitions

Within an object, the control of operations can be described in terms of state transitions, where events trigger transitions from one "major state" to another and corresponding actions are performed in the course of such transitions. The triggering events can be operations invoked by external objects, the completion of operations invoked on other objects, or internal events, such as timer expiry. Actions are typically modifications to data within the object or the invocation of operations on other objects.

The general structure of a state transition is as follows:

```
FROM        current major state
TO          next major state
WHEN        event
PROVIDED    enabling condition
BEGIN
  action
    .
    .
    .
  action
END
```

A tabular or graphical notation is used typically to represent state transitions.

The "enabling condition" in the above is a constraint on a transition that specifies the conditions under which the transition is allowable. This enabling condition typically reflects some constraint on the event that has occurred, e.g., whether the parameters of an operation are valid, or expresses a necessary link between this transition and past events within the object as reflected in the value of particular data elements. For example, an enabling condition for a certain transition could be the requirement that the last executed operation be of a particular type.

The state of an object at any time depends not only on its major state, but on all the data contained within the object.

14.2.6.2 State Record

This data structure includes all the information that is relevant to the processing performed by the object. It includes the value of the object "major state" and reflects where on the processing tree the object currently sits. It includes the identification of the subjobs, transactions, or dialogues that have been completed and those that are still active. It may also include references to any other data structures that are particular to the current job and may influence the future behavior of the object.

14.2.6.3 Completion Records

In most cases, the actions performed by a state machine are static and can be described using composed statements in some programming language, e.g., Pascal. However, in some applications, a more elaborate mechanism for describing actions may be helpful, e.g., when the nature of the state transitions is consistent among the objects of a class but the details of the actions vary from one object to the next. For example, two objects performing the same job in different parts of the country could have the same set of state transitions governing their behavior, but they might interact with different external objects (of the same type but geographically distinct). It may be useful in such cases to set parameters for the behavior of objects. The term *completion record* refers to a data structure that contains information that "customizes" the behavior of an object of a particular class. This information might specify the enabling conditions for certain state transitions (e.g., a job is to enter the "completed" state when the specified actions have been completed), it might be in the form of a language specification for the actions an object is to perform, or it might consist of data values that control predefined action rules. An example of the last type is a set of data values that specify the initial values for certain fields of a data entry screen.

An advantage of the use of the concept of completion records is that it allows for remote manipulation of the behavior of objects via OSI management protocols.

Note that when a completion record consists of definitions of actions that an object is to perform, it takes on characteristics comparable to the work specification of the OSI job transfer and manipulation application. Such work specifications are interchanged between systems participating in a job and therefore are considered as forming part of the application data.

It may be useful to consider a state machine specification as a behavior specification for an object class. The completion record together with the state machine specification defines the behavior of a specific object, i.e., an instance of the object class.

14.2.6.4 Operation Group Record

Where a job includes subjobs, transactions, or dialogues, a separate data structure may be defined to describe the details of each such operation group. This data structure would be linked by reference to the state record. Each operation within an operation group may in turn be described by a separate data structure linked to its appropriate operation group structure. Figure 14.3 illustrates the various control structures and their interrelationships. As both the state record and the operation group record contain historical information, they would typically be used for generating performance, statistical, and other management data.

Note: Of the data structures described above, the state transitions and the state record are most significant; the completion record and the operation

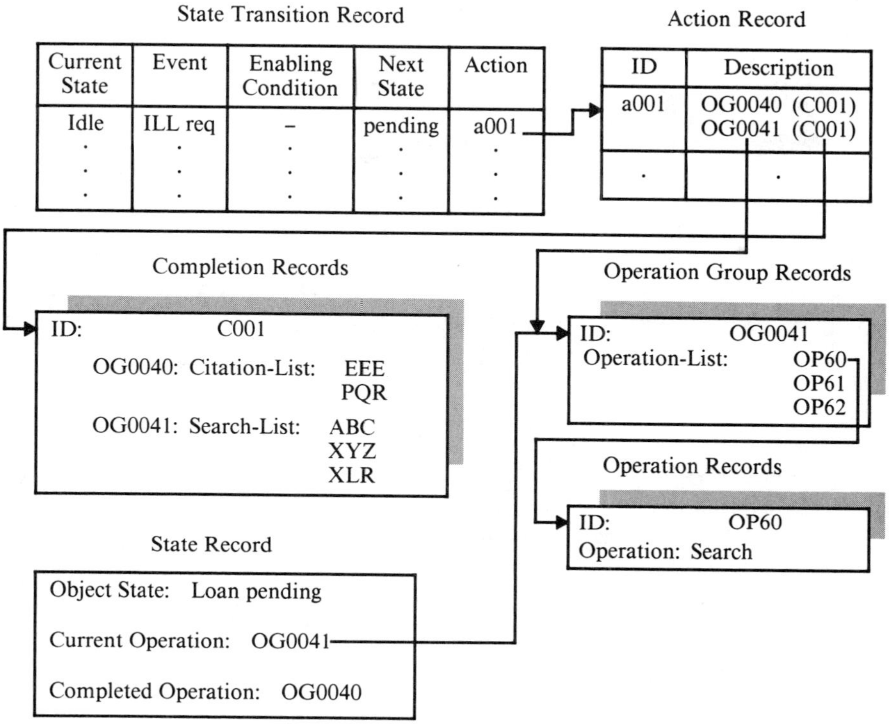

Figure 14.3: Example of control structures associated with an object.

group record are data structures that reflect implementation-dependent approaches and could readily be supplanted by other mechanisms.

14.2.7 Operation Support Environment

When operations are invoked by one object on another, a mechanism is needed to support the transfer of operation parameters and results between the objects. This support is provided by the operation support environment.

The operation support environment provides a set of services to interacting objects to permit operations to take place in a location-independent manner. This is shown abstractly in Figure 14.4A, where object *A* wishes to invoke an operation *X* on object *B*. The permissible operations are defined by the operational interface; the actual transfer of information is achieved by object *A*'s making an operation execution request to the operational support environment. This environment is responsible for ensuring that the information is passed to object *B*, execution of the operation is initiated, and the results are passed back to object *A*.

The operation support environment includes the necessary provisions for security, reliability and performance, etc.

When this environment is mapped onto a single computer system, as shown in Figure 14.4B, the operation support environment can be viewed as

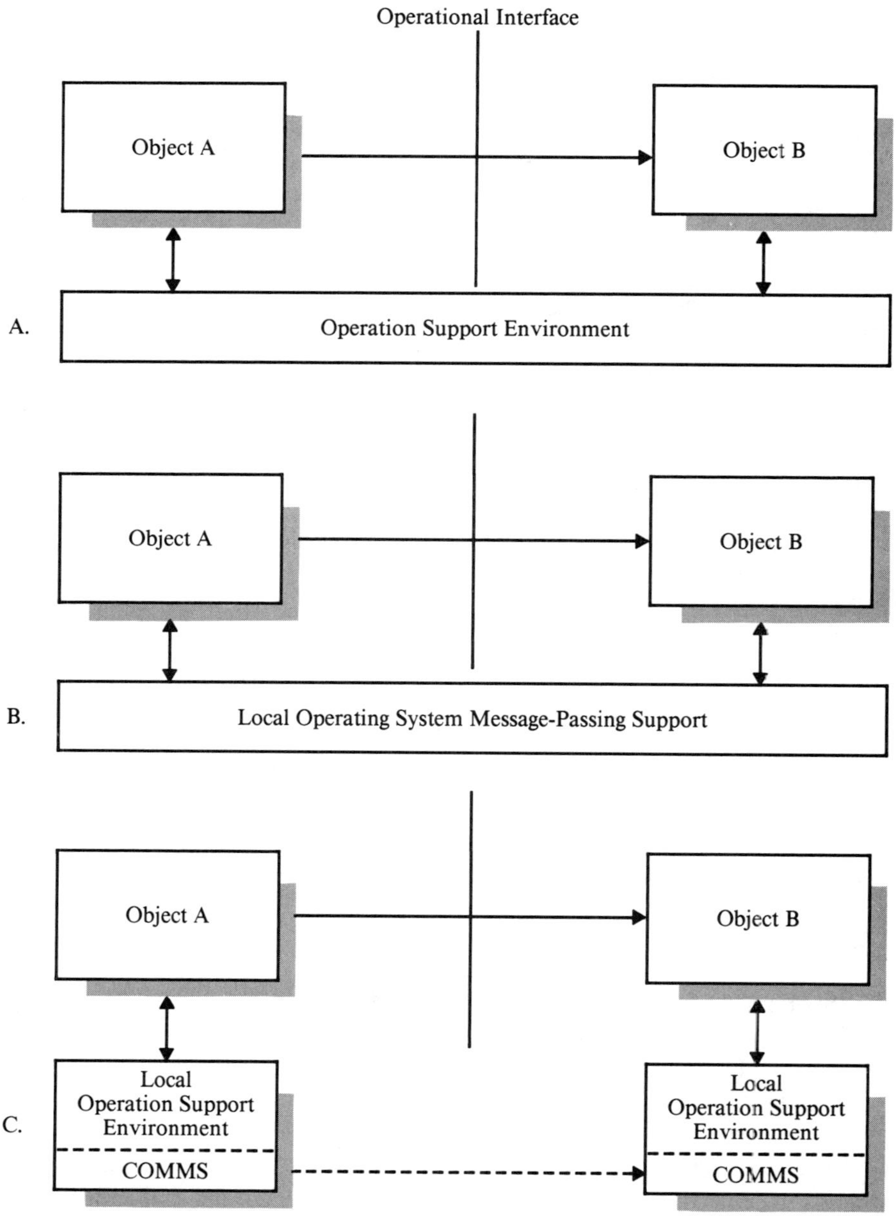

Figure 14.4: A. General model of operation support environment. B. Mapping of operation support environment to local environment. C. Mapping of operation support environment to distributed environment.

the underlying operating system that provides message passing services in support of interprocess communication. When two interacting objects are located on physically different systems, the operation support environment consists of the operating systems of the respective systems, plus the communications subsystem linking the two systems. When an operation is invoked, the local operation support on the invoking system accesses the communication subsystem to effect the transfer of information between systems. This is done transparently to the objects concerned. (See Figure 14.4C, which has universal applicability; it applies equally to connection-mode, connectionless-mode, and store-and-forward communication.)

Depending on the implementation, the operation support environment could be configured so that bind–unbind operations are explicitly visible to objects or are made transparent; i.e., the operation support environment performs these operations on behalf of objects in a manner invisible to them.

From an OSI perspective, there are a number of possible mappings between the OSI protocol stack and the operation support environment. The latter includes:

- OSI layers 1 to 4, with layers 5 to 7 located within individual objects.
- OSI layers 1 to 6, plus the basic application-independent service elements, e.g., Association Control and Message Transfer, of layer 7. The remaining, application-specific part of layer 7 would be located within individual objects.
- All OSI layers.

CHAPTER 15

MOVING TOWARD AN OPEN SYSTEMS WORLD

No introduction to OSI would be complete without at least a cursory examination of what it takes to make OSI successful. OSI has already become a well-known example of how standards can be produced quickly (relatively speaking) and efficiently using a consensus process. The experiences gained from OSI standardization are now being applied more widely; areas of standardization like system software interfaces, office document processing, database systems, and distributed processing are progressing more rapidly as a result. Completion of the basic set of OSI standards can, and should be, considered as a major milestone in the quest for an open systems world. Unfortunately, the mere existence of the standards is not the complete answer; their widespread use in products and the adoption by users of the products are the real measures of success.

What, therefore, is required for OSI to achieve its aims? Four factors are deemed to be critical to a successful evolution to an open systems world:

- The *business need* for OSI must be recognized (everyone should need it).
- Cooperation and commitment to the goal of *openness* is necessary (the vision must be clear).
- Overall system *economics* must be favorable (there should be at least some quantifiable financial incentive).
- *Confidence* that OSI works should be backed up by testing.
- Ongoing operational support must be guaranteed.

In this chapter we stand back for a moment and look at today's realities and tomorrow's vision. No one knows exactly how a standard will turn out until the last vote has been cast, and no one can really mandate the use of standards of this type.

15.1 THE CHALLENGES OF STANDARDIZATION

No one would ever claim that it is easy to make a standard take hold. Thus, it is quite difficult to anticipate the contents of standards for product development purposes, and it certainly takes more effort to achieve product differentiation.

There are challenges at every stage of the standardization process. One that appears to be common to all stages is education. Developers must learn what standards are required and how user requirements are changing. Standardization organizations must learn how to optimize the process itself and must become much better at promoting their products. Product implementors must learn to work within the new constraints imposed by a standards environment (including the need for formal conformance testing). Finally, users must learn to participate actively in standardization and must learn to make better use of the results.

It has been said that the concept of open systems marks a shift to a new paradigm, a new way of thinking. There are bound to be many pitfalls, and just as many opportunities.

15.2 THE COMPLEXITIES OF MOVING TO OSI

Each individual OSI standard, as we have seen, is complex. These complexities, unfortunately, are compounded when the standards are implemented and assembled into real systems; we saw (in Chapter 11) that functional profiles, registration authorities, and implementor agreements must be used to reduce the number of options and harmonize independent implementations.

Having had a glimpse into the "standards industry," the reader may find it surprising that interconnection among systems is ever actually achieved. Of more concern, however, is the potential confusion for a user who simply wants to get a development task completed on time, within the budget, and with a minimum of stress. It is critical that the techniques of OSI become well known and well understood.

It is assumed, correctly, we believe, that an "open world" cannot be mandated and will never appear in sudden "big bang" conversion. Imagine what would happen if every telephone had to be turned off in order to change the network technology! Too much time and effort has been invested in applications that use today's proprietary communications solutions to modify them all at once, even if the eventual benefits are very clear. The need to coexist with existing communications will be a fact of life for a long time to come.

Clearly, OSI is not the only viable approach to communications. In fact, proprietary communications architectures, such as IBM's SNA and Digital Equipment Corporation's DNA, became very well established during the 1970s and today dominate the data processing world. They are rich in functionality and are designed to take best advantage of the vendor's specific hardware and software platform. OSI, on the other hand, was developed as a vendor-independent solution that can be implemented in any system. Early implementations may suffer from a lack of developer experience, may not be supported by mature testing services, may run into defects, and will most likely not be optimized.

Despite these risks and complexities, OSI-based communications products are already beginning to take their rightful place in the system designer's toolkit. During its tenth anniversary in 1988, OSI demonstrated its potential at the Enterprise Networking Event in Baltimore and was well on its way to becoming a success. Most major communications suppliers have decided to support OSI and have chosen either to integrate OSI into their architecture or to provide gateways that interface to it.

Major users have claimed, for a number of years, that connectivity and manageability are key result areas for networking in the late 1980s and 1990s. Many of these users are now looking for OSI-based products. Some large user groups have defined their needs through OSI functional profiles (Manufacturing Automation protocols for factory automation and Technical and Office protocols for office systems, for example). Other potential users are still deciding whether the "business case" for OSI is sufficient to warrant the conversion effort. Policies encouraging the use of OSI for government systems have been formulated; Government OSI Profiles (GOSIP) in the United States and the United Kingdom and Canadian Open Systems Application Criteria (COSAC) in Canada are examples.

Any new technology goes through a life cycle that includes introduction, growth, maturity, and decline phases. The OSI standards themselves are now in the growth phase, with the problems of maintenance becoming important and many extensions in the planning stages. OSI products are barely into the introduction phase, but they would be classified by most buyers as being at the leading edge in communications technology. Business applications that exploit OSI facilities are still considered to be on the "cutting edge." The standards committees need feedback from users in order to provide improvements leading to a mature suite of OSI services and protocols.

Change always involves both risks and rewards. The implementation of OSI, especially when the products are new, is certainly no exception. One risk is that the products are not complete and that further change (which is costly) will be needed. The other risk is that various implementations will be incompatible. The potential rewards are improved communications with lower costs, improved performance, and rich new function.

15.3 OSI IN REAL LIFE: TODAY'S PRODUCTS

The tenth anniversary of OSI standardization in 1988 can be considered the first year of serious OSI implementation. Standards became available for all seven of the OSI layers, functional profiles had been completed, and the first wave of products from major manufacturers and carriers became commercially available.

The "entry cost" to an open world is relatively high. OSI products are new to most users, technical experts are scarce, and new systems need to be developed to exploit the new capabilities. Although initial training and education can be expensive, the investment will prove profitable if training for each new installation can be reduced or avoided. Technical expertise will become available when university and industrial courses begin to teach OSI more thoroughly. Changing to new systems and providing transition strategies has a definite cost, but taking "the big step" to OSI should reduce future conversion costs and eliminate the need for multiple gateways. The potential is enormous; the benefits, however, do not come free. A commitment to OSI is necessary.

Although critics ask when OSI will be "complete," the reality is that standardization will never be complete as long as new requirements appear and technology changes. There is no best time to jump onto the OSI bandwagon, since both the standards and the products will always be subject to extension and improvement. The key is to determine when the products will satisfy requirements and, when they do not, to push for change. OSI has already been shown to be useful and valuable for a number of applications, but it must be remembered that OSI is not an end in itself. OSI is not trendy; it is a trend because it satisfies requirements.

OSI has become a powerful "megatrend" in information-processing systems and is influencing manufacturers more, perhaps, than any external influence has ever done. The widespread adoption and implementation of OSI promises to make universal connectivity—the "infophone"—a reality.

15.4 THE NEXT GENERATION: OPEN SYSTEMS

The scope of OSI is limited to the interconnection and interworking aspects of systems. OSI makes no attempt to define or standardize the internal operations of a system. The success of OSI has, however, demonstrated the value of information technology standards in general and has increased industry focus on areas of standardization such as programming languages, graphics, databases, operating system and user interfaces, application portability, and expert systems. Openness can, and likely will, be extended to include the use of standards for many other aspects of systems, the result being "open information systems."

The Reference Model for Open Distributed Processing (ODP), described in Chapter 14, promises to be the first step in a new wave of standardization for information systems. At its simplest, ODP will extend the OSI concept of "openness" to distributed processing. One of the important goals of ODP is to provide a framework for various existing standards initiatives.

Given the increased scope of information technology standards, it is becoming vital that users, manufacturers, and carriers cooperate in defining standards. This is especially true of the users who are the ultimate beneficiaries. So far the process for determining specific requirements and for prioritizing the development efforts has been too informal and is often influenced by too few people.

15.5 ADVICE TO THE "HITCHHIKER"

OSI is neither easy to introduce nor to understand. For many people the details will be unnecessary: It is the effects that are important. For a few, especially systems developers and telecommunications providers, the details are critical. As a megatrend, however, OSI is important to everyone because it promises to change the way we live and work.

A final question to be answered might be, "OK, I'm convinced, but how do I get started with OSI?" Three basic strategies for standards implementation that can be considered are the half-closed-eyes strategy, the manufacturer-oriented strategy, and the gradual conformance strategy.

The *half-closed-eyes strategy* is essentially a case of avoiding the subject altogether. The idea is to ignore OSI and hope the problem either goes away or gets solved by someone else. This avoids up-front research and planning overheads. This strategy might be appropriate if information and systems were not important; even so, it would eliminate many opportunities. This strategy is not appropriate for most businesses, especially those that are information intensive.

The *manufacturer-oriented strategy* involves simply putting your faith in a single manufacturer and waiting for that one to supply the answers. This was the approach often used in the 1960s and 1970s for the introduction of computer automation. During this era most computing was done in isolated data centers, and distributed processing was a rarity. Today, it is normal for users to assemble their systems from the best available components, and usually no single manufacturer can supply all the necessary parts. This strategy involves the risk of trusting one manufacturer—putting all your eggs in a single basket.

A *gradual migration strategy* is becoming increasingly attractive for many users. A gradual migration towards OSI-based networks of systems permits existing technology investments to be preserved and ensures that the risks associated with introducing any new technology are minimized. It also implies that a user can "get started" without a massive commitment of time and resources. For industries like banking, it is important both to gain experience with new technologies as early as possible and to avoid unnecessary risk. This strategy will prove most suitable for the vast majority of OSI users.

APPENDIXES

APPENDIX I

ACRONYMS

OSI RELATED

AA	Application-association
AC	Association Control
ACSE	Association Control Service Element
AE	Application-entity
AFI	Authority and Format Identifier
AK	Acknowledgment
ALU	Application Layer User
AP	Application-process; or Agent Process
APDU	Application-protocol-data-unit
ASDC	Abstract Service Description Conventions
ASE	Application-service-element
ASN.1	Abstract Syntax Notation One
ASP	Abstract Service Primitive
BNF	Backus–Nauer Form
CASE	Common Application-service-element
CC	Connect Confirm
CCITT	International Telegraph and Telephone Consultative Committee
CCR	Commitment, Concurrency, and Recovery
CCS	Calculus of Communicating Systems
CEI	Connection-endpoint-identifier
CI	Connect Indication
CIGOS	Canadian Interest Group on Open Systems
CMISE	Common Management Information Service Element
CNLS	Connectionless Network Service

CO	Connection-mode
CONS	Connection-mode Network Service
COS	Corporation for Open Systems
CR	Connect Request
DAD	Draft Addendum
DAP	Directory Access Protocol
DCS	Defined Context Set
DIS	Draft International Standard
DLC	Data Link Connection
DLSAP	Date-link-service-access-point
DLSDU	Data-link-service-data-unit
DML	Data Manipulation Language
DSP	Directory System Protocol; or Domain Specific Part
DFR	Document Filing and Retrieval
DSA	Directory Service Agent
DTAM	Document Transfer, Access, and Management
DUA	Directory User Agent
ECMA	European Computer Manufacturers Association
Estelle	Extended State Transition Language
FDT	Formal Description Technique
FP	Functional Profile
FTAM	File Transfer, Access, and Management
GKS	Graphical Kernel System
GR/PR	Graphical Representation/Phrase Representation
G-LOTOS	Graphical-LOTOS
IDI	Initial Domain Identifier
IDP	Initial Domain Part
IEC	International Electro Technical Commission
IONL	Internal Organization of the Network Layer
IOS	Intermediate Open System
IPM	Interpersonsal Messaging
IPS	Information Processing Systems
ISDN	Integrated Digital Services Network
ISO	International Organization for Standardization
ISP	International Standardized Profile
IUT	Implementation Under Test
JTC	Joint Technical Committee
JTM	Job Transfer and Manipulation
LAN	Local Area Network
LAP	Link Access Procedure
LM	Layer Manager
LOTOS	Language of Temporal Ordering Specification
LSE	Local System Environment
LT	Lower Tester
MACF	Multiple Association Control Function
MIB	Management Information Base
MIS	Management Information Services
MHS	Message Handling Systems

MOTIS	Message Oriented Text Interchange System
MP	Machine Processable; or Managing Process
MPDT	Multipeer Data Transmission
MR	Message Retrieval
MS	Message Store
MT	Message Transfer
NCM	Network Connection Management
NCMS	Network Connection Management Subprotocol
NIST	National Institute of Standards and Technology
NPAI	Network-protocol-address-information
NPDU	Network-protocol-data-unit
NSDU	Network-Service-Data-Unit
ODA	Office Document Architecture
ODIF	Office Document Interchange Format
ODP	Open Distributed Processing
OPDU	Operation-protocol-data-unit
O/R	Originator/Recipient
OSI	Open Systems Interconnection
OSIE	Open Systems Interconnection Environment
PCEI	Presentation-connection-endpoint-identifier
PCI	Protocol-control-information
PCO	Point of Control and Observation
PDAD	Proposed Draft Addendum
PDTR	Proposed Draft Technical Report
PDU	Protocol-data-unit
PICS	Protocol Implementation Conformance Statement
PIXIT	Protocol Implementation Extra Information for Testing
PM	Protocol Machine
POSI	Promoting Conference for OSI
PR	Printing
PSAP	Presentation-service-access-point
PSTN	Public Switched Telephone Network
QOS	Quality of service
RDA	Remote Database Access
RIB	Routing Information Base
RO	Remote Operations
SACF	Single Association Control Function
SAO	Single Association Object
SAP	Service-access-point
SASE	Specific Application Service Element
SC	Subcommittee
SDL	Specification and Description Language
SDU	Service-data-unit
SGML	Standard Generalized Markup Language
SMAE	System Management application entity
SMAP	System Management application process
SNAc	Subnetwork Access
SNIC	Subnetwork Independent Convergence

SNPC	Subnetwork Dependent Convergence
SU	Service User
SUT	System Under Test
TC	Technical Committee
TM	Terminal Management; or Test Management
TP	Transaction Processing
TPDU	Transport-protocol-data-unit
TSDU	Transport-service-data-unit
TTCN	Tree and Tabular Combined Notation
UN	Use of Network
UT	Upper Tester
VT	Virtual Terminal
WG	Working Group

BANKING RELATED

ATM	Automated Teller Machine
IA	Interactive Authorization
POS	Point-of-sale

APPENDIX II

RELEVANT INTERNATIONAL STANDARDS

UPPER LAYER ARCHITECTURE

ISO DIS 9545 Information Processing Systems—Open Systems Interconnection—Application Layer Structure
ISO 9545 PDAD1 Connectionless Operation

OSI REFERENCE MODEL

ISO 7498-1 Information Processing Systems—Open Systems Interconnection—Basic Reference Model
ISO 7498-2 Information Processing Systems—Open Systems Interconnection—Security Architecture
ISO 7498-3 Information Processing Systems—Open Systems Interconnection—Naming and Addressing
ISO 7498-4 Information Processing Systems—Open Systems Interconnection—OSI Management Framework
ISO 7498 AD1 Information Processing Systems—Open Systems Interconnection—Addendum to Reference Model for Connectionless Operation
ISO 7498 PDAD2 Information Processing Systems—Open Systems Interconnection—Addendum to Reference Model on Multipeer Data Transmission

SERVICE CONVENTIONS

ISO TR 8509 Information Processing Systems—Open Systems Interconnection—Service Conventions

ABSTRACT SERVICE DEFINITION CONVENTIONS

ISO 10021-3 Information Processing—Text Communication—Message-Oriented Text Interchange System—Part 3: Abstract Service Definition Conventions

APPLICATION LAYER STANDARDS

ISO 8649 Information Processing Systems—Open Systems Interconnection—Service Definition of the Association Control Service Element
ISO 8649 PDAD1 Authentication Service
ISO 8649 AD2 A-UNIT-DATA Service
ISO 8650 Information Processing Systems—Open Systems Interconnection—Protocol Specification for the Association Control Service Element
ISO 8650 PDAD1 Authentication Protocol.
ISO 10035 Information Processing Systems—Open Systems Interconnection—A-UNIT-DATA Protocol
ISO 9804 Information Processing Systems—Open Systems Interconnection—Commitment, Concurrency, and Recovery Service Definition
ISO 9805 Information Processing Systems—Open Systems Interconnection—Commitment, Concurrency, and Recovery Protocol Specification
ISO 8571 Information Processing Systems—Open Systems Interconnection—File Transfer, Access, and Management—Parts 1 to 5
ISO 8571 AD1 Overlapped Access
ISO 8571 AD2 Filestore Management
ISO 8831 Information Processing Systems—Open Systems Interconnection—Job Transfer and Manipulation Concepts and Services
ISO 8832 Information Processing Systems—Open Systems Interconnection—Specification of the Basic Class Protocol for Job Transfer and Manipulation
ISO 9040 Information Processing Systems—Open Systems Interconnection—Virtual Terminal Basic Class Service
ISO 9040 AD2 Additional Functional Units
ISO 9041 Information Processing Systems—Open Systems Interconnection—Virtual Terminal Basic Class Protocol
ISO 9041 AD2 Additional Functional Units
ISO 9041 AD3 PICS Proforma
ISO DIS 10026 Information Processing Systems—Open Systems Interconnection—Distributed Transaction Processing—Parts 1 to 3
ISO DP 9579 Information Processing Systems—Open Systems Interconnection—Remote Database Access

ISO 9072 Information Processing Systems—Text Communication—Remote Operations—Parts 1 and 2
ISO 9066 Information Processing Systems—Text Communication—Reliable Transfer Service—Parts 1 and 2
ISO 10021 Information Processing—Text Communication—Message-Oriented Text Interchange System—Parts 1 to 7

PRESENTATION LAYER STANDARDS

ISO 8822 Information Processing Systems—Open Systems Interconnection—Connection-Oriented Presentation Service Definition
ISO 8822 DAD2 Symmetric Synchronization
ISO 8823 Information Processing Systems—Open Systems Interconnection—Connection-Oriented Presentation Protocol Specification
ISO 8823 PDAD1 PICS Proforma
ISO 8823 DAD2 Symmetric Synchronization
ISO 8824 Information Processing Systems—Open Systems Interconnection—Abstract Syntax Notation 1 Specification
ISO 8824 AD1 Specification Addendum
ISO 8825 Information Processing Systems—Open Systems Interconnection—Basic Encoding Rules for Abstract Syntax Notation 1 (ASN.1)
ISO 8825 AD1 ASN.1 Encoding Rules Addendum

SESSION LAYER STANDARDS

ISO 8326 Information Processing Systems—Open Systems Interconnection—The Basic Connection-Oriented Session Service Definition
ISO 8326 DAD1 Symmetric Synchronization
ISO 8326 DAD2 Unlimited User Data
ISO 8327 Information Processing Systems—Open Systems Interconnection—The Basic Connection-Oriented Session Protocol Specification
ISO 8327 DAD1 Symmetric Synchronization
ISO 8327 DAD2 Unlimited User-Data

TRANSPORT LAYER STANDARDS

ISO 8072 Information Processing Systems—Open Systems Interconnection—Transport Service Definition
ISO 8072 AD1 Information Processing Systems—Open Systems Interconnection—Transport Service Definition—Addendum 1: Connectionless-mode Transmission

ISO 8073 Information Processing Systems—Open Systems Interconnection—Connection-mode Transport Protocol Specification

ISO 8073 DAD1 Information Processing Systems—Open Systems Interconnection—Connection-Oriented Transport Protocol Specification—Addendum 1: Network Connection Management Subprotocol

ISO 8073 DAD2 Information Processing Systems—Open Systems Interconnection—Connection-Oriented Transport Protocol Specification—Addendum 2: Operation of Class 4 over Connectionless Network Service

ISO 8602 Information Processing Systems—Open Systems Interconnection—Protocol for Providing the Connectionless-mode Transport Service

DP 10025 Information Processing Systems—Open Systems Interconnection—Transport Layer Conformance Testing

NETWORK LAYER STANDARDS

ISO 8208 X.25 Packet Level Protocol for Data Terminal Equipment

ISO 8208 AD1 X.25 Packet Level Protocol for Data Terminal Equipment—Addendum 1: Alternative Logical Channel Number Allocation

ISO 8208 AD2 X.25 Packet Level Protocol for Data Terminal Equipment—Addendum 2: Extensions for Private and Circuit Switched Use

ISO 8208 AD3 X.25 Packet Level Protocol for Data Terminal Equipment—Addendum 3: Packet Level Static Conformance Requirements

ISO 8348 Information Processing Systems—Data Communications—Network Service Definition

ISO 8348 AD1 Information Processing Systems—Data Communications—Network Service Definition—Addendum 1: Connectionless-mode Transmission

ISO 8348 AD2 Information Processing Systems—Data Communications—Network Service Definition—Addendum 2: Network Layer Addressing

ISO 8348 AD3 Information Processing Systems—Data Communications—Network Service Definition—Addendum 3: Additional Features of the Network Service

ISO 8473 Information Processing Systems—Data Communications—Protocol for Providing the Connectionless-mode Network Service (Revision 2)

ISO DIS 8473 PDAD2 Information Processing Systems—Data Communications—Protocol for Providing the Connectionless-mode Network Service—Addendum 2: Formal Description of ISO 8473

ISO DIS 8473 DAD3 Information Processing Systems—Data Communications—Addendum 3: Provision of the Underlying Service Assumed by ISO 8473 over Point-to-Point Subnetworks
ISO DIS 8648 Information Processing Systems—Open Systems Interconnection—Internal Organization of the Network Layer
ISO 8878 Information Processing Systems—Data Communications—Use of X.25 to Provide the OSI Connection-mode Network Service
ISO 8878 PDAD1 Information Processing Systems—Data Communications—Addendum 1: Protection and Priority
ISO 8878 PDAD2 Information Processing Systems—Data Communications—Addendum 2: Support of Additional Features of the Network Service
ISO DIS 8880-1 Information Processing Systems—Data Communications—Specification of Protocols to Provide and Support the OSI Network Service—Part 1: General Principles
ISO DIS 8880-2 Information Processing Systems—Data Communications—Specification of Protocols to Provide and Support the OSI Network Service—Part 2: Provision and Support of the Connection-mode Network Service
ISO DIS 8880-3 Information Processing Systems—Data Communications—Specification of Protocols to Provide and Support the OSI Network Service—Part 3: Provision and Support of the Connectionless-mode Network Service
ISO TR 10029 Information Processing Systems—Data Communications—Operation of an X.25 Interworking Unit
ISO DIS 8881 Information Processing Systems—Data Communications—Use of the X.25 Packet Level Protocol in Local Area Networks
ISO DIS 8882-1 Information Processing Systems—Data Communications—X.25-DTE Conformance Testing—Part 1: General Principles
ISO DIS 8882-3.3 Information Processing Systems—Data Communications—X.25-DTE Conformance Testing—Part 3: Packet Layer
DP 9068 Information Processing Systems—Data Communications—Provision of the Connectionless Network Service Using ISO 8208
ISO DIS 9542 Information Processing Systems—Data Communications—End System to Intermediate System Routing Exchange Protocol for Use in Conjunction with ISO 8473
ISO DP 10030 Information Processing Systems—Data Communications—End System to Intermediate System Routing Exchange Protocol for Use in Conjunction with ISO 8208
ISO DP 9574 Information Processing Systems—Data Communications—Provision of the OSI Connection-mode Network Service by Packet Mode Terminal Equipment Connected to an ISDN
ISO DTR 9575 Information Processing Systems—Data Communications—OSI Routing Framework

ISO DP 10028 Information Processing Systems—Data Communications —Network Layer Intermediate System Functions

ISO DTR 9577 Information Processing Systems—Data Communications —OSI Protocol Identification in the Network Layer

DATA-LINK LAYER STANDARDS

ISO 3309 Information Processing Systems—Data Communications—High-Level Data Link Control Procedures—Frame Structure

ISO 3309 PDAD1 Information Processing Systems—Data Communications—Addendum 1: Start/Stop Transmission Operation

ISO 4335 Information Processing Systems—Data Communications—High-Level Data Link Control Procedures—Elements of Procedure

ISO 4335 AD1 Information Processing Systems—Data Communications—Addendum 1: Consolidation of Previous Addenda

ISO 4335 AD2 Information Processing Systems—Data Communications—Addendum 2: Enhancement of the XID Function Utility

ISO 4335 AD2 Information Processing Systems—Data Communications—Addendum 3: Start/Stop Transmission Operation

ISO 7478 Information Processing Systems—Data Communications—Multilink Procedures

ISO 7776 Information Processing Systems—Data Communications—High-level Data Link Control Procedures—X.25 LAPB-Compatible DTE Data Link Layer Procedures

ISO 7809 Information Processing Systems—Data Communications—High-level Data Link Control Procedures—Classes of Procedures

ISO 7809 AD1 Information Processing Systems—Data Communications—High-Level Data Link Control Procedures—Classes of Procedures—Addendum 1: UI Consolidation of Previous Draft Addenda

ISO 7809 AD2 Information Processing Systems—Data Communications—High-Level Data Link Control Procedures—Classes of Procedures—Addendum 2: Description of Optional Functions

ISO 7809 AD3 Information Processing Systems—Data Communications—High-Level Data Link Control Procedures—Classes of Procedures—Addendum 3: Start/Stop Transmission Operation

ISO 8471 Information Processing Systems—Data Communications—HDLC Balanced Classes of Procedures—Data Link Layer Address Resolution/Negotiation in Switched Environments

ISO 8802-2.2 Information Processing Systems—Local Area Networks—Part 2: Logical Link Control

ISO DIS 8802-2.2 DAD1 Information Processing Systems—Local Area Networks—Part 2: Logical Link Control—Addendum 1: Flow Control Techniques for Multisegment Networks

ISO DIS 8802-2.2 DAD2 Information Processing Systems—Local Area Networks—Part 2: Logical Link Control—Addendum 2: Acknowledged Connectionless-mode Service, Type 3 Operation

ISO 8802-3 Information Processing Systems—Local Area Networks—Part 3: Carrier Sense Multiple Access with Collision Detection

ISO DIS 8802-3 DAD1 Information Processing Systems—Local Area Networks—Part 3: CSMA/CD—Addendum 1: Medium Attachment Unit and Baseband Medium Specifications for Type 10BASE2 Networks

ISO DIS 8802-3 DAD2 Information Processing Systems—Local Area Networks—Part 3: CSMA/CD—Addendum 2: Repeater Set and Repeater Unit Specification for Use with 10BASE5 and 10BASE3 Networks

ISO DIS 8802-3 DAD3 Information Processing Systems—Local Area Networks—Part 3: CSMA/CD—Addendum 3: Broadband Medium Attachment Unit and Broadband Medium Specifications, Type 10BROAD36

ISO DIS 8802-3 DAD4 Information Processing Systems—Local Area Networks—Part 3: CSMA/CD—Addendum 4: Starlan IBASE5

ISO 8802-4 Information Processing Systems—Local Area Networks—Part 4: Token-Passing Bus Access Method and Physical Layer Specifications

ISO 8802-5 Information Processing Systems—Local Area Networks—Part 5: Token Ring Access Method and Physical Layer Specifications

ISO DIS 8802-7 Information Processing Systems—Local Area Networks—Part 7: Slotted Ring Access Method and Physical Layer Specifications

ISO 8885 Information Processing Systems—HDLC Procedures—General Purpose XID Frame Information Field Content and Format

ISO 8885 AD1 Information Processing Systems—HDLC Procedures—General Purpose XID Frame Information Field Content and Format—Addendum 1: Additional Operational Parameters for the Parameter Negotiation Data Link Layer Subfield and Definition of a Multilink Parameter Negotiation Data-Link Layer Subfield

ISO 8885 PDAD1 Information Processing Systems—HDLC Procedures—General Purpose XID Frame Information Field Content and Format—Addendum 2: Start/Stop Transmission Operation

ISO 8886.3 Information Processing Systems—Data Link Service Definition for Open Systems Interconnections

PHYSICAL LAYER STANDARDS

ISO DIS 10022 Information Processing Systems—Data Communications—OSI Physical Layer Service Definition

Note: Various connector standards exist (e.g., RS-232C) but have not been listed.

REGISTRATION PROCEDURES

ISO 9834-1 Information Processing Systems—Open Systems Interconnection—Procedures for Specific OSI Registration Authorities—Part 1: General Procedures

ISO 9834-2 Information Processing Systems—Open Systems Interconnection—Procedures for Specific OSI Registration Authorities—Part 2: Registration of Document Types

ISO 9834-3 Information Processing Systems—Open Systems Interconnection—Procedures for Specific OSI Registration Authorities—Part 3: Joint Registration Authority Procedures for Object Identifier Values

ISO 9834-4 Information Processing Systems—Open Systems Interconnection—Procedures for Specific OSI Registration Authorities—Part 4: Procedures for Abstract Syntax

ISO 9834-5 Information Processing Systems—Open Systems Interconnection—Procedures for Specific OSI Registration Authorities—Part 5: Procedures for Transfer Syntax

ISO 9834-6 Information Processing Systems—Open Systems Interconnection—Procedures for Specific OSI Registration Authorities—Part 6: Procedures for Application-Process and Application-Entity Titles

ISO 9834-7 Information Processing Systems—Open Systems Interconnection—Procedures for Specific OSI Registration Authorities—Part 7: Procedures for Application-Contexts.

ISO 9834-8 Information Processing Systems—Open Systems Interconnection—Procedures for Specific OSI Registration Authorities—Part 8: Procedures for System-Titles

ISO 9834-9 Information Processing Systems—Open Systems Interconnection—Procedures for Specific OSI Registration Authorities—Part 9: Procedures for VT Profiles

ISO 9834-10 Information Processing Systems—Open Systems Interconnection—Procedures for Specific OSI Registration Authorities—Part 10: Procedures for VT Control Objects

FORMAL DESCRIPTION TECHNIQUES

ISO 9074 Information Processing Systems—Open Systems Interconnection—Estelle—A Formal Description Technique Based on an Extended State Transition Model

ISO 8807 Information Processing Systems—Open Systems Interconnection—LOTOS—A Formal Description Technique Based on the Temporal Ordering of Observational Behavior

ISO JTC1/SC21 N 933 Guidelines for the Application of Formal Description Techniques to OSI

ISO JTC1/SC21 N 3249 Estelle Tutorial

ISO JTC1/SC21 N 1539 A Tutorial on LOTOS

CONFORMANCE TESTING

ISO 9646 Information Processing Systems—Open Systems Interconnection—OSI Conformance Testing Methodology and Framework—Parts 1 to 5

OSI MANAGEMENT

ISO 9595 Information Processing Systems—Open Systems Interconnection—Common Management Information Service Definition

ISO 9595 PDAD1 Cancel Get

ISO 9595 PDAD2 Add/Remove

ISO 9596 Information Processing Systems—Open Systems Interconnection—Common Management Information Protocol Specification

ISO 9596 PDAD1 Cancel Get

ISO 9596 PDAD2 Add/Remove

ISO JTC1/SC21 N 2066 Information Processing Systems—Open Systems Interconnection—Management Information Services—Structure of Management Information

DIRECTORY SERVICE

ISO 9594 Information Processing Systems—Open Systems Interconnection—The Directory—Parts 1 to 8

OFFICE SYSTEMS STANDARDS

ISO 8613 Information Processing Systems—Text and Office Systems—Office Document Architecture (ODA) and Interchange Format—Parts 1 to 8

ISO 8613-2 PDAD1 Formal Specification of ODA Document Structures

ISO DP 10033 Information Processing Systems—Text and Office Systems—Recording of Documents Conforming to ISO 8613 on Flexible Disk Cartridges Conforming to ISO 9293

ISO 8879 Information Processing Systems—Text and Office Systems—Standard Generalized Markup Language (SGML)

ISO 9069 Information Processing Systems—Text and Office Systems—SGML Support Facilities—SGML Document Interchange Format (SDIF)

ISO DIS 9070 Information Processing Systems—Text and Office Systems—SGML Support Facilities—Registration Procedures for Public Text Owner

ISO DTR 9573 Information Processing Systems—Text and Office Systems—SGML Support Facilities—Techniques for Using SGML

ISO DP 10031 Information Processing Systems—Text Communication—Distributed Office Applications—Parts 1 and 2

CCITT Recommendation T.432 Document Transfer, Access, and Manipulation—Services and Protocols—Service Definition

CCITT Recommendation T.441 Document Transfer, Access, and Manipulation—Operational Structure

BANKING STANDARDS

ISO 8583 Bank Card-Originated Messages—Interchange Message Specifications—Content for Financial Transactions

ISO DIS 9955 Applications of OSI in Banking—Methodology and Guidelines for the Development of Application Protocols for Banking Information Interchange

LIBRARY STANDARDS

ISO DIS 10160 Documentation—Interlibrary Loan Service Definition

ISO DIS 10161 Documentation—Interlibrary Loan Protocol Definition

ISO DIS 10162 Documentation—Application Service for Information Systems—Search, Retrieve, and Update Service Definition

ISO DIS 10162 Documentation—Application Service for Information Systems—Search, Retrieve, and Update Protocol Specification

MANUFACTURING AUTOMATION STANDARDS

ISO DIS 9506 Manufacturing Message Specification—Parts 1 and 2

ELECTRONIC DATA INTERCHANGE STANDARDS

ISO 9735 Electronic Data Interchange for Administration, Commerce and Industry (EDIFACT)—Syntax Rules

ISDN RECOMMENDATIONS

I.110 Preamble and General Structure of the I-Series Recommendations for ISDN

I.111 Relationship with Other Recommendations Relevant to ISDNs

I.112 Vocabulary of Terms for ISDNs

I.113 Vocabulary of Terms for Broadband Aspects of ISDN

I.120 Integrated Service Digital Network (ISDN)

I.121 Broadband Aspects of ISDN

I.122 Framework for Providing Additional Packet Mode Bearer Services
I.130 Method for the Characterization of Telecommunication Services Supported by an ISDN and Network Capabilities of an ISDN
I.133 Static Description of the Service Using Attributes
I.140 Attribute Technique for the Characterization of Telecommunication Services Supported by an ISDN and Network Capabilities of an ISDN
I.142 ISDN Charging Attributes and Values
I.210 Principles of Telecommunication Services Supported by an ISDN and the Means to Describe Them
I.211 Bearer Services Supported by an ISDN
I.212 Teleservices Supported by an ISDN
I.220 Common Dynamic Description of Basic Telecommunication Services
I.221 Common Specific Characteristics of Services
I.230 Definition of Bearer Services
I.231 Circuit-mode Bearer Services Categories
I.232 Packet-mode Bearer Services Categories
I.240 Definition of Teleservices
I.241 Teleservices Supported by an ISDN
I.250 Definition of Supplementary Services
I.251 Number Identification Supplementary Services
I.252 Call Offering Supplementary Services
I.253 Call Completion Supplementary Services
I.254 Multiparty Supplementary Services
I.255 Community of Interest Supplementary Services
I.256 Charging Supplementary Services
I.257 Additional Information Transfer Supplementary Service
I.310 ISDN—Network Functional Description
I.320 ISDN Protocol Reference Model
I.324 ISDN Network Architecture
I.325 ISDN Hypothetical Reference Connections
I.326 Reference Configurations for Relative Network Resource Requirement
I.330 ISDN Numbering and Addressing Principles
I.331 Numbering Plan for the ISDN Era
I.332 Numbering Principles for Interworking Between ISDN and Dedicated Networks with Different Numbering Plans
I.333 Terminal Selection in ISDN
I.334 Principles Relating ISDN Numbers/Subaddresses to the OSI Reference Model Network Layer Addresses
I.335 ISDN Routing Principles
I.340 ISDN Connection Types
I.350 General Aspects of Quality of Services and Network Performance in Digital Networks Including ISDNs
I.351 Recommendation on Other Series Including Network Performance Objectives That Apply at S/T Reference Points of an ISDN
I.352 Network Performance Objectives for Call Processing Delays

I.410 General Aspects and Principles Relating to Recommendations on ISDN User–Network Interfaces
I.411 ISDN User–Network Interfaces—Reference Configurations
I.412 ISDN User–Network Interfaces—Interface Structures and Access Capabilities
I.420 Basic User–Network Interface
I.421 Primary Rate User–Network Interface
I.430 Basic User–Network Interface—Layer 1 Specification
I.431 Primary Rate User–Network Interface—Layer 1 Specification
I.440 ISDN User–Network Interface Data Link Layer—General Aspects
I.441 ISDN User–Network Interface Data Link Layer Specification
I.450 ISDN User–Network Interface Layer 3—General Aspects
I.451 ISDN User–Network Interface Layer 3 Specification
I.452 General Procedures for the Control of ISDN Supplementary Services
I.460 Multiplexing, Rate Adaptation, and Support of Existing Interfaces
I.461 Support of X.21 and X.21 BIS-Based Data Terminal Equipments (DTEs) by an Integrated Services Digital Network (ISDN)
I.462 Support of Packet Mode Terminal Equipment by an ISDN
I.463 Support of Data Terminal Equipments DTEs) with V-Series Type Interfaces by an Integrated Services Digital Network (ISDN)
I.464 Multiplexing, Rate Adaptation, and Support of Existing Interfaces for Restricted 64 Kbit/s Transfer
I.465 Support by an ISDN of Data Terminal Equipment with V-Series Type Interfaces with Provision for Statistical Multiplexing
I.470 Relationship of Terminal Functions to ISDN
I.500 General Structure of the ISDN Interworking Recommendations
I.510 Definitions and General Principles for ISDN Interworking
I.511 ISDN-to-ISDN Layer 1
I.515 Parameter Exchange for ISDN Interworking
I.520 General Arrangement for Network Interworking Between ISDNs
I.530 Network Interworking Between an ISDN and a Public Switched Telephone Network (PSTN)
I.540 ISDN/Circuit Switched Public Data Network Interworking
I.550 ISDN/Public Switched Packet Data Network Interworking
I.560 ISDN/Telex Interworking
I.601 General Maintenance Principles for ISDN Subscriber Access and Subscriber Installation
I.602 Application of Maintenance Principles to Subscriber Installation
I.603 Application of Maintenance Principles to ISDN Basic Access
I.604 Application of Maintenance Principles to the Primary Rate Access
I.605 Application of Maintenance Principles to the State Multiplexed Basic Rate Access

INDEX

Page numbers in **bold** face refer to tables or illustrations.